I0187493

SIX STRINGS AND A NOTE

SIX STRINGS AND A NOTE

LEGENDARY GUITARIST AGYA KOO NIMO IN HIS OWN WORDS

ERIC OBENG EDMONDS

FOREWORD BY EMERITUS PROFESSOR J.H. KWABENA NKETIA

Copyright 2016 Eric Obeng-Amoako Edmonds, Ed.D

All Rights Reserved. Without limiting the rights under the copyright reserved above, this book may not be reproduced, in whole or in part, stored in a retrieval system, or transmitted in any form or by any means (electronic, mechanical, photocopying, recording, or otherwise) except for brief quotations in critical reviews or publications without the prior permission of the publisher or author.

Library of Congress Cataloging-in-Publication Data

Six strings and a note: Legendary guitarist Agya Koo Nimo in his own words / Eric Obeng Edmonds

ISBN
978-0-9973519-0-3 Hardback
978-0-9973519-1-0 Paperback
978-0-9973519-2-7 Ebook

Includes bibliographical references and index
1. Memoir   2. Ethnomusicology   I. Title

Editor: Clare Higgins

First Edition
Printed in the United States of America
Library of Congress Control Number: 2016903481

Disclaimer: The author has tried to recreate events, locales, and conversations from his memories of them. In some instances, the author has changed the names of individuals and places in the interest of privacy. The author may also have changed some identifying characteristics and details such as physical properties, occupations and places of residence.

Rights for publishing this work in English or in non-English languages are administered by the publisher.

Dedicated to my children,
in whose strength and faith I found my own.

Kwabena Ampomah, Kwasi Gyawu, Kwaku Gyasi, Akua Kwartemaa,
Kofi Nimo, Ama Tutuwaa, Nana Yaa, Ama Kobi and Yaw Asare.

- Agya Koo Nimo

CONTENTS

ACKNOWLEDGEMENTS

"It is very easy to start writing a book, but very difficult to finish," Dr. J.B. Danquah wrote. Now, as I reach the point where my memoirs have transformed into a literary work, my hope is that my sincere gratitude will find its way to the many remarkable individuals I have encountered along my life's journey.

Over the years, I have met countless people with whom I shared my life and my dreams. The joy of writing this book lies in having the opportunity to thank all of them, and many more whose names may escape me but for whom my appreciation is genuine.

To God, who, in His infinite wisdom and grace, gives life and has guided my steps for nearly a century. To my father, Kwame Amponsah, and my mother, Akua Fokuo, who lived exemplary lives for me to emulate. My family became my greatest supporters and critics, and the love they shared gave me the strength to pursue my dream with a guitar.

I wish to express my deep gratitude to my late wife, Theresa Afua Owusuwaa, and my current wife, Comfort Joyce Manu. Without their unwavering support, the sun might never have risen on my many ambitions. I am also thankful for the late Kwabena Onyina, a man whose life and influence I have always cherished.

I thank Emeritus Professor Albert Mawere Opoku, Professor of Dance and Choreography at the University of Ghana, Legon. In him, I have always had both an advocate and my best critic, every step of the way. I owe a debt of gratitude to Professor Emeritus J.H. Kwabena Nketia, Director of the Institute of African Studies, who celebrated everything I did. There were times when he would invite me to Legon to perform at events, simply to give me a chance to play authentic traditional music to audiences across the country.

My life and career may have taken a different turn if I had not met Mr. J.B. Butali, who served as Director of the Mordernaires Band; Vice Chancellor Robert Patrick Baffour; Professor William Neizer Laing, a pathologist and the first Dean of the School of Medical Sciences at KNUST; and Emeritus Professor F.A. Kufuor. Emeritus Professor Ebenezer Laing, a geneticist, has always been a man I have been honored to call my friend. I hope that someday, when people reflect on my life's work and the depth of my character, the impact of men like Professor Laing and Professor F.A. Kufuor on everything I dedicated my life will be recognized, making it a life well-lived.

I am deeply thankful to Mr. Owusu Prempeh, Mr. Osei Mensah Bonsu of the Kumasi branch of the Ghana Broadcasting Corporation, Nana Osei Owusu, Dr. J.P. Andrews, and Dr. W.E. Duncanson, both of whom served as Principals at the Kumasi College of Technology; Dr. A.A.Y. Kyerematen, the first Director of the Ghana Cultural Center in Kumasi; Dr. E.K. Osei Kofi; Professor W.E. Abraham; Professor Kwasi Wiredu; and Professor Kwame Arhin.

A special thank you to my friend, Professor Andrew Kaye, a Fulbright scholar, who wrote about my music in *Koo Nimo and His Circle: A Ghanaian Musician in Ethnomusicological Perspective* as his Ph.D. dissertation. My sincere appreciation also goes to the joy that friends like Clark Terry and Cat Anderson brought into my life, and a heartfelt thank you to Professor Ellingson at the University of Seattle, Miss Adelaide Amegatcher, Mrs. Diana Rheindorf, the late Dr. Ofosu Baako, the late Professor Kwasi Andam, Dr. Glen Wood, and Dr. Sir Wireko Brobby and family.

Much of my life has been shaped by the Ashanti royal courts, where the values and principles I have upheld throughout my life took root. To Opanin Kyirifufuo, Nana Opoku Ware II, Nana Kwame Bonsu, Nana Akua Mansa, Queen Mother Nana Amma Serwaa Nyarko II, her daughter Nana Ama Serwaa, Nana Kwaku

Mensah, Nana Kwasi Ansah, Nana Osei Kofi, Lawyer J.F. Cobbina, and the elders in the royal palace, my gratitude to you all is endless.

My sincere gratitude extends to Asantehemaa Nana Afua Kobi Serwaa Ampem II, who took pride in my success and has been an extraordinary influence on my life. I hope my profound thanks will reach Otumfuo Osei Tutu Ababio, the Asantehene, for all his encouragement and the countless opportunities he provided me to showcase my work. The great honor you have bestowed on me over the years, your unwavering support for musicians across the country, and your exceptional vision for Asanteman and Ghana will continue to inspire our society for generations. Otumfuo, please accept my humble appreciation.

I thank Mr. D.K. Sam, a Fante catechist at the Foase Methodist Church from 1934 to 1942, who first taught me to play the church organ. By the age of six, I was playing the organ during church services, thanks to Mr. Sam's wonderful support. Ambassador H.V. Sakyi taught me piano at Adisadel College, and Mr. Albert Hammond taught me Latin and Greek. Dr. Ato Taylor, Professor Wuddah Martey, and Dr. P.A. Owiredu were my math teachers, and their influence on my life extended far beyond arithmetic formulas.

I am grateful to Yaw Nkwantabisa III, my brother-in-law, who paid my airfares and those of my children to the United States, a gesture that has meant a great deal to me through the years. I can only say thank you. I also thank young Francis Gyaba, whose future I pray will be bright, as he worked tirelessly as my private secretary to help make my own journey so much easier.

My sincere gratitude goes to Teacher Mante, Mr. Atenka, and Attorney Kwaku Bonsu, all of whom expressed such joy in teaching a curious Koo Nimo at Kumasi Presbyterian Middle School between 1944 and 1947. Before attending Adisadel College, I had known Mr. Abaka, who lived near the royal palace and once advised me to be mindful of how often I apologized, as it could imply a feeling of guilt, which is not a trait of an outstanding person. Like Mr. Abaka, people such as Owusu Akyaw, Yeboah Nyamekye, Okyere Darko, and Dr. Agyei Barwuah, all of whom I met at the Center for National Culture, sowed seeds of faith, affirmation, and reassurance into my life and career. These seeds have guided me throughout my journey.

I thank people like Professor Robin McCabbe, Chris Lesser, Mr. Berkovitz, Stella McKenzie, Janet Buckenham, Mrs. Peggy Appiah, Ms. Hannah Schreckenbach, Archbishop Emeritus Peter Kwasi Sarpong (Chairman of Adom Society), Mrs. Valerie Sackey, Justice D.F. Annan, Nat Amarteifio, Attorneys Hayfron Benjamin and Nanabayin Dadson, Laddie Nylander, classical guitarist Gilbert Addy, Joe Pass, my guitar student James Whetzel, drummer Kofi Annan, Sowa Mensah, Akosua Addo, and Professor of Guitar Leo Brower. I thank the late Dr. Mrs. Efua Sutherland, Esi Sutherland Addy, the late Willie Amarfio, sculptor Saka Acquaye, Dr. Amegatcher, Stanley Jordan, Laurindo Almeida, Boo Hinkson, Len Boogsie Sharpe, Fitzroy Coleman, Bill Marshall, and Mr. Bampoe at NAFTI, as well as Christopher Laird at Banyan TV in Trinidad and Tobago, Professor John Collins, and Art Bennin. They have all been invaluable on my journey, and I thank them profoundly.

My deep appreciation extends to Dr. Mary Hark, Dr. Henry Drewal, Ben Mandelson, Bill Kubeczko (who produced my *Roots Revival* record), Professor Kwame Addoh, George Lee, Professor Kwasi Ampene at the University of Michigan in Ann Arbor, Dr. Atta Kwami and his wife Pamela Clarkson, Emeritus Professor Owusu Sarpong (Osagyefo Ampem Anye Amoampon Ataberako II, Wenchihene), banker Mr. Manu Sarpong, singer Maame Afua Abasa, Kwaku Duah, Okyeame Kwame Nsiah in Ayeduase, Kumasi, and Professor Kofi Asare Opoku, who worked as my consultant on Akan Ethics and Religion.

I thank Nana Aboagye Dacosta – Nana Gyinadu Kufuor II, Maame Yaa Manu, Mary Debra, Major Boateng and his brother

Kwame Owusu, Mr. Kojo Simmons, Mr. David Asomaning, Mr. Tsatsu Tsikata, Kantinka Dr. Donkoh Fordwor K.S.G., Dr. Adrian Oddoye, the honorable Kojo Yankah, and Professor Kwesi Yankah. Edwaasehene Nana Opoku Agyemang Barwuah Nsafoa, Nana Kranim of Foase Atwima, Nana Kwadwo Nyantakyi III (Asantehene Sanaahene), Akwasi Donkor, Bosie Amponsah, Professor Peter Gyawu, Adu Danquah, Kojo Twumasi, and Kow Ansah - your contributions have greatly enriched my life and added my voice to a universe filled with art. For this, I owe an incredible amount of thanks.

I have been eternally grateful for the thoughtfulness and backing of people like Dr. Evans Anfom, Professor Kwame Adarkwa, Professor Kwasi Andam, Professor Bamfo Kwakye, Professor F. O. Kwami, Professor E.H. Amonoo Neizer, Professor Ayim, Professor Otoo Ellis, Mr. A.S.Y. Andoh, and Mr. Kobby Yebo-Okrah.

Some of the wonderful people I had the great pleasure of working with include Professor Emmanuel Akyeampong, Professor Kay Shelemay at Harvard University, Professor Opoku Agyemang, Professor Naana Jane Opoku Agyemang, Dr. Beulah Brown, Janet Akosua Edge, Dr. Mariama Ross, Julialynne Walker, Dr. Emily Owusu Ansah, Professor Cynthia Schmidt, Professor Kofi Anyidoho, Dr. Esther Afreh, Mr. A.A. Amoako, Brigit Ellinghaus, Anna Cottrell, Professor F.O. Akuffo, Kwaku Opuni Ofosuhene, Lt. Col. Alex Aryeh, Professor Carnita Groves, Esther Cobbah, Tete Kobla, and Dr. Gayle McGarrity.

I have had the good fortune of meeting Drs. Anderson, Gorman, Ayisi Boateng, and Amanama at Komfo Anokye Hospital, as well as Dr. J.G.A. Wood, Mercy Boateng, and Sister Martha, all of whom were a tremendous help to me when I needed their counsel. I truly appreciate the work of Mrs. Gifty Bright, Akosua Adoma Kyerekuaa, and Edwina Adjei in organizing my library. Amara Hark Weber, Nana Yaa Asantewaa, and Phada Simone, thank you for your excellent work.

I am very grateful for all the extraordinarily selfless help I have received from my great friends Mr. Michael Nyamekye, Mr. S.O. Larbi, Mr. Kwaku Boakye, Madam Yaa Asantewaa, Mr. Sarpei Nunoo, and Professor Kofi Agawu at Princeton University. I would also like to thank Papa Baah, Dr. Seidu Karikacha, Sowah Mensah, Dr. Akosua Addoh, Professor Kwami Addoh, Mr. Oscar Doe, Professor Philip Schyler, Professor Dudley Shannon, Marc Seal, Obo Addy, Tetteh Mustapha Addy, Minna Zhou, Dr. Akua Duku Anokye, Maame Donkor Wawase, Mr. Kow Ansah, Nana Kwaku Kunadu Ayeduase Manwerehere, and Nana Kwarteng. You have all been truly remarkable.

Classical guitar tutor Professor Robinson at the Manchester School of Music in the late 1960s helped me refine my craft, and Professor Adele Kramer of the London Guildhall College of Music has been an exceptional teacher, demonstrating a level of patience I will never forget. Mr. Dick Moore, who once served as the Director at the U.S.I.S., displayed genuine support for my work, taking the time to organize workshops with American jazz musicians like Pharaoh Sanders. He would also bring jazz guitar manuals for me to study when he was traveling to Ghana.

Musicologist Jon Kertzer is the epitome of selflessness and reassuring friendship. Dr. Rick Welty worked tirelessly at Jack Straw Studios on the *Tete Wo Bi Ka* record, and Dr. Thomas Kruppa has been incredibly instrumental in shaping the creative artist I would become. I thank all of them dearly. To Dr. Henrick Bettermann, thank you for your hard work in Music Therapy, and to Tom Fryer and Liam Freeman for introducing me to some of their favorite jazz music.

Thank you also to Leo Sarkisian and Rita Rochelle's *Voice of America* program for helping me tell my story to an audience, many of whom I may never meet. The work of the indefatigable and truly special Laurel Sercombe, archivist at the University of Washington-Seattle, meant a great deal to me, and I am grateful to you.

I can never find enough words to thank Mr. Faisal Helwani, who dedicated much of his energy and personal resources to helping me during the ten years I served as president of MUSIGA. I am deeply grateful for the time he invested in getting me to where I stand today. My friend and great English classical guitar composer, Jack Duarte, wrote, "Someone has to bring the guitar to Ghana as a musical instrument. May this guitar manual help my friend Daniel Amponsah to be the one who does it." I have been incredibly fortunate to have had people like him in my life. Mr. Kwabena Fosu Mensah and Apogee produced my first-ever CD in Ghana, *Osabarima*, and I will always thank them for such an expression of kindness and excellence.

I am eternally grateful to my childhood friends and fiercest rivals in music, Robert Owusu and the late Dr. Harry Opoku. I may never have had the urge to pick up a guitar if I hadn't met both of you. I treasure the friendship I have been blessed to share with you over the years. Thank you to Professor Steven Friedson at the University of North Texas for your excellent and tireless work in ethnomusicology and for the privilege of sharing in it, even in a small way.

Throughout it all, there has been the remarkable work of my attorney, Bernard Katernor Nana Bosumprah. A man who shared his skills and passion so that musicians could chase their dreams, without concern for applause or adulation. He served as my attorney for the ten years I was president of MUSIGA and played a crucial role as the copyright administrator when international recording artist Paul Simon applied to use "Yaa Amponsa" in his *Rhythm of the Saints* album. I owe him a great debt of gratitude.

My music career would never have become what it did without the great partners I found along the way. Kofi Twumasi, one of the greatest guitarists in Ghana, performed with me for about 30 years. Other remarkable musicians whose collective talent carried me through the years include Kwao Sarfo, J.K. Barwuah, Hanson Obeng, Yaw Nimo, Kojo Nyamekye, Kojo Kusi, Yaw Poku, Yaw Badu, and

Sammy Kweggir. There were also Kwabena Donkor, Osei Assibey, Bonsu, Moro, Dwumaa, Emella Fosuaa, Nana Yeboah Abeyle, Baffour Abeyie, Badu, Gifty Ghartey, Faustina Akyeampong, Tawiah, Akosua Frimpomaa, Abena Felicia Manu, Yaw Manu, Anyanor, Yaw Asare, Osei Korankye, the seperewa virtuoso, John Amponsah, Stella Amponsah, and Kwabena Ampomah.

To my brothers and sisters - Grace Boah-Agyarko, Victoria Amponsah, Hannah Amponsah, Reverend Rockson Amponsah, Abraham Adusei Amponsah, Paul Amponsah, Mama Akua Fosuaa, and Amma Asibuo, - and to my nephews and nieces - Kwasi Teng, Yaw Boama, Kojo Bonsu, Nana Ama Serwaa, Nana Akua Achiaa, Sallah, Nyarko, and Beatrice Addoh - I express my deepest gratitude.

Finally, my utmost gratitude goes to Eric Obeng-Amoako Edmonds for being the perfect person to bring this work to life. Your integrity and focus helped turn many hours of conversation into a beautiful piece of art, something I had yearned to do for many years. Most importantly, thank you for the never-ending line of questions that often made me jog my memory and travel several decades into my past. I know it took extraordinary patience to listen and great devotion to writing to peel through the layers of my life.

To all my friends around the world whose well wishes kept me alive and whose smiles gave me the strength to become an artist, I thank you. I am deeply grateful for the opportunities I've had every step of the way over all these years. My words will live longer than I will, and my hope is that my work will leave behind a legacy for future generations.

– Koo Nimo

FOREWORD

It is both a great pleasure and an honor to write the foreword to *Six Strings and a Note*. Although I am not a performing member of Koo Nimo's band, I am confident that they are aware of the strong intellectual and artistic ties I share with Koo Nimo himself.

This journey began through the initiative of Mawere Opoku, who appreciated my approach to verbal and musical communication grounded in our tradition, which I learned from Ephraim Amu. Mawere believed that Koo Nimo could follow suit, as we were birds of the same feather. We maintained close contact and drew from our shared traditional sources, although we did not form an independent Asante Trio band. Instead, we were content with the inspiration that fueled our work as concerned artists, deeply rooted in the creative traditions of our forebears while exploring individual paths within our ancestral heritage, all in new and creative contexts.

Because of the quality of Koo Nimo's creative and practical approach to tradition, it was easy for him to broaden his perspectives. He successfully forged a connection between his practice of traditional music, his knowledge of Western music, and the discipline of Ethnomusicology—now vigorously pursued in the United States and beyond by members of the Society for Ethnomusicology and the International Society for Music Education, both of which I am an Honorary Member.

As a result, Koo Nimo is prominently featured in the textbook *World Music: A Global Journey* (Routledge, 2006), compiled by Terry Miller and Andrew Shahriani. Moreover, Ghana has become one of the key centers for study abroad programs in Ethnomusicology and Music Education. This is why I am pleased that Koo Nimo has taken the time to narrate not only his autobiography but also to share a glimpse of his creative work and the ideas that drive him as a concerned citizen of Ghana. His narrative also highlights the reciprocal contributions of those who have benefited from his work or shared his insights.

I am delighted that Koo Nimo makes every effort to keep our lives in touch. Whenever my phone rings and I hear the voice saying "Agya Koo ni oo" (This is Agya Koo), I can't help but thank the Good Lord for the renewal of our fellowship, which began modestly during the Mawere Opoku period.

So, permit me at this juncture not to embark on a tedious review of the entire content of *Six Strings and a Note*, which you can explore at your leisure. Instead, I will conclude my foreword with heartfelt words of appreciation.

I congratulate Koo Nimo and Obeng-Amoako Edmonds, not only for compiling this invaluable collection of works, which I treasure as a voluntary associate of Koo Nimo, but also for renewing the connection with the breadth and depth of the Koo Nimo experience that this work provides.

– Emeritus Professor J.H. Kwabena Nketia

FROM THE AUTHOR

Writing is often a solitary pursuit, but when the words resonate with the songs you have heard and enjoyed, the project becomes worthwhile at every turn. When a story comes to life easily in your mind, and the lessons spark intellectual curiosity, the long nights are filled with smiles and fascinating reflections on your own life. *Six Strings and a Note* was an exciting project from the start, and the real challenge was condensing almost nine decades of experiences and memories into one book. The stories could very well have filled volumes, each one equally inspirational, making this journey enjoyable for me as well.

As I worked with Agya Koo Nimo on this book, my primary goal was to delve into his mind and life to uncover what made him tick. We spent many hours researching and took several trips down memory lane, exploring more routes than he had initially imagined. A memoir truly comes to life as an honest reflection of events tucked away in the years gone by. I never knew anyone who could recall events as vividly as Agya Koo Nimo did, and he ensured we did not miss any of the details.

Producing this literary work required a curious mind and intellectual clarity. What made it all possible - and easy - was the fact that Agya Koo Nimo continues to impress audiences with his vast knowledge of culture and history. He consistently made connections between the lessons he learned in his youth and the man he would become over the years.

I have many people to thank, some of whom I have never met in person. Yet, their words and photographs provided invaluable insights into the legendary Koo Nimo. I am deeply grateful that, in their own way, they captured snippets of an extraordinary life and its impact on the world. To a large extent, I viewed writing this book as a long-overdue exercise, as if it had been waiting for me to come along. My generation, and those after me, will read about what I learned through conversations, guitar sessions, and stories about life.

If I must give credit to one person for convincing me of the significance of this project, it is my best friend and wife, Julliet. She transformed my every question and thought into words and envisioned this work long before I sat down to write. My wife shares this praise with my sons Akrofi and Amofa, who patiently listened to their father read drafts of every manuscript over and over when they could have been listening to nursery rhymes like any other baby. You were my most reliable audience, and although I'm convinced you don't remember a word of what you smiled through, I'll thank you someday soon when you can understand it all. I am truly blessed to have you both in my life.

I thank my family, especially my father, who made me appreciate highlife music as a young boy by playing guitar chords. My mother, who tolerated the noisy highlife band sessions of her sons; and my brothers, who found it exciting to record highlife music on cassette players and made us take turns memorizing lyrics as a hobby. Even when the meaning eluded me, I enjoyed songs by artists like Nana Ampadu, George Darko, Pat Thomas, and their contemporaries. Now, I am grateful for what sparked my genuine interest in pursuing this project.

To Agya Koo Nimo's children, especially John and Eugene, thank you for your patience during the lengthy conversations late into the night when the journalist in me needed every bit of information I could find. Your support and encouragement meant a great deal to me. I hope my work is close to what we envisioned at the start, and I gladly pass on to all of you every accolade and praise I receive from this project.

To my friends Nana Yaw Anobah, Frank and Bernice Adu Gyamfi, Nana Yaw Sarpong, Joe Union, and Eddu Oparie Addoh, thank you for your feedback and honest insights into this creative project. Mrs. Charlotte S. Akyeampong, Professor F. Andoh-Baidoo, Dr. Rosemarie Andoh-Baidoo, Yaw and Lucy Boadi, thank you for your encouragement to keep working, even when the days seemed to be running out with all of life's competing priorities.

I am humbly indebted to Josiah Osei and his wife, Jeanette. This project would not have been possible without people like you, who create unexpected blessings. It is impossible to fully express my gratitude to you on paper, but I will try nonetheless. To my friend, Dr. Cindy Kwarteng, I could not have asked for a more honest critic and friend, with a treasure trove of ideas. Nana Owusu Addae Munumkum I and Madam Ophelia Owusu, I am deeply thankful for your kindness and generosity. There have been many hours of research that sparked long conversations about Asante culture and Akan traditions, and I thank you for helping me connect the dots.

I am grateful to people like Joe Latham and Andrew L. Kaye, who took a keen interest in Agya Koo Nimo's message and career over the past decades. Your articles and references provided a framework for me to create a bridge between an accurate biography and a compelling memoir. In writing this book, if there is one discovery I can share, it is that there is much more to a folk singer than just music and much more to a teacher than the lessons in a song.

Clare Higgins, you are God-sent and a brilliant editor, much more than any author could wish for. The hardest part of writing this book fell on your shoulders, and I am truly grateful that you came along on this journey and worked tirelessly on this project. Elena Reznikova, another heartfelt thank you for your genuine patience and truly amazing creativity.

I thank Agya Koo Nimo for choosing me to write this book. What began as a lesson in semitones and augmented notes turned out to be a lesson on life itself. The greatest blessings in writing this book have been what I learned from you and the wisdom and ideas I will carry with me throughout my life. I have done my best to capture every fact and message.

Ghana and Africa will forever celebrate a legendary guitarist, a leading folk musician, a veteran ensemble organizer, an energizing educational thinker, a scientist, a role model, and a cultural ambassador. Mr. Daniel Kwabena Boa Amponsem made a commitment to excel in the path he chose - and he did. This has been a literary journey, and I will be the first to say that listening to Koo Nimo's memories firsthand has been an absolute labor of love.

My only hope is that my choice of words will bring clarity to a remarkable life and the notes he leaves behind for generations to come. The task came with specific instructions from Agya Koo Nimo - that the diction should be as straightforward as our conversations, not like a thesis. His greatest wish is that his words and thoughts about culture and heritage will not fade with time. In a small way, I am glad to have had the opportunity to be part of a journey to preserve the wisdom and ingenuity of this remarkable person.

Finally, and most importantly, I thank God for His unrelenting grace and for the chance meetings that alter the course of a life.

"I started my musical career the first day I was born.
I sang my first song when I cried.
A man is born as a self-contained musical instrument."

– Agya Koo Nimo

1

A DREAM FROM A DISTANCE

Early Memories in Foase and the Early Years

If we all begin our lives with the end in mind, our hopes and doubts, as well as our thrills and burdens, will find meaning over time. The longer a person lives, the clearer life's complex picture becomes, and the joy of a life lived as best as we know how shines through every moment we remember.

If there was ever one prayer I said more than any other, it was for "my Creator to allow me to live longer than my mind's eye could see. There are so many things that I would like to do." From everything I've lived through and seen in my lifetime, I think it's fair to say that my prayer has been answered, and my wishes have come true beyond my wildest dreams. Maybe I will live as long as my grandfathers, who lived for over a century and saw their great-grandchildren thrive in a future they could never have imagined for themselves. At one point in life, I prayed that I would live to be 150 years old and witness the sunset in the distant future.

The small village of Foase, where I was born, was filled with beautiful scenery. There were long stretches of plantain, cassava, and oil palm trees under clear skies. The land was dotted with coffee and cocoa trees, providing shade under large trees on sunny days, where one could lie and gaze into the beauty tucked behind the clouds. Foase did not have many opportunities for a person to try their hand at a trade, especially in my early years. We had to learn quickly to embrace every glimmer of hope and find joy in every little thing we had. The village was in Atwima No.1, about 12 miles from the major city of Kumasi, in Ghana's Ashanti region.

At the time, my father could not afford to send me to school, and I was fortunate to have my uncle's help. Wofa George Agyei Kyem enrolled me in the local Methodist primary school in 1939. He was also a blacksmith in the Bogoso Mines, and throughout my adolescence, I was grateful for the educational opportunities he provided. Wofa Agyei Kyem became one of the most influential and intellectual figures in my early life. I saw how he made discipline a central part of his lifestyle and would often say, "Order is the first law in Heaven; without it, there is no life."

Ever since I can remember, I grew up with a sense of awareness and purpose that had been deeply ingrained in me. In a world where people might easily ignore basic social concerns, I was fortunate to have a family that paid attention to even the smallest details in everything we did. There were things I found unappealing long before I had any real reason to do so. I often recall walking past people urinating in public areas, on walls, and behind trees. There was a sense of decency and responsibility instilled in me, and even as a boy, I never found anything desirable about those actions.

From the very beginning, I was fascinated by how, when I set my mind against indulging in a particular action, the mere thought of it became uncomfortable. Even when no one was around to see, I had, in a way, become my own honest judge of character. Somehow, I found myself resisting the urge to follow the crowd. In a place seemingly untouched by the chaos and relentless pace of nearby towns, it felt as if nature had shielded us from life's grind, waiting until we were ready to face it.

For some strange reason, I also disliked sleeping anywhere away from home. I had restless nights whenever I had to do so. Maybe this instinctive reaction had something to do with the thought that admiring another person's belongings was essentially devaluing my own, even the little that I had. Other times, when visiting a home, I would learn too much about the family's unpleasant attitudes and traits that were not admired in society. I would rather sleep in my own house with nothing than be part of a home that had everything but potential for an immoral character. Eventually, I would come to understand that these inclinations helped shape whatever skills I had and pushed me to strive every day.

Life in the village taught sons and daughters to be extremely cautious of characters and attitudes that were frowned upon in society. The safest place in the world would be our own home. As a generation from whom not much would be expected, children my age did not often dream of traveling around the world or leaving their story behind. Hidden in the quiet shade of oak trees, we knew there was a bigger world out there, beyond Foase and Kumasi, where children dreamt of who they would become and how far they would go someday.

As children, nothing in our environment made us fathom the limitations of our lot in life. Our first role models were the men and women who had earned the utmost respect from everyone in the village. Maybe someday, we too would follow in their footsteps, but it wasn't something we spent much time dreaming about.

Miles away from Kumasi's bright lights, Foase was primarily a society where survival was one of the most important things in life. The pursuit of ambition often came as an afterthought. Nevertheless, the elderly were actively involved in every facet of life that affected the community. I remember thinking as a boy that someday it would be my generation's turn to do the same. We just didn't know how.

In the year I started Methodist primary school, I moved in with Mr. Daniel K. Sam, who taught me to play the organ. He was a Fante catechist, a Christian missionary who worked in neighboring villages. Whatever music lesson he taught me, I had to be ready to play in church on Sunday morning. My fascination with the organ and church music was almost immediate. We would visit the villages, clean the churches, and often wake up early enough to ring the bell and invite the villagers to services. I had ample opportunity to serve local communities and play musical instruments, and it never once felt like a chore.

Through this experience and training with Mr. Sam, I had a unique early musical upbringing. Every village had its own story to tell. Luckily, Mr. Sam noticed my curiosity during these encounters and did his best to unveil the value of every moment in a way my young mind could understand. I was fortunate to live the stories that my friends only heard about, so my sense of reality was awakened at a very early age. I was studying under the tutelage of people who were prominent in their professions and equally passionate in their commitment to serve.

Back in Foase, my grandmother, Nana Akosua Mansah Tutuwaa, lived to be over 100 years old. She was as protective as she was incredibly insightful and wise. She taught me many valuable lessons. One thing I will never forget is how she stressed the importance of respecting women in any society. In her words, insulting any woman is no different from insulting your own mother, who carried you in her womb and brought you into this world. That would be the ultimate gesture of disrespect. Conversations with Nana Mansah were filled with some of the most fundamental lessons any young person would need to hold dear.

I remember the days when something would happen in the neighborhood. At the onset of any chaos or loud noise, my grandmother would hurriedly get all the children inside the house and close the door. She made sure her family stayed far away from trouble, not lingering outside to watch the chaos unfold. In her own way, she warned us to avoid trouble beyond our doors and not be lured outside by curiosity. "Kwanhyia wuo," she would remind us often, an Akan phrase meaning "death by accident," a tragedy that befalls someone simply by being in the wrong place at the wrong time. And that could happen to anyone.

My life in Foase became a vital foundation of lessons that have accompanied me throughout my life and across the world. What's truly amazing is that no matter how far life takes us, we can always recall the invaluable treasures of knowledge and wisdom instilled in us at a young age. Even the scent of the air and the gritty sand beneath our feet formed memories that replayed in our minds over and over through the years.

Whether I was in Foase or traveling the world, what probably made the most difference in my life was the company I kept. I did not have many friends my age. For some reason, I gravitated toward older men who understandably had very different viewpoints on life than I did. Perhaps I wanted to grow up quickly, or maybe I was an old soul trapped in a young body. In those early years, I met Mr. C.E. Osei, who later became the Governor of the Bank of Ghana. I spent many Sundays visiting him, learning as much as I could. He was one of the most knowledgeable people I had ever met and was profoundly adept in traditional proverbs. To this day, I speak of him with deep respect for his incredible insight.

I was very fortunate to have encountered Mr. Osei at such an early age. Many people visited him and recorded his wise words and proverbs for cultural research documents. His primary passion was imparting wisdom to young people who cared enough to seek to understand the meaning behind various aspects of our culture. Mr. Osei understood the Asante language perhaps better than anyone I've known over the years. As a student of the culture and history of which I'm a part, this encounter and the opportunity to learn from him were undeniably some of my most defining moments in life.

In late 1980, I was attending a music conference in Martinique when Mr. Osei passed away. Losing one of the most inspirational and learned individuals I've met, someone with a profound depth of cultural knowledge, was untimely. It remains one of my greatest honors to have been invited to perform *kete* music at his funeral.

When I was a teenager, 90 years seemed like an advanced age. In Foase, I recall that most of the elderly men had been farmers for much of their lives. The manual labor and long days spent farming had taken a toll on their bodies, and their life expectancy reflected that. The wrinkles on their faces and the cracks in their palms told their stories vividly. Yet, their calm smiles often reminded us of the hard work that would become a significant part of our own lives. Despite this, many lived much longer, doing all they could to continue teaching and inspiring others until they were too weak to speak. In my own extended family, Nana Akwasi Gyawu lived to be 103 years old, and Nana Efua Nsema passed away at 105.

The people of Foase came from diverse backgrounds, and the village gradually evolved into a cosmopolitan community. Many of the residents had come from the Denkyira region, as well as from places like Akropong, Akyem, Kofikurom, Kaase, and surrounding villages. Each group brought with it unique skills and talents, and as a result, the village became a socially eclectic mix of artisans, craftsmen, and intellectuals. The craftsmen produced *nkuaba*, an important art form that told African stories through carved images and cultural philosophies in Adinkra symbols. These artifacts depicted culture and morals through their intricate decorations.

Even as young boys, we were captivated by the artwork that surrounded us in the village. The wooden carvings everywhere were particularly impressive. Many craftsmen used their skills to sculpt stools, dolls, and various other imaginative wooden creations. One striking element in our surroundings was the abundance of art, which ignited our imaginations. We marveled at how ordinary logs were transformed into beautiful sculptures, each telling a unique story.

In hindsight, however, the unfortunate outcome of this artistry was that some young men who took to crafting and sculpting lost interest in formal education. While this may not have been a problem in other parts of the world, in our village, some of the brightest young men limited their potential, focusing solely on their craft within the village.

The quiet casualty of this was the inability of these young men to use their skills to reach a broader audience. Even the most skilled craftsmen confined their focus and understanding of opportunity to earning just enough to get by each day and week. I often wondered how much further their creativity and art could have flourished if they had encountered fewer obstacles in life. Though no one may ever know their names, I hope they did not carry their unexpressed creativity to the grave.

Outside my village, I can probably count on one hand the number of people in the world who knew me as Kwabena Boa. Perhaps what truly matters in life is not the name we are given but the value of the moments we live. Many documents record my life's beginning as Wednesday, October 3, 1934. I've often been curious to travel back in time and witness my first day at Methodist Primary School, when my uncle Agyei Kyem must have written my birthdate on a piece of paper. Whatever the school recorded was who I became.

The date serves as a reference to the year and day he must have been told, as people often remembered a child's birth in relation to some popular or historical event. During those years, Nana Prempeh I had become Asantehene, and that might have been the only connection my mother made with my birth. Why my uncle chose that specific day in October remains one of life's mysteries.

Wofa Agyei Kyem also gave me the Christian name Frederick. I thought he must have encountered the name while reading about prominent British nobles like Prince Frederick of Wales. Whatever his reason, I disliked the name.

As a young boy, I wasn't fully aware of the impact a name could have, but I knew I wanted one that I could admire and honor. Frederick didn't resonate with me. From my early exposure to the Bible, I had come across the name Daniel, and I was immediately captivated by it. Daniel's faith in God was remarkable. Despite serving some of the most powerful pagan kings of his time for many years, he never lost his love and loyalty to the true God of his fathers - Abraham, Jacob, and Isaac. I was deeply inspired by such faithfulness. I wanted a life in which I could stand for something memorable, allowing my actions and convictions to speak for themselves. That's why I chose the name Daniel.

I later came across one of the most intriguing parts of my life when I visited my father in Brong Ahafo. My father was a farmer in Kukuom. I was an inquisitive little boy, always looking for something new to play with. My father's house was a small mud structure, known in Ghana as Atta Kwame Edan, with remnants of its original muddy joints still spilling over the blocks. On the wall hung my father's trumpet, and when I approached it, I noticed my name written in charcoal. The date next to my name was January 27, 1931, as though it was written by a farmer who wasn't sure how long he would live or whether his memory would fade over time.

This encounter, etched into my memory, remains vivid, a reminder of how fleeting time can be. I wasn't the only one whose birthdate or significant moments might have been forgotten or erased by the passage of time. Yet, we were fortunate to be surrounded by countless artifacts of history and by people who helped guide us, helping us understand who we were and where we came from. Perhaps, in the end, that was all we truly needed, to have our identity rooted in something deeper than mere dates and events.

Kwabena Boa-Amponsem was my name, given to me on a Tuesday, as boys born on that day inherit the Akan name Kwabena. But even at an early age, I was mindful of something greater: perhaps the Creator had given me an assignment to accomplish, regardless of the day I was born. I was born to be part of history in my own small way. Everyone enters this world with purpose, and we spend the rest of our lives discovering what has always been inside us.

I grew up around people like Nana Nframa, Wofa Kwaku Agyei, and Nana Danso. They were mostly farmers but also strict disciplinarians in society. More importantly, they were men of substance who saw themselves as role models and embraced the responsibility that came with it. We saw them working hard, rain or shine, on their farms in the village. The memories of people like Nana Kwabena Taa, Nana Akwasi Gyawu, Wofa Kwaku Agyei, Wofa Kwaku Owusu, Wofa Kwame Mosi, Wofa Kwaku Du, Opanin Mua, Nana Mensa, Amanpesee, Adwoa Afra, and Akua Manu feel as fresh as yesterday.

The elders in the village had earned the respect of everyone because we witnessed their exemplary lives. Their influence shaped every moment of our lives. The greatest blessing we had in our village was that our community was filled with men and women who became our role models. For every historical figure we admired from afar, there was someone in our own backyard who embodied that person's qualities.

I often reflect on stories about Napoleon Bonaparte, the French military and political leader who rose to prominence during the French Revolution. He is famously quoted as saying, "Every good leader must be a dealer in hope." The leaders in our village embodied this idea, offering us hope in ways both big and small. For those whose wisdom guided us through our formative years, I am eternally grateful. Their prudence not only shaped our lives but also gave us the courage to dream, even from a distance.

When I speak of a man like Nana Kwaku Fori, I remember someone whose encouragement shaped our inner monologue when we were too young to have a voice of our own. He would often start his day early, working on his farm, but made sure to return home in time to visit every house, ensuring that every school-aged child was indeed in school. Even when a child played truant, every parent could rely on Nana Kwaku Fori to stop whatever he was doing and take the child back to school. The village raised us all, and we never lost sight of this. The people cared.

Education was a privilege our fathers and grandfathers never had, which is why they made every effort to ensure that the children of Foase wouldn't be deprived of it. It wasn't just the responsibility of parents, it was a collective effort. The whole village shared in the task of raising a child to become a meaningful and contributing member of society. This sense of community shaped us, creating an environment where each child's future was everyone's concern.

Through my travels, people often ask me how different my village was from others. Foase was a community where respect for authority, commitment to hard work, and reverence for human life pervaded everything we did. I've shared many stories of how a student disciplined for misconduct in school would return home only to be disciplined again by their parents. The elders talked about who we were as a people, the pride in our blood, and what we represented. We were *adehye*, the Akan word for royalty.

As boys, we found this sense of responsibility uncomfortable, unnecessary, and even strange; nevertheless, we accepted it as part of life. There was nothing better to do than play all day and into the night. We basked in the joy of our innocent lives. I grew up in a society where neighbors became extended family members, and everyone shared in both happy and sad moments. I recall how my uncle, Wofa Agyei Kyem, once took a young woman who had left her husband back to their marital home and urged them to resolve their differences instead of walking away. There was nowhere else in the world I would rather have called home.

As I grew older, I came to realize the richness of our seemingly simple lifestyle. I look back at some of my happiest moments spent along the narrow paths in the village woods, daydreaming about a distant future. With every turning point in my life, I met new people whose influence continued to shape my outlook. Nana Kwame Bonsu and his older brother, Nana Opoku Ware II, were passionate about education and learning.

When I first moved to live in the royal house in Kumasi, I watched them closely. When the time came for me to choose between prominent secondary schools like Achimota, Mfantsipim, and Odumase-Krobo, Nana Opoku Ware strongly recommended his alma mater, Adisadel College. That was the school I had already set my heart on, so it did not take much to convince me it was the best option.

At that time, Ghana - then the Gold Coast - was still under British colonial rule, and there were only a few secondary schools scattered across the country. I had completed the Standard 7 School Leaving Certificate examination at a Presbyterian Middle School in Adum, Kumasi, in 1947. The following year, in 1948, I returned to Foase as a pupil teacher for subjects like English, geography, and music. I had told myself that one day, I would also attend Adisadel and pursue my ambitions. I enjoyed working as a pupil teacher, even though my salary of three pounds, one shilling, and eight pence was not much.

In the same year, I passed the Common Entrance Examination and was accepted as one of 26 students at Adisadel College. I had read about notable Ghanaian figures such as Dr. Kyerematen, Lawyer Torto, Robert Gardiner, Kojo Botsio, and Komla Gbedemah, all of whom had attended the school. It was this prestige that first inspired my admiration for Adisadel. The next four years of my life would immerse me in Western-style education, and for children in the Gold Coast before 1957, we learned everything there was to know about the British.

Adisadel College in Cape Coast, located in Ghana's Central Region, was founded in 1910 under the auspices of the Society for the Propagation of the Gospel (SPG), an English missionary group whose origins date back to 1701. The school's founder, Reverend Nathaniel Temple Hamlyn of the Anglican Church, started Adisadel to provide a grammar school education for children of Anglican parents, later extending it to children throughout the region. The beginnings of Adisadel College, originally known as St. Nicholas Grammar School, were to serve as a training ground for church personnel.

Before attending Adisadel, I had already played the organ in Foase and developed a strong love for it. Upon joining the school's choir, I found a new avenue for creative expression, and it became one of my greatest passions. I also developed an interest in jazz music and grew to appreciate that musical form. If there was one thing the next four years would cement for me, it was that I wanted to make music.

As I grew older, I became a firm believer that healthy competition breeds excellence, even when it feels uncomfortable. In 1951, during my third year at Adisadel College, I met Robert Owusu and Harry Opoku, who became my first fierce competitors, long before we knew the value of a spirited rivalry. They were the two people whose every action I studied closely, striving to surpass them. It did not matter how well I did unless I had done better than Robert and Harry. Rivalry and a dedication to excellence, forged through friendship, encouraged us to push ourselves harder than we would have without the competition. And for us, it worked.

Harry excelled in every activity as a student, and I did my best to match his achievements, particularly in Latin and Greek. The only thing I wanted to be sure of was that if there were anyone who scored higher in a game, earned better grades, or played an instrument better than I did, it wouldn't be Robert or Harry. Neither of the two boys wanted to be second to me in anything, either.

This strange desire to outdo one another somehow forged a deep bond between the three of us, making us the best of friends, yet we never lost sight of the competitive spirit that fueled us. Harry was in Canterbury House, and I was in Elliot House, but we always found ways to cross paths, eager to see what the other was practicing. I never understood the root of our rivalry, but whatever its source, it pushed both of us to want to give our best. These early challenges led me to a turning point in my life.

At this stage of my teenage years, I had learned to play the organ and loved every part of it - the keys and pedals. I can't remember exactly, but I am almost certain that I thought, one day, I would return to Foase and make Mr. D.K. Sam proud of the skills I had acquired since he had last seen me. Then, one afternoon in early 1952, I saw Harry standing near the bathhouse, playing an E.K. Nyame tune on his guitar. The melody was beautiful. He had taken the time to learn music theory, allowing him to play with a special technique.

It was as if I had been struck by lightning. My love for the organ immediately vanished. From that moment, I would never play the organ again. I was obsessed with the guitar. My only wish for the next few months was to play better than Harry. One thing was certain - if I was going to succeed at this new goal I had set for myself, I had to practice endlessly, and my life would revolve around guitar strings and chord progressions. This was the birth of Koo Nimo, the classical guitarist.

Life in the village was pure. Our joy stemmed from the simplest things, long before the village occasionally transformed into a busy town and before playing in the rain ceased to be fun. If music became my first love, it was due to the environment I lived in and the opportunity to come home and share what the larger world had taught me. My most cherished memory from that time was that I managed to start a small library with my meager salary to assist local students. I didn't know how far my gesture would go, but I was convinced that it might open a new world for the children.

In Foase, I discovered that our creative limits were stretched in the absence of luxury, so we created what we could imagine. The process of innovation demanded close attention to detail to ensure that the sound we produced was usable for our music. One such sound was the rhythm instrument *asratoa*, named after *"asra,"* the Asante word for powdered tobacco made from the *asra* tree, and "toa." When the tree ripened, we would carefully cut the fruit to avoid damaging the pods. We then poked holes through the sides of the pod large enough to insert small sticks into the fruit.

We learned to wait patiently for several days while the fruit rotted. None of us knew how long the pods should lie in the hot sun, so we learned to trust our instincts. In this important exercise, the least useful parts of the fruit were the seeds and pericarp. We scraped out the rotten parts and left the pods in the sun to dry. What was once an edible fruit was now filled with small pebbles.

We used strings and small sticks along the sides to give the instruments their distinct acoustic qualities. For the boys in the village, finding the perfect pebbles to place inside our instruments added another layer to the sound, even if it meant long walks through wooded paths in search of them. The *asratoa* became a canvas for the creativity and uniqueness of the young boys who spent days transforming fruit into acoustic instruments. That was our life, - the best years of our lives.

We also played the *adenkum*, made from *adenkum* gourds with long necks. Then there was the instrument *sraka*, which we made by cutting down a small tree with small seeds and covering its sides. We would then cut an opening at the tip of the tree, known as the resonator, and insert a stick underneath. We gradually rattled the two together, wrapping the resonator around the instrument to give it its sound. The sound waves traveled through the instrument, and this discovery was made possible only by our curiosity.

As a little boy, I was particularly fascinated by these handmade instruments. My mind was always focused on making sounds with objects we found in our environment, which probably weren't created for those purposes. When I hummed *abibindwom* alongside the sounds of the instruments, I liked what I heard. The art of creating sound waves and music in ways where we controlled the outcome and excellence of the instrument left a lasting impression on me.

I often reflect on those days, combing through the quiet woods with only the songs of birds and the hisses of snakes to keep me company. That was how I nurtured my craving for music. *Mmoguo*, Asante story songs, consumed my mind, and that was what I would later use to develop lyrics. The experiences with these handmade instruments helped me understand African rhythms in an authentic way. Later in life, I came to appreciate how these encounters had profoundly impacted my musicianship and the lure of the acoustic guitar.

While the nostalgia of those golden years in the village always brought a smile to my face, the value of these simple instruments provided a unique and challenging yet rich path to understanding music. Who can say, perhaps with different circumstances, more children might not have dared to share their ideas with the world through sound and music? In those years, we didn't have money for toys or instruments. Providing for basic needs consumed every parent's attention; they wanted to give their children what they did not have themselves. Everything we did in our spare time revolved around using the natural resources that surrounded us, filling the dull moments with ingenuity, the best we knew how. That was our substitute.

Years later, some of my peers joined brass bands and easily transitioned to other popular instruments. Despite the differences, all of the instruments shared similar fundamental sound theories. It became even clearer that the foundational years with the *asratoa* and *sraka* had been incredibly instructive. It was many decades after I left Foase that I looked back and realized how those years had prepared me for something far greater than I had anticipated. Life often places value on each stage of our journey, and the greatest gift we can give ourselves is to make the most of what we have - no matter how insignificant it may seem at the moment.

Back in Foase, I had learned from the elders that many in the village had once suffered from influenza. Fortunately, my generation escaped those painful epidemic years. We heard stories of family members carrying a loved one's casket to a cemetery, only to meet a neighbor who had just buried their own relative. It had been a heart-wrenching time for the entire village, but the people found solace in relying on each other during the chaos. Musicians, for their part, created songs that brought comfort and, even through the pain, allowed people to remember the good years and preserve pleasant memories.

At times, accidents found us, and even the comforting words of a caring village couldn't soothe the pain. One afternoon at Methodist primary school, I was with a group of boys weeding the compound when tragedy struck. We used sharp iron machetes to clear grassy areas and create walkways or prevent snakes and other animals from hiding in the short bushes. Because I am left-handed, my left leg stayed in front when I weeded to maintain my posture.

Kwaku Adiyea, a boy in my class, was right-handed, so as he weeded, he unintentionally moved closer to me. It was an accident, and in that instant, the world seemed to freeze. Suddenly, his machete struck my left knee, and the sharp sting pierced through my whole body. I immediately collapsed in excruciating pain, and my friends rushed me home.

My family, believing I didn't need immediate medical attention, decided not to take me to a hospital. Instead, they treated my injured knee with herbal medicine. They applied *agyen aduro* leaves to my leg and tied them around my knee. Although there was no noticeable progress, they hoped the knee would heal over time. *Agyenaduro* was first used by Nana Agyen in Denkyira to treat gunshot wounds in battle, but it did not do much for me. When my brother-in-law, Nana Kwame Bonsu, came to visit the village and saw the wound, he insisted that I be taken to Okomfo Anokye Hospital in Kumasi.

The bones in my knee joint were fractured. I had suffered worse wounds than anyone initially thought. My saving grace came when the doctors performed timely surgery to reconstruct my knee with plaster of Paris (POP), the standard treatment at the time. After a few days in the hospital, they sent me home with my knee in a cast. Dr. Jones Quartey performed the surgery, and the doctors told my family I would wake up by 4:00 PM. I must have slept soundly, despite the pain, because the chatter by my bedside didn't wake me.

When I didn't wake up on time, news quickly spread through Bantama and the village that I had died. A few hours later, I woke up, but the accident had left a lasting impact that would linger for years. It was a stark reminder of how swiftly life can change in the blink of an eye. Despite the pain, I found a way to see the brighter side and became deeply grateful for the life I still have, even with its discomforts. The pain remains a constant companion, but I am alive - and I am determined to make the most of what I have left.

Looking back, I could have resented the incident, but it wouldn't have changed anything. Participating in any physical activity became an uphill climb, but I was still alive and determined to do my best with what I had. In my teenage years, boys in my town did not spend their days obsessing over their futures. Perhaps that was because I grew up in a society and culture where people understood their tacit responsibilities and roles, no matter what vocation they chose. Any achievement for the youth in Foase, no matter their chosen path, was expected, though no one had specifically defined it for us.

As I grew older, I came to realize that living my ambition is a deeply personal journey, one that each of us defines in our own way. While people may attempt to outline the components of success, I've learned that true fulfillment ultimately resides within the individual. In any village or town, young men and women were never held back from dreaming, even from a distance. I came to understand that if, at the end of the day, we can look back and know we gave our best effort at every turn, then we've truly succeeded. This understanding became my own, and I learned not to rush toward tomorrow, but to savor the journey and the process along the way.

At Adisadel College, I realized that one crucial component of success is integrity. For most people I encountered, life had been little more than a stage where they performed to the best of their ability until the curtains closed. The audience might marvel at such performances, but the only people who were never impressed by such a life were our own selves. I was beginning to understand the importance of honestly examining what mattered most and making it my priority to excel at it. This is how I came to understand success. It did not matter where a person was born or the size of their dream.

The greatest lesson from my childhood was that we didn't need to be famous to change our world. No one from Foase had their name written on the world's tallest buildings, and perhaps no famous person even called Foase home, but we were prominent in our own eyes. The late Dr. Busia, in his work *The Position of the Chief in the Modern Political System of Ashanti*, was once asked where the intellectuals of Ghana could be found. He replied that the true intellectuals could be found in the villages.

From the men and women he met on his visits to some of Africa's most remote areas, Dr. Busia saw firsthand their untainted perspective on nature and the wisdom that filled their hearts. It was amazing to discover how much knowledge lived in the hearts of people who had never stepped into a British classroom, never read a word of Shakespeare or Aesop, but were masters of the world that surrounded them.

People in the cities seemed to have become consumed by the busyness of life, losing touch with the simple, yet profound lessons nature offers. In the remote villages, however, the idea of intellect and success was deeply rooted in how well one connected with and gave back to the earth. Dr. Busia often spoke of how the wisdom that came from living a rich, peaceful life in a village was far more valuable than any material wealth or formal education one could buy. It made me appreciate on the depth of knowledge that comes from a life lived in harmony with the natural world, a wisdom often overlooked in the rush of modern life.

As I left home and began visiting towns around Kumasi and other major cities, I encountered the stereotype that people in the villages were unintelligent. Sure, in the midst of poverty and the lack of educational facilities, many had never had the opportunity to attend school. Yet, many outside their world failed to recognize that, just as knowledge isn't the same as wisdom, education isn't the same as intelligence. Much of life unfolds every day, regardless of the academic preparation we believe will teach us everything we need to know.

I had no way of knowing what would become of every small step I took, nor could I have predicted the twists and turns my winding paths would follow. A heart like mine could only move forward, trusting that everything I hung on to, no matter how small, would somehow lead me somewhere meaningful. In places like Foase, where the world often felt distant and the future uncertain, we allowed ourselves to dream. We even dared to imagine lives beyond our circumstances and far beyond the narrow confines of our present. And perhaps, in hindsight, that liberty to dream was the most daring thing we did. Imagination cost very little, and that was something we could always afford, no matter how little we had.

We were never oblivious to what we lacked, even the emptiness that sometimes threatened to dampen our spirits. Over time, I came to find that whatever we didn't have didn't matter as much as we once thought. Our hopes for tomorrow weren't anchored in material possessions but in our belief in possibility.

It was only through the slow and sometimes painful passage of time that I came to cherish the significance of every moment in my life. Each experience, whether joyous or painful, had its place. Even the misfortunes and accidents, those events I once wished I could erase, began to reveal their purpose. They had a way of breathing life into the ambition I had yet to fully understand. In the turmoil and disappointments I faced, it was impossible to see any silver lining. I could hardly find the energy to search for one. My heart was sometimes too broken, and my spirit too weary to imagine that anything good could come from the chaos.

But healing came. It came from the dreams we tucked deep into our hearts. Time, though slow and often painful, allowed me the space to find the clarity I needed to look up again, to search for the light that had seemed so elusive. In my darkest moments, when hope felt like a distant memory, time gently reminded me that I could begin wherever I stood. I began to hope that no matter where I looked, perhaps it would be the warmth of the sun, beckoning me to step into yet another moment filled with possibility.

When I was nearly 80 years old, a young man I met in the United States asked if some innate desire from my childhood had driven me to pursue my dream. I had never thought of success as a desperate desire to become famous. In the words of Horace Greeley, "Fame is a vapor, popularity an accident, and riches take wings. Only one thing endures, and that is character." The value of a life, for me, has everything to do with a person's character. Whatever my dream may have been, it should not have distracted me from the man I was working to become.

I had come from a place where every challenge offered hope for a future. Hope made us believe that someday we too could become whoever we wished. In a place with few material possessions, hope was abundant, passed down from elders and parents whose faith in the future rested on the shoulders of their sons and daughters. A humble life in Foase had taught me much about a world I had yet to see.

And I was ready.

2

WATER FOR ROOTS

NATURE, SCIENCE AND A CURIOUS DESIRE TO CREATE

The applause was deafening. The makeshift audience of students was spellbound by my guitar performance. I was a young student, and my colleagues had never imagined that the boy they knew as Kwabena Boa could play the guitar with the skill of much older men. Their heads swayed from side to side as my fingers leapt from fret to fret. That evening, when the students refused to leave my performance to do their chores and requested an encore, the entertainer in me had found his voice.

The news quickly spread throughout the school that I was entertaining a group of students in the assembly hall. What began in a simple and unsuspecting way had drawn the attention of some of the most discerning audiences I would ever know. It took a lot to impress my peers, and perhaps It was that desIre to find an extra nerve within myself to prove my talent to a potentially merciless crowd that unleashed a passion to excel.

I looked up and saw Professor W. E. Duncanson, who briefly muttered something about what had captivated a few of the students earlier. Then, with a grin and an amazed look on his face, he said, *"My son, this is your life."*

"Why would this man talk to me like that?" I wondered quietly to myself. I reasoned that it was how most people would naturally react to a stranger's observation. I imagined he meant well, perhaps seeing a potential in me that I hadn't fully recognized in myself. He saw a musician with a natural gift for communicating through song and was kind enough to encourage me to pursue it further.

In my heart, the song never stopped. I kept playing, and for the next seven decades, those words never faded from my memory. But it was in that moment in the assembly hall that I thought to myself, "I will pursue this." Any time I played the words back in my mind, it felt as though I heard them for the first time - *"My son, this is your life."*

Ultimately, it was people with different perspectives on who I was and what I could become that helped shape me into who I turned out to be. All the situations and people I encountered watered my roots, and helped my guitar take me to places I never dreamed I would go. I have to thank Professor Duncanson for planting a seed that could blossom, because, as they say, words have incredible power to affect both the heart and mind. Looking back, I can see that his reassuring words to me were like water for my creative roots.

My earliest exposure to science came in 1949. As intriguing as some of the innovative ideas we had heard about were, I never grew up believing that science and creativity were reserved for only a select few. I didn't have any particular admiration for scientists, and for my part, I stumbled into that field of work. In a rather strange way, the creativity that arose from that environment stimulated my instinctive tendency to create.

I had been playing music long before I set foot in a laboratory, but there was always a sense that I could perfect my skill with the same meticulous approach. Nothing happened in a vacuum. It was a series of gradual actions, each delicately dependent on the one before. But there was still fear and doubt in my mind anytime I wondered about what I could do that would be novel and exciting. Perhaps it had something to do with the fact that no one usually leaves Foase, a remote village in Ghana, to invent anything. But that had not stopped us from dreaming and watching the rain fall on our imaginations. Whatever we imagined as children - no matter how far-fetched - was the currency that bought us a ticket into the world we had heard about but never seen.

My creative influences took a different turn in a boarding school several miles from home. I was among a group of 26 students admitted to Adisadel College from different regions of the country in 1949. Some of us were placed in the arts classes, while the rest were assigned to science courses, without much choice in the matter. I was selected to be among the science students, so I had to take courses like biology, physics, chemistry, and mathematics.

I wasn't thrilled to be in a chemistry class or any science course. As with most academic work, I gradually found my footing in the definitions and jargon. I certainly hadn't gone to Adisadel with the singular ambition of becoming a scientist or a doctor. Occasionally, other boys would talk at length about their dreams of becoming famous surgeons or pursuing other wild ambitions in medicine, and I wondered how I had mistakenly ended up with that bunch.

I worked hard at almost everything and desperately wanted to excel in everything I was involved with. That was my saving grace: a desire not to fail. I knew I either had to learn quickly, or I would drown in chemical reactions and lessons on human anatomy. My love for science came with time. A genuine curiosity kept me going. The strangest thing was that, while science occupied my mind, my heart never strayed too far from the arts. I was particularly drawn to English literature very early in my education.

Literature was engaging. Philosophy was mesmerizing. I found that the writers' choice of words were occasionally confusing or even strange. Often, they were both. However, the language and thoughts expressed through imagery were beautiful and enlightening. Even more, the arts interpreted life in ways I had never known.

Long before I could understand every word or meaning of any poem, I was incredibly fascinated by the eloquence of some early writers and their sheer mastery of words. For literature, there was a connection that I didn't have to try hard to make. The curriculum at Adisadel was structured so that students could study subjects like Greek and Latin early in the school year. We were all allowed to take other elective courses much later. Naturally, I picked literature. This would be my chance to let my imagination run wild and travel with the words of world-renowned writers and remarkable thinkers.

I read a lot about the Romantic Era and considered the artistic and intellectual years that began in Europe. The 19th century produced popular names like Edgar Allan Poe and Charles Dickens, among others. All of these writers left indelible marks on scholarship and what would soon become world culture. I was equally absorbed in the writings of great Greek philosophers like Socrates, Plato, and Aristotle. To this day, I remember how I would come alive, lying peacefully on a bench in the corridors of the royal palace or in the empty hallways of Adisadel College, reading Aristotle's works.

Looking back, I think I was more fascinated by the Greek philosophers because of some unusual similarities with my own background. I spent the most formative years of my life in the Ashanti courts with much older men as close friends. I did not pick them; they picked me.

They knew about some of these philosophers and would occasionally reference them in passing. They had stories about their past lives and what they had seen in Manhyia Palace through the years. I found their choice of words rooted in the Asante nomenclature curiously appealing. This was their home, and they knew everything a person ought to know about their homeland.

The conversations with the elders were filled with brainteasers and wise sayings that would often force a listener to think beyond the words they had just heard. After decades of training under the tutelage of other statesmen, the elders' choice of words was so clever that their meaning could be entirely different from what an ordinary person might hear.

Early Greek philosophers wrote with such wisdom and intellect, and the Ashanti elders spoke with the same remarkable mastery over words. Philosophy had a way of asking some of life's simplest questions, only to find that there were no easy answers. A love of such wisdom found another admirer in me.

Even at an early age, I was convinced that men like Aristotle and Socrates took time to think through any thought before they spoke. Their words were weighty, and the wisdom was piercing. They knew perhaps the value of their language and that their writings might one day become what the world would remember them by. As a teenager, I did not have to understand every word to know that they offered great insight into everything we saw around us and into elements of life that we lived through. Seventy years later, my quiet evenings reading *Plato's Republic* became cherished moments I wish I could relive. I would give anything to hold the torn edges of the books one more time.

Science gave birth to my inquisitive mind, but literature nurtured it every step of the way. A genuine curiosity opened the door. The attitudes of these studious men in Athens had a profound effect on me long before I held a guitar in my hand. It is no surprise that I started my music career with my final act in mind and legacy as my North Star. When all that is known of Koo Nimo the musician and all that remains of my life are my words through music, will the next generation find any value in the meaning of my lyrics?

The irreplaceable awareness for me, looking back, was that Koo Nimo was not from Athens or Corinth. I could be inspired by philosophers' works, but I would have to express my creativity through my own lens. Will all that I have said through song leave indelible marks on the minds of people around the world? For some, it could be a smile or a thought to ponder. It may even be a simple nudge. But maybe all these early influences helped me shed light on life and its nuances in ways most people would not ordinarily imagine. Just as science takes an idea and gives it life, words and rhythm give life to a song.

My earliest inspirations had set the stage to nurture my talents into a passion that would gradually outline my footsteps for the rest of my life. Somehow, I managed to become both my own worst critic and my most ardent enthusiast. I wanted to be perfect, and as a teenager, I was convinced that perfection might be within reach for someone who committed themselves wholeheartedly to any activity. It was much later in life that I realized that what I thought was perfection was, in fact, excellence. I had set out with a simple objective in life — to excel in everything I did. I wanted to master anything I touched. Excellent moments are worth all the time and energy it takes to achieve them. My mother said that too often for me to forget it.

In my teenage years, I was very fortunate to meet people whose faces and voices gave me the reassurance to push further. Creativity often possesses a person as a conduit with a message yearning to be heard. There is a story told of a musician who stood in court on an allegation of reckless driving. Something had distracted him, and even behind the steering wheel on a busy road, he could not take his mind off it. The only case he could make in his defense was that he constantly heard a sound - a B flat note - in his head while he drove. The musician claimed that he had been possessed by the sound, in B flat, to such an extent that he could not ignore it.

As strange as the claim may have seemed, it felt true to the life of a genuine artist, composer, and creator. A heart is often filled with thoughts and sounds that the mind doesn't always have the luxury of time to fully interpret or decipher, wondering which ideas will resonate with an audience and which ones may fade away. My own world, too, was gradually evolving, shaped by the profound influence of the creative mind. It was as though I was becoming more attuned to the unspoken connections between thoughts, sounds, and the emotions they would eventually stir.

Gradually, I was learning that all of us are born with elements of creativity and creative intelligence. We have the innate capacity to be creative if only we can dedicate ourselves to it and stretch our minds to harness it. The human brain is remarkably complex and absolutely fascinating in the way it develops, captures information and transforms it into messages. Many neuroscientists and neuro-biologists will quickly explain how the interaction of genetics and social environment affects the way the human brain develops. None is more fascinating than the truth that we are all equally capable of being creative; the difference is that few people actually make the time for doing so.

As the depth of my own experiences and lyrics deepened, I often wondered how each musical note could add color to the words and inspire the listener even more. If the roles were reversed, would Socrates, Plato, and his peers pause to be inspired by my words, just as I was by theirs? If music were to become my life, it should represent everything in life that I saw, felt, and wished for. The songs had to touch lives and be true. Before I knew it, that drive for perfection had crept into everything I did.

Years ago, I told a story about my late father. In the village where we lived, we washed clothes by hand, usually in large pans filled with water. The important thing was to be sure the water was used wisely because there was not much to waste. We would then hang the clothes on drying lines made of copper wire with rubber coverings. We trusted the sun to dry the clothes and hoped the accompanying dust didn't find its way onto them. I remember how, whenever we left the clothes hanging overnight, the rain would splash dirt from the ground back onto them. It was an excellent metaphor: the best ideas, left unprotected, would soon lose their grandeur.

My father was a perfectionist, and he would always say that he was the easiest person to please - if only we were willing to work hard. On the days when he came home to see his clothes still hanging on the drying lines, his world would fall apart. The norm was to remove clothes at sunset before the evening's cold air blew in. My father would inspect them thoroughly, as if he had never seen his own clothes before. When he saw anything that resembled a stain or a dirty spot, he would wash the clothes all over again.

It took a while for me to truly understand why he was so consumed with excellence, but he was aware that he had young minds watching his every attitude and did not want them to miss some of life's most important lessons. Maybe his hope was that his children would also find the same value of distinction in every fleeting moment, just as he did. Strangely, and in spite of how often that happened - and it happened often - my father never complained. In many ways, I observed him and wondered why he had such seemingly high standards, even for the most trivial things. I may never remember everything he told me or every song he sang to me, but the picture of him sitting next to the large pan washing his clothes is as vivid as if it were yesterday.

In my father's eyes, how a person treated the most trivial and inconsequential actions would have a lot to do with how they approached the big events in life. In fact, much of life is sparked by seemingly unimportant events, yet they often make the biggest differences. My father never asked his children to be perfect. All he wished for was that we would give our best and pay attention to the underlying rhythms of life that we could easily overlook. Little did I know that those same tense lessons from my father would be my first lessons in the pursuit of excellence.

In 1962, I went to England on a study leave. A few days after I arrived, I strolled into a bookstore and walked out with two books: the Holy Bible and the Oxford English Dictionary. I believe it was the late Nana Opoku Ware who once advised me that if I never read anything else faithfully, I should make time for those two. His admiration for the Bible and the dictionary likely stemmed from the fact that both had been widely used by scholars around the world and remained undeniably excellent literary works. I had first read the Bible in Methodist School and in church, but this was the first time I picked it up to explore the stories for myself.

The dictionary, in particular, became an invaluable tool in my journey of learning new words, their meanings, and pronunciations. My mind absorbed knowledge like a sponge, and I found great joy in the process. It was during this time that I was introduced to publications like *Reader's Digest* and the *London Calling* journal, both of which captivated me with their unique blend of language and imagery. These publications not only broadened my vocabulary but also deepened my appreciation for the power of storytelling and the ways in which words could paint vivid pictures, sparking my own creativity.

My friend, Professor Kwasi Wiredu, now a professor at Tampa University, was one of my early motivators to expand my knowledge through literature. Kwasi had been a few years my senior in both the Presbyterian school and Adisadel College. At Adisadel, we joined a reading club where we cultivated an interest in a range of literary works. Ultimately, reading and learning became permanent companions.

Some of my most impactful moments have come from quiet reading days. It's probably easy to say this now as an adult, but for as long as I can remember, I loved to read almost anything. Biographies, especially those of people whose lives offered a great deal of encouragement, had special value for someone like me who dreamed a lot. Every word sparked a thought, every thought spurred an idea, and every idea nurtured my imagination. They seemed to give me a glimpse into the lives of people I would otherwise have known nothing about.

Creativity is bringing something new into existence, and years after I left Adisadel College, I realized that creativity was even more fascinating in a world filled with infinite ways to convey an idea. Unlike objects like gold, diamonds, and precious minerals, which are ultimately finite, imagination is not. The notes and tones that combine to form music will never end. There is infinite potential for music to produce something novel.

When an idea travels through the mind, our response to it and ensuing actions yield a creative moment that may reveal something the world has never heard. That is creativity to me. A musical instrument has an unending capacity to bring such moments to life. However, such an adventure requires a great deal of time, effort, and dedication. Coming from Foase's creative milieu, these notions became remarkably impactful early in my life.

The sources of creative inspiration were abundant. Both pain and joy offered moments that called for reflection and admiration. In times when my heart was weighed down with sorrow, words would often flow from within me. Years ago, a strange moment of creativity emerged from the aftermath of my father's death. A heavy sadness lingered over my family, and while I hoped that, in time, I would find the strength to move forward with a song, that moment was not yet.

The grief was too fresh, and the words, though there, needed more time to take shape.

Opanin Kwame Amponsah died in 1970. I had just arrived home from Manchester, United Kingdom, when I received the unfortunate news. As was our tradition, the family went to the cemetery to perform the final rites. It had rained earlier in the day, and the ground was so muddy that we could not dig to fill the grave with dirt. The last thing we wanted was to walk away from an open grave and leave my father at the mercy of the rain and dew. I would have to return to the cemetery with my nephew, Kwadwo Bonsu, with a pickaxe and shovel to cover the grave.

On my way home, I couldn't shake off a nagging discomfort. I had not been able to leave my father's grave in the honorable way any son would want. The most inexpensive thing, the dirt we never thought of, had become the most important thing. It was in this somber, grieving contemplation that I wrote the song "Maame Me Papa Wo He?" This tribute to my late father translates to "Mother, Where is My Father?"

"Maame Me Papa Wo He?" tells the story of a wealthy man who fell ill with a terminal disease. He left all his wealth to his wife to use in raising their only child. The woman mourned the loss of her husband and wept bitterly, hiding her own pain from her young son. Wealth and material possessions could not keep a grieving widow company in the way any person -especially one whose heart had been closest to us could.

On a rainy Christmas morning, the little boy sat quietly, watching his lonely mother at the window. She gazed out at the falling raindrops, her eyes fixed on the sky as if it held the answer to something she longed for. Each drop fell softly, lingering for only a moment before it disappeared, washed away as quickly as it had come.

It was Christmas morning, and the trees outside still held their green life. The poorest children in the village had received warm embraces and little Christmas gifts from their parents, who could not afford much more. The little boy, however, ached for that same experience. All the riches his father had left behind could not fill that simple void, a loving embrace. So he asked, *"Maame Me Papa Wo He?"* The words meant, "Mother, where is my father?"

His mother did her best to explain to her son that his father had died in a way that a little boy would understand.

"Your father is gone," she said.

"Gone… where?" the little boy asked.

"Unfortunately, he has passed on. He is no longer at home and has been buried at the cemetery."

The little boy looked even more confused as his mother tried to explain. Then, as he managed to wrap his mind around what his mother had just told him, he wondered aloud, *"So, would the falling rain make my father wet and cold?"*

In a life where mortality is fragile and the most precious things cannot be bought, all the wealth the rich man had accumulated in his lifetime and left behind for his family could not buy him an umbrella at the cemetery. Tears began to run down the mother's cheeks as she listened to her son's innocent attempt to make sense of the mystery of death and the brittleness of life itself. In death, a wealthy man leaves behind tears and pain just as piercing as the man without any material possessions.

When I wrote "Maame Me Papa Wo He?" one thing I had learned early in life was that the true measure of a life is found in the legacy we leave behind. In the end, when our life is helpless against the proverbial raindrops, the smiles we leave behind are much of what our life's purpose and value will be counted by. Who will watch raindrops and relive the joys we had brought to their lives? My father had lived a rich life, filled with memories and lessons that no one else could have taught me. How I wished he were here to listen to me play one more song.

Another of my biggest musical influences was the traditional proverbs, *Mmebusem*. Proverbs were woven into Asante history in what we called *Abakosem*. Whenever I created music, I couldn't help but weave such thoughts and ideas into the song. At a very early stage, I decided to let the meanings hang onto the rhythms as if to give a listener a way to pluck word after word and interpret my lyrics in their own way.

Proverbs and cultural oratory were my ways of infusing the genuineness of who I was and where I came from into my songs. Even for people who would understand the lyrics, there was always a deeper meaning embedded within. I had learned about Asante culture throughout my teenage years, but I also found that everywhere I had been and everyone I had known had prepared me for this moment in time. It had been water for my roots. My incentive as a creative artist has always been to transcend rhythms and sounds and to offer an even richer musical experience that is uniquely African and inspiringly universal.

The thought of creating music for a world far beyond my immediate surroundings has always been the driving force behind my self-criticism. I believed that it had to carry meaning not only for the creator but also deeply resonate with the listener. It wasn't enough for the music to simply exist. It had to evoke something real, both in the emotions of the one who created it and in those who experienced it.

I remember a song my group was to perform in 1981. A gentleman who had been part of my group used words that I didn't find appropriate. It seemed catchy or even popular at the time, but I thought it sent an unattractive message. I never released the original song. Even as a young man, I had become very cautious. If my audience were the men and women who had encouraged me to become a guitarist and the teachers who poured long days into my training, would my song make them smile, or would it make them quiver? It started with the simple concern that people would hear the song, and I didn't want to spend the rest of my life explaining what it meant.

That feeling of responsibility evolved into the kind that I placed upon myself, knowing how my unique influence in society ought to serve a greater function than just entertainment. Odomankoma Nana Nyankopon had blessed me with an amazing platform, and I could not afford to miss the opportunity. Koo Nimo, the musician, may not be around someday to explain the lyrics and meanings behind the songs, so the only way I can pass on a priceless thought is to see my actions today as if they would be for posterity. Nothing would bother me more than if I did anything that would shame my family or dishonor my people.

Another prickly song I wrote with a friend was titled *"Onipa Nua ne Nkanka"*. The words literally translate to "Human beings are kin to termites." The main reasons I never grew fond of the song were its premise and the comparison to termites. I quickly expressed my disagreement with the association between humans and termites.

Despite the metaphors and personifications, the song simply didn't sit right with me. For me, a song was never just a song, it had to carry something deeper. What others might have viewed as a creative or artistic expression didn't resonate with me on that level. There was a part of me that felt uneasy about it, so I felt compelled to push for a change in the title. It wasn't just about the words, it was about making sure the song truly reflected what I felt inside.

Early in my career, one of my advantages came from being surrounded by a close-knit group of thinkers - sages in their own right - whose intellect and wisdom I could rely on. These were the men and women with rich life experiences and knowledge of both Asante and world cultures. They made all the difference in my work as an artist and had a significant influence on the rest of my life.

It was always a blessing during the creative process to have people to turn to when I needed to think through lyrics and receive valuable insights. I called them my "think tank," and they lived up to the name. One friend, Kwame Nsiah, had started writing proverbs at a very young age and had mastered Asante culture and diction. He had devoted much time and effort to learning, to the point where there were few things about tradition that he didn't understand.

There were days when Kwame and I would sit back, contemplating unusual words and their meanings. We would dissect Asante words and delicately play with phrases, as gently as a mother cradling her infant. Those long hours with Kwame served as a reminder that whatever I created, I was doing so for posterity. That sense of impacting generations and influencing thoughts long after I was gone drove me to pursue music with uncompromising passion.

As a creative artist finds solace wherever life leads him, I held on to the hope that any moment could inspire a thought. I spent much of my adult life working in quiet rooms, where I had ample time to reflect on life around me. I had fallen in love with the orderliness and the magic behind the uncertainty. The knowledge I gained sparked curious and novel thoughts throughout my training, because the nature of science gave causality to events we might otherwise consider ordinary or coincidental. There was a remarkable appreciation for how seemingly unconnected actions in life are all interrelated and how we create outcomes.

Later in life, much of what I did followed this same pattern of thought. The foundation for my creative path had been different from anyone I knew, perhaps because my roots were different, which made my branches unique and able to create their own shade. I would spend many decades finding new connections between guitar strings and deriving joy from turning harmonies into artistic expressions of life's many emotions. The curiosity to create is often born from a myriad of experiences, and mine was no different.

Looking back, if there were any artistic period I would envy, it would be the days of the great Duke Ellington. Those exciting years in music profoundly influenced my own life. Ellington is widely regarded as one of the greatest jazz musicians and composers of all time. Alongside him, the jazz pianist and composer Count Basie remains one of my favorite musicians, a figure of immense influence in music. I admired their creative instincts and how they transformed sound and music into masterpieces.

In my later years, I met some musicians from Duke Ellington's band in Manchester, England. Whenever they were on tour in London, I would find a way to see them perform at venues like Hammersmith, Odeon, and the Astoria theaters. It was these bands and great musicians that inspired me to hone my own skills and gave birth to my genuine passion for sharing life through guitar strings.

I quickly learned that ingenuity in music is a powerful avenue through which perfection and excellence can be brought to life. I remembered my years in Foase and Adisadel. All that I had witnessed during those years gave me a unique perspective on life. I made many mental connections in ways I could not have if the colors of my life experiences had been shaded differently.

It was early in my music career that I began to appreciate the sculptors and craftsmen whose work I had seen growing up. Back home in Foase, I observed how sculptors went to great lengths to ensure each piece was carefully created from unique pieces of wood. The grains and knots were always different, much like the melodies and rhythms that lived in the heart of a composer. The beauty of a wood carving was gradually unveiled from its natural imperfections.

Much like sculptors, not many people take the time to admire a piece of wood in its raw, natural state. It doesn't seem beautiful at first glance, just rough, discolored bark with an earthy scent. But only someone who understands its true potential can look beyond that exterior and see what lies within. Every time I held a guitar, I became that sculptor, holding not just an instrument but an opportunity to transform something ordinary into something beautiful. I wasn't just playing music; I was shaping something that, to me, had the potential to resonate on a deeper level.

As a young boy, I learned from Mr. D.K. Sam, the Fante catechist, that creativity took practice. I sometimes tell the story of an American student who visited me from Seattle, Washington. He had come to Kumasi to learn guitar theory and, importantly, the unique African sounds we infused into it. Maybe traveling more than seven thousand miles to come to me wasn't proof of enthusiasm on its own, but it certainly was a start. The student, committed to learning, found a joy only the guitar's strings can give. He practiced every day and every night. His fingers lived on the strings. He was full of appreciation for the creative energy surrounding him and the passion he saw in the young men he practiced with.

The longer I lived, the more I discovered how talent could not blossom without an unwavering commitment to learning and the pursuit of distinction. It is amazing how many people I met in my small world who wanted something but were unwilling to make the necessary sacrifices. It is the long hours spent practicing a skill, especially on a guitar when fingertips are sore with pain, that turn a student into what he envisions for himself. When you've pushed yourself as far as you can go, you may have reached that tipping point where you discover something new, even about yourself.

While I nurtured my own passion for music, I learned that excellence is born in the moment when the best advice you receive is a whisper to play through the calluses. The pursuit of accomplishment finds its strength when it hurts to practice and a person is on the verge of walking away from the guitar's strings. That is when I realized I would have to dig deep to find the inspiration to keep trudging along. Creative people do not have the luxury of idleness.

When the legendary Oscar Peterson died in 2007, the Canadian pianist was remembered for many things in his life and career, but none was more powerful than his devotion to learning. Oscar and his four siblings learned to play the piano from their father, a self-taught musician. Most people, however, do not remember him for playing with popular orchestras as a teenager or even his glory days performing for international celebrities like Ella Fitzgerald and Louis Armstrong.

In the 1970s, Peterson won his first Grammy with his talented trio, bassist Niels-Henning Ørsted Pedersen and guitarist Joe Pass, and went on to win seven more. At the height of his illustrious musical career, one trait that defined Peterson was his relentless practice. He immersed himself in the instrument, and just as a sculptor works through the night to transform a piece of wood into a work of art, Oscar Peterson discovered that talent alone would not make him a genius. He mastered the piano to such an extent that he was often said to have played 100 notes where other pianists might have used ten.

After Peterson suffered a stroke in 1993, he could no longer practice as often as he would have liked. Physical therapy helped him regain strength in his left hand, but he probably never went a day without experiencing the sacrifice that comes with working through pain and discomfort. Perhaps he lived every day with the same mantra that another innovator, Jascha Heifetz, lived by: "If I don't practice one day, I know it; two days, the critics know it; three days, the whole world knows it." Oscar Peterson's story taught me an invaluable lesson early in my career. Until everything in us forces us to stop learning and practicing, we can all push ourselves to go the extra mile.

While I was pursuing my music, I was also quietly shaping my career as a laboratory technician. In a way that I hadn't fully antici-pated, success in one area began to influence and enhance the other. My training at the Korle Bu Teaching Hospital in Accra, followed by my time at the Medical Research Institute until 1954, laid a foundation I would carry with me. When I returned to Kumasi to work at the Okomfo Anokye Hospital, I realized how the discipline and precision required in science had, in subtle ways, shaped my approach to music.

As a young laboratory technician still learning to find my feet in a vocation that didn't leave much room for creativity, I followed instructions rather than invent them. But when I held a guitar in my hand, I was in charge of the consequences. Perhaps those seemingly frozen hours in the laboratory were a perfect complement to my life as a musician because there was always an idea stirring deep inside me.

I was placed in the pathology laboratory, alongside a group working in the biochemistry department. The next six years found me at Okomfo Anokye Hospital, working as both an assistant and a technologist. I resigned from the hospital on the night of October 31, 1960. Less than 12 hours later, I had a new position at the Kwame Nkrumah University of Science and Technology (KNUST), also in Kumasi. At that time, it was called the Kumasi College of Technology.

Much of my earliest influences as a musician and a person had to do with the people with whom I shared moments and spaces. Some of my fondest memories about science come from working in the chemistry department under the supervision of Professor Emeritus Francis Addo Kufuor. I was in a world where precision and diligence were ideal traits. My roots had found a home, and my career had, unbeknownst to me, been planted in fertile ground that would bloom in its season.

In 1962, I earned the opportunity to pursue additional training at Paddington Technical College and Imperial College in London. I used every chance to discover new things in a new environment. I returned to Ghana in 1965 and later traveled to the University of Salford in Manchester, England, for courses in laboratory instrumentation, radiochemistry, and instrumental analysis.

Throughout my academic journey, I never truly saw myself as a scientist. Yet, after years immersed in that environment, I had unconsciously absorbed the work ethic of dedicated researchers, a mindset that would serve me well later in life. I found myself surrounded by scientists and individuals whose minds were brimming with tales of molecules and the wonders of organic chemistry. Their words deepened my own understanding, adding weight to my perspective and teaching me the art of seeing the many layers within every action, every sound.

The beautiful experiences for me were the opportunities to solve problems and sit next to thinkers as they brainstormed complex concepts. Gradually, my personality was refined in the laboratory in Kumasi. My genuine appreciation for creativity had found its nurturing soil. Creativity, as much as it is an art, may very well be a science. I have occasionally paused to wonder how I learned to play the guitar and how much I learned during the time I spent away from it.

Interestingly, there is an element of self-efficacy in the process of acquiring knowledge. Once you learn an instrument, it is likely that you will develop the aptitude for others. That may very well be the result of the creative root. Like any seed that is planted, my creative roots found their way through the winding maze of life, its ups and downs, and through what had been teaching moments for me. The artist Koo Nimo was soon to find his voice and confidence.

I met Dr. J.L. Latham in the small market town of Chorley in Lancashire, England. When I lived in Manchester for a few years, I would visit him on weekends to learn mathematics. In retrospect, these experiences with men like Dr. Latham, who explained mathematical concepts in ways any mind could easily digest, laid a strong foundation in my mind for scientific reasoning. My curiosity was about how traditional African drums, like the *atumpan* and *dondo*, could infuse the underlying principles of science and mathematics.

I dreamt of a day, not too distant in the future, when mathematicians in Ghana would explore the equations of sound. It would be a complicated undertaking, given the wide variety of instruments, all with distinctive sound characteristics. It would take a great deal of devotion and creativity. Music research has the potential to provide great insight into musical instruments and the science behind their sounds.

In the late 1990s, Kwame Nkrumah University of Science and Technology proposed that I turn my house into an extension of their Math and Physics Department. Part of me saw this as a welcome opportunity to assist in the development of African music in a way that would preserve the authentic value of our creative process. I met with the Forestry Commission in Kumasi soon after. I requested that they find a way to grow trees for a new purpose. The trees often used to create drums were mostly *tweneduro* or *tweneboa*, the local names for *Cordia millenii*. This could become the first step toward realizing the dream and setting the stage for future generations to delve even deeper.

My hope was that whenever the Forestry Commission cut down these trees, rather than discarding the unused portions, they would give them to the university. It could prove immensely beneficial to search for trees with similar acoustic properties to the ones used in drum-making. My audacious intent was that the Forestry Commission could invest in such trees and use limited resources in a way that would ultimately benefit our people.

I never went to school to study music formally. In Ghana, music students often received their formal training at institutions like the Winneba School of Music, the University of Ghana, or Cape Coast University. My humble beginnings had a rather unique starting point because I had to learn to play the guitar from any mentor who would teach me and seek any idea that could spur my creativity. When you are both your own favorite teacher and student, you can connect with the medium of learning much more quickly than most people. One lesson I took away from those years was that composing music is foremost an inspirational act.

Beyond inspiration, talent and effort take over. I found wings to fly when I met Professor J.H. Kwabena Nketia, from Asante Mampong in the Ashanti region. The influences that helped me excel in a music genre considered timeless and rich with cultural symbolism and significance continued. My professional relationship with Professor Nketia gradually developed through several invitations he extended for me to share my talent with any audience he was a part of. He spoke about what he knew and taught me everything he could. From this rich happenstance, which evolved into a friendship, I have always said that Professor Nketia was certainly more of an inspiration to me than I could have been to him.

His colleague was another creative genius whose experience I greatly tapped into: Professor Albert Mawere Opoku. I met him in 1960. He was the one who gave me the simple but life-altering insight that if I wanted to play guitar, I would be better off starting with a classical guitar. He believed the nylon strings would be easier for a learner to practice with and would also produce a richer sound. I found this thought appealing, long before I knew enough about guitars to appreciate the insight.

Long before Koo Nimo became a household name in Ghana, the two professors gave me a moment I would forever cherish. They invited me to a seminar at the University of Ghana in Accra. Shortly after the event, they asked me to come to a private office, where they handed me a gift. Draped in green gift-wrapping paper was the traditional Asante black cloth, *Brisi*. Traditionally, the *Brisi* cloth is worn in mourning, not something one would ordinarily expect to receive as a gift. There had to be some deeper meaning behind it.

Standing in the middle of the room, Professor Mawere Opoku explained that one of their greatest wishes was for me to live many years. Their prayer was that I would live long enough to give both of them a fitting burial when they passed away someday. This was a gesture that spoke to how they respected my work and my sincere effort to honor our traditions and culture. Receiving the gift remained one of the most touching moments of my adult life. For the two men, it was their way of passing on a proverbial torch and urging me to pursue whatever gifts and talents I had been blessed with. In doing so, I would live my life with a sense of purpose.

"Time has its boundaries, and no one can plough beyond them," Professor Nketia said. We are all mortals, rushing through time with every passing moment and day. Someday, when our life's work is done, we will leave behind a world we once had the opportunity to be a part of. Unlike me, Professor Nketia was an only child. His perspective on life took a different path, one where he had to learn as much as he could from his own experiences since he didn't have a brother or sister watching his every step to challenge and encourage him. He learned many of the songs he would later teach from his grandmother in Ashanti Mampong.

Despite his many accomplishments throughout his career and life, his grandmother's words stayed with him. I was fortunate to be one of the recipients of the wisdom passed down to Professor Nketia by those who lived in a time when children cherished quiet evenings spent with elders around a fireside.

Perhaps nothing was more important than having a heart capable of finding wisdom, not just in the grand, transformative moments but also in the quiet, ordinary ones. It was in those subtle instances that life often revealed some of its deepest lessons. Dr. Duncanson's words, though simple, carried a profound weight: *"My son, this is your life."* In a simple and unassuming moment, what I heard served as both an affirmation and a gentle reminder, one I would carry with me always. It was my choice to not take the words for granted, just as I appreciated the fact that the talents I possessed were not merely gifts to be taken for granted. It was my duty to nurture these talents, to protect them, and to devote my energy to allowing them to grow, to flourish in ways I had yet to understand. The journey wasn't always clear, but it was mine, and that alone gave it meaning.

As I moved through life, I realized that every encounter along the way held significance. Each person I met and every conversation served as an important marker on the path I was walking. Some encounters would offer words of reassurance, others would challenge me in unexpected ways, but all would shape my journey. There were times when I didn't find the clear and unmistakable signs I hoped for, and the messages of encouragement would be all that I had to nudge me forward. It was in those moments, though, that I learned the most. I came to understand that reassurance would not always come in the form I expected. It might be found in the lyrics of a song that resonated with my soul, or in the pages of a book that spoke to my experience. It might be a story shared by a stranger or the reflection of my own struggles mirrored in someone else's journey.

For every conversation I shared with people like Professor Mawere Opoku and Professor Kwabena Nketia, moments of learning, growth, and connection, there would be many more individuals whose paths I would cross. Some of these people would inspire me, others might challenge my views, and some would simply offer a kind word at just the right time. But all would contribute in some way to the richness of my journey. It was in keeping my heart and mind open that I would allow these encounters to deepen my understanding of the world and of myself.

There are times when I write songs, reflecting on composers like Mr. Entsuah Mensah, who, by all standards, would be considered one of the greatest songwriters of his generation. He was a major inspiration in my early career. His style and methodology have stayed with me. Unlike most songwriters, Mr. Mensah would often modulate, making it difficult to learn or teach his songs.

Modulation is the process of changing the key from one tonal center to another. Not many people successfully mastered the art, and Mr. Mensah's unique skill made him one of the creative master-minds and a favorite of mine throughout my adult life. Even now, years later, I still find myself aspiring to learn his songs, to share those remarkable tunes with a new generation who may otherwise never hear his name. His music continues to resonate with me, and I feel a deep sense of responsibility to ensure that his legacy lives on, through my own understanding and the stories I pass along.

Everything my early years taught me became the foundation upon which I built the rest of my life. In making music, I believe the words come alive first, before the sounds transform them into a song. Despite my brief time at the Manchester Music School, much of my style developed from not having the formal training that many of my peers had. As a classical guitarist, I initially learned by playing the songs of other musicians. Over time, when creating my own music, I started with the simple words and conversations I heard throughout the day.

The simplicity of this process created an outlet for honest dialogue with myself, and before I knew it, it became the inspiration for my next song. My guitar gently draped the words, and I allowed the sounds to flow freely, without restraint. Throughout this journey, I made sure to be grateful for every random event that sparked a tune in my heart. It was the simplest things that influenced me the most. Whether it was something I heard in a church, at a market, or in any random place I happened to be, the music I created spoke to situations and events that people could relate to.

I found that audiences not only listened to the songs, but also paid close attention to the movements of my fingers between the guitar frets. The musician I became had not set out to simply play the guitar on stage, but to communicate with a world beyond entertainment. The creative artist in me had much to say about life and its many facets, and it became clearer through the strings of the guitar. I made every effort to forge complex connections with the strings and frets, just as a scientist might mix chemical compounds in a laboratory. None of those years were in vain.

Perhaps the strings of the guitar helped me tell my stories in ways I never could have on my own. Each note seemed to carry more meaning, more depth, than my words alone could express. All of my influences and musical inspirations played a role in guiding me toward finding my voice, discovering my sound, and, ultimately, experiencing the true joy that music brings.

3

ALL IN A NAME

FAITH, FAMILY AND A HEART TO SURVIVE TIME

Ever since I was given my name, my life's path was carved. My faith and courage, along with my pain and tragedy, all came together drop by drop, like rain into a hollow pond. My life's most fortunate adventure was the opportunity to step through some of the most exciting years in Asante culture, customs, and traditions. I look back on my life, and I am grateful for every chance I've had. Like the fragrance of flowers plucked from a quiet morning field, all of life's colors and discolors, its sadness and laughter, come together to turn an otherwise ordinary life into one filled with beauty and joy.

I am a Denkyira, named after my grandfather Kwabena "Kokoo" Boa. I learned that the Denkyira people often added the name

Amponsem to every person named Boa. Much of our social and cultural identity arose from a need to express both the uniqueness and the native roots of a person. *Boa Amponsem* was the name by which my forefathers were known.

Foase Atwima, where I was born, had leaders who truly cared about our customs and legacy. Hence, whenever my family traced our roots, it led us back to a heritage where the only extravagance in our hearts was in our service to our people. The pursuit of music flourished in this environment, surrounded on all sides by drums, horns, flutes, and other musical instruments. The chief of the Denkyira at the time, Nana Boamponsem, made culture and tradition a priority for a nation that had existed long before the Ashanti. For many years, its people remained staunch supporters of customary sounds, traditional drumming, and cultural dances. We seized every opportunity to display the symbolism of human existence through artistic performances during celebrations and festive occasions.

In an effort to make his kingdom and power known to the surrounding regions, Nana Boamponsem ordered that the rhythms from beating the large gourds - what we called *mpintin toa* - loudly say *am-pon-sem*, *am-pon-sem*. The rhythm indeed spoke: *am-pon-sem*. The sound of the drums calling his name was meant to signal the strength, splendor, and spirit of the Denkyira to nearby kingdoms.

My family came from Nsuayem in the Denkyira kingdom, a village near Dunkwah, on the Offin River. My grandparents, Nana Mansa Tutuwaa and Kwame Tumfoo, did all they could to keep our family together. I learned from my father that not long after they arrived in Foase, a dispute led my uncle, Wofa Agyei Kyem, to the royal palace. Nana Prempeh II, who was the Asantehene at the time, ordered my family to return to where they had originally come from. After long days of travel on foot, my grandparents ended up in Nsuayem No. 2.

The only thing I vividly recall from my uncle's recollection of their seemingly endless journey was the sparkle in his eyes as he spoke. It was as if to say, "We survived." It was perhaps his way of reassuring me that no matter how life's adversity might push my faith beyond what I thought I could bear, I belonged to a family that had survived incredible odds. I was a *Boa Amponsem*, and I was never to forget that. It was in our name.

Later, I discovered that some of my family members had become heirs to the custodial seat in Nsuayem. It felt as though I was destined to become the ambassador of the culture I had been so blessed to be immersed in. Perhaps that was where it all began, a weight placed upon their shoulders to shape the family's destiny and impact generations to come.

As a young boy in Foase, I encountered many people who left indelible marks on my memory. There were men and women of character, like Nana Mansah and Maame Akua Fokuo, whose grit and audacity gave me courage. Their life's architecture became a blueprint for how I would build my own ambitions and remember my roots. In their unique ways, they made a profound impression on a young boy with a strong desire for music and culture.

Perhaps the luckiest element of my life was being born to parents who had a fondness for rhythm and music. My father, Opanin Kwame Amponsah, had been a guitarist and a trumpeter in the village brass band. He had lost some of his fingers in his youth while cutting kola nuts from a tree, so he had to creatively improvise where others would easily play an instrument. He only played music to entertain himself, and I never thought it occurred to him to make a career of it. My mother, Akua Fokuo, sang in a choir at a local Methodist Church. There was always music as the ideal companion to their long workdays. Soon, I found myself humming the words along with them. I listened closely, and even as a young boy, I gradually turned to the songs that replayed in my head for companionship. Music quickly became part of my childhood.

I was born into faith. My parents, like my grandparents, were active members of the Methodist church. In a home with devout Christians, I grew up with a clear understanding of God and faith. My reverence for God's omnipotence brought me unimaginable peace in my heart and comfort amidst the chaos that would unfold in my later years. As a young boy, I listened intently to *Twere Kronkron* - the Holy Bible - which established the foundation of my own belief.

Later, in my youth, I began developing my own perception of God. I had a deep conviction that God had created me, and there was always a reassuring calm that came with that thought. Even then, I knew my life would not be without its share of heartaches, but I also knew I would sail through them, just as my fathers had done before me. The Methodist songs I learned as a little boy echoed in my mind through the years, and they occasionally took on new meaning with every new life encounter.

Faith gave hope, even in the rain, and through much of life's deepest pain. I came to find that the ache in a heart is often subdued by a hope for the sun's ray. I quickly learned that one of life's often-ignored blessings is having lived through its ups and downs, and still having the energy to live a full life. Despite the tragedies of the years, I would not change anything if I had to do it all over again. I am thankful to have lived a life in which I can sincerely say I have no regrets. I certainly wouldn't change the people who were closest to me, who saw me through my successes and shortcomings.

Faith was what carried my young heart along trails where I otherwise wouldn't have known which way to turn. When my parents died, I didn't know much about life, but I certainly felt death's cruel sting. Over and over, it pierced me, each time sharper and more crippling than before. Then came a crushing tragedy in 1973, as I laid my eyes on my wife for the final time before she returned to the earth.

Overwhelmed by grief, I spent many Saturdays sitting by her grave, wishing I could hear her voice just one more time. In those years, five of my children also made their journey to the grave, each loss piercing a man's heart and gripping him with a pain no words can describe. But faith brought comfort.

In my youth, the religious works of prominent thinkers impacted my life greatly, especially in times of adversity. Through some of the readings, I found gentle reminders of the creator's intent for me not to stand alone. I had a family who carried me when I could not stand on my own so that sadness didn't drench my heart. I came across nuggets of inspiration, all of which made it so I didn't endure the sorrow of tragedy alone. I had a family to lean on. Whether in the village or in the Ashanti royal courts, there wasn't a feeling in the world that clouded the bright sun of a family's love. For this reason, no matter how far life took me, that was the one reassuring reality I would cling to.

Who I was wasn't an accident, and neither were the places where I spent some of the most instrumental parts of my life. Having grown up in Foase, I witnessed captivating elements of African traditional religion. At its core, I thought it was not too different from other religions around the world, and it piqued my curiosity early in life. I was surrounded by a fascinating shell of cultural awareness, something I would not have known in any other way. I was moved by the wealth of knowledge that walked along the quiet paths, and by how every conversation was a father's chance to pass on our ancestors' journey to his children. Many people didn't get the chance to walk in the steps I did and perhaps didn't see Asante tradition from where I stood.

Much of the traditional religion I knew marveled at God's creation and imagined how all of us were nothing but a tiny dot in an infinite universe. The countless stars, each holding stories of its own, were a reminder that beyond everything we knew, there was an unfinished journey that would take a lifetime to fathom. Perhaps, with a guitar in hand, Koo Nimo the artist could also add one more chord to this universe's song.

God was Twereduampon and Toturobonsu. In our reverence for God's awe and omnipresence, we called Him Ahunta-hunu. For the rest of my life, these foundations would guide my ambitions, like vaulted ceilings and ancient writings would guide another artist in another part of the world. Nothing could change what God, in His might, had in store for a man's destiny. When the tragedies of life knocked at my door, I was forever thankful that my heart didn't let the pain nurture any ambivalence. As a creative artist, everything that happened in my life was a chance to recreate a thought.

Traditional songs and rituals acknowledged a certain majesty, which expressed itself in the nature around us. We sang:

Ɔkwan atware asuo
The path has crossed the river
Asuo atware kwan
The river has crossed the path
Opanin ne hwan
Which of you is the elder?
Yebɔɔ kwan kotoo asuo no,
We cut a path and it went to meet the river
Asuo yi firi te te,
The river came forth long long ago
Asuo yo firi odomankoma oboadeɛ
It came forth from the creator of all things.

My family members were my first teachers in every aspect of life. My boundless curiosity was never discouraged, even when it filled a day with more questions than my parents had answers to. As a boy who would later become a musician, I was surrounded by a wealth of knowledge in the home where I spent my early years. There was a high expectation of excellence for all children, and it didn't surprise me that my father, who worked as a tailor, also sought to excel as a builder, farmer, and even a blacksmith.

My father bore the pride of a people whose history drove them toward ingenuity and brilliance. He taught me a little about everything he knew. At the time, I didn't fully grasp the tremendous value of those years, nor the significance of overcoming the odds stacked against our lives. In hindsight, I was fortunate to grow up in a place where men and women were constantly learning and striving to pass on their knowledge to their children.

Much of life in Foase was rooted in a matriarchal society, where family remained paramount over individual pursuits and dreams. No one stood alone. Our failures and triumphs were shared. The collectivist attitude ensured that we never forgot those who had made sacrifices for us to live our dreams. As I traveled in my later years, I came to greatly appreciate the pillars of this outlook on life. Long before Dutch sociologist Geert Hofstede shared his observations on the traditional African family in his Cultural Dimensions theory, the people around me were already convinced of the rewards inherent in interwoven dependencies in our social structure.

For us, the remarkable part was not merely thinking or living socially but knowing that our lives had not become isolated islands. We could not fight and dream solely for our own benefit. Contrary to the notions from the outside world about our Akan attitudes toward life, I grew up in a secure society where an individual's passion and uniqueness were celebrated unabashedly. I desperately wanted to contribute in any way I could, like the many men and women I had seen do the same. At the time, I couldn't imagine how far music would take me, but the passion to give my best effort drove every inch of my being. For the Ashanti, collectivism was an awareness of the social fabric and a recognition of how our actions affected the lives of those around us.

Every time I introduced myself with my birth name, people often wondered - sometimes aloud - how I came to be called Agya Koo Nimo. It was back in 1955 when I returned home to Kumasi and joined Antobre's Band. I truly enjoyed every performance, as though I were my own audience, and it never felt like work. A year later, the Ghana Broadcasting Company offered me a fantastic opportunity to join a trio whose work would be featured on the national radio. The group was named the Koo Nimo Entertainment Trio.

For the Akan people in Ghana, "Koo" is short for Kofi, meaning a boy born on Friday. However, in some regions, especially in the villages, "Koo" was also a term of endearment for a true child of the community. I also knew that "Nimo" referred to someone who stands in and takes the blame for others - a meaningful name to live up to. My identity would soon come to embody everything that the name represented - woven together with strands of culture and song.

Adjekum T.D.B.'s stage name appealed to the producers, so they kept it. As author Andrew Kaye puts it, "Koo Nimo is an Asante sobriquet with ironic and rustic overtones. The name well-matched the mix of guitar band music, highlife, folk songs, and comedy which the group performed." Two years after our first performance, Adjekum left the group. The remuneration for a 30-minute program was 7 shillings and 6 pence, which was barely enough for a musician to live on, and it often took a long time for us to get paid, adding to the frustration. I occasionally led the group and carried on the band's name, so I became Koo Nimo.

Koo Nimo the musician is a product of a village no one knew about. Koo Nimo the artist came from a world not many people would have reason to visit, and my lyrics would someday become their window into what Foase had been for me. From the very start, I found it incredibly important that my name, my words, and my songs found a home in the hearts of the people I wanted to connect with through music. The stage and spotlight gave me a platform larger than I had imagined. The six strings grew louder year after year. My only wish was that I never created a rift between my sincere heart and my wildest ambitions.

The name Koo Nimo kept me connected to elements that represented the simple life. The authentic relationships and the genuine interest in the world around me were signs of the man I was to become. Every time I returned to the village, I cherished every opportunity to play music for the local elders and their chiefs. The music had become my compass, guiding me home. It was a rare chance to learn about our history and wisdom from those who had lived it.

Destiny wanted me to reassure the younger generation of a life we held in our own hands and to transform our work into a voice that would be loud enough for the world to hear. Standing here and looking back on my life's journey, nothing gives me greater satisfaction than knowing I did not forget my village, my roots, and my people.

I will be the first to say that I learned much about my history from people whose lives were fully immersed in it. These encounters and experiences redefined my life, and perhaps that's because they painted a clear picture of how nothing in my life had been a coincidence. As it turned out, Kwabena Boa-Amponsem and Daniel Amponsah became Koo Nimo. Later in life, the term "Agya" (meaning "father") - an expression of admiration for an elderly man - was used by many to introduce me. I had become a father to a culture whose son I would always be.

Like most people, my journey was not without pain. I bore deep scars and shed many tears. The bright days brought sunshine, while the darkest nights left their agony. Yet, I have always attributed everything I am and everything life has allowed me to become to God, Nana Nyankopon. My gifts and talents became the foundation of a life I never imagined. At every turn, I encountered people who nurtured my passions and fueled my most audacious expectations.

Whenever the people closest to me believed in my dreams, I believed in them even more.

Before I decided to become a musician, I was a boy walking the dusty paths of a village, humming songs. My life's path has been just as dusty, with every new day and turn revealing my life's true potential. It was often the simplest gestures that made the biggest difference in my life. In the lives of the people I met and read about, I found the strength to forge ahead. The men and women in my community became like family to me, and in their words and embraces, I found comfort.

From a distance, I admired Dr. J.B. Danquah and his grey hair. It seemed as if every strand bore its own story, wisdom, and lesson of a remarkable life. I prayed that I too would live long enough for every hair on my head to turn grey and that my life's journey would encourage someone else. I was privileged, even as a young bystander, to witness the leadership and conduct of Nana Prempeh II, Nana Opoku Ware II, and Akroponghene Nana Ansere Ababio. They were great men who inspired a people as they built a nation.

As a boy, I also admired Sir Winston Churchill of England. Everything I knew about Churchill came from books and newspapers, but it almost felt as though I had walked beside him for a brief moment in time. I thought of him as remarkably sophisticated, eloquent, and learned. Coincidentally, in 1965, my son, Barima Kwaku Gyasi, was born in the same hospital where Sir Winston had been born—Saint Mary Abbott's Hospital in London. If there's such a thing as serendipity, that is one coincidence I always found interesting.

Much of how I saw my family evolve became the foundation of my own yearning for a family that believed in each other's dreams. More than anything, I wanted a family whose hands would guide weary feet and encourage a dreamer to stretch his imagination, even along the gloomy pathways of life. I took a cue from my early years to shape my own.

Life took a sudden turn when my sister married the Asantehene's brother, Nana Kwame Bonsu, in the early 1940s. The late Otumfuo Opoku Ware II was the Asante king at the time. All I knew about the royal family came from what we heard in the community or saw on television, just like any outsider. I moved to live with my sister in Kumasi. My life was no longer filled with an empty routine, as it would have been for other boys. I had been immersed in tradition and a rich culture. I would grow up in a royal court and in the company of profound wisdom, gaining a new perspective on life and the world.

To this day, I remember the days before important festivals and celebrations like the Adae and Odwira. Large crowds would gather to celebrate our heritage and history. One after another, ceremonial horns and master drummers would entertain the crowd with tributes to the rulers. I felt an incredible sense of belonging and hoped that one day, I too would take my turn.

Fortunately for me, the people with whom I spent most of my days understood the significance of our culture and took the time to explain it to the children. Little did I know that I had been thrust into a life-changing training that would shape my worldview and provide a foundation for my ambition throughout the next decade. Everything I would become as a man had been ingrained in the deepest parts of my heart.

Like the waves in an ocean, my dreams were swept toward a perfect shore where I stood hand in hand with the woman I loved. I married Theresa Afua Owusuwaa from Asante Domenase near Tanoso. She was a beautiful woman whose smile brought comfort to a young, ambitious musician. The best partner for a dreamer is one who understands that much of life's story has yet to unfold, just like the songs I was to write. Love is always a journey into an unfamiliar world. Her smile kept the dreamer alive when all else seemed to drown around him. Her hands held the joy in my heart when the day's troubles left a void.

A person is never fully prepared for all of life's joys and sorrows, but a life partner makes even the most unexpected and sharpest pains worth enduring. Afua Owusuwaa became that partner for me. Together, we had ten children, all of whom were a reminder that the most precious thing in life is having a family as your anchor. What joy it was to share even the most uneventful moments with those we are blessed to have in our lives, even for a short time. What death took from us, only Nyankopon's unchanging hand gave us the grace to live through.

I soon discovered how life never has much meaning until you look into your child's innocent eyes and catch a glimpse of a pure heart. I loved being a father, and each child's uniqueness made this feeling almost impossible to describe in words. Tragedy showed its cruel hand when we lost five of our children. The pain, which didn't ease with time, left a father with songs of despair.

Even after many years, I'm convinced that one of the toughest ordeals anyone can endure is the loss of a child. It creates an unbearable pain and a void in a man's heart that lasts a lifetime. The only comfort for me, if there was any, was that despite such tragedy, Nana Nyankopon's watchful eye nursed a father's wounds and helped him stand strong.

I could never have imagined that my journey in love would end so soon. Afua Owusuwaa died on 21 September 1973. She had just given birth but lost her life. What gave life, took hers. Afua's death left a deep emptiness in my heart that only the grace of time and a family's love could soothe. I spent many days sitting by her graveside, wishing that my memory of her would be enough to comfort a grieving heart. Even after the tears settled, my heart remained too heavy to be still. Perhaps fate knew I would survive again.

At first glance, life seems to be nothing more than a simple sequence of events. But nothing could have prepared me for Owusuwaa's death, neither my father's passing nor, certainly, my mother's. When you take the time to peel away the layers of each day and moment, you realize how unpredictable everything truly is. No one can foretell the lonely days or predict when the sunny days will return. The joy in each moment is what we peel away. If life is anything like a tangerine, the bitter days of our past will eventually give way to beautiful moments. This metaphor came to me years ago, and I find it a fitting expression of life's uncertain paths.

In 1974, I traveled to St. Monica's Training College in Mampong. Professor Hyland and his wife had been teaching piano to students and invited me to come and teach guitar and traditional music. It was a quiet afternoon when we sat down, the wind blowing peacefully. I leaned back in the chair, my hands resting on the guitar's frets, my mind sifting through memories.

When I first played the song *"Odo Akosomoeei,"* Professor Hyland insisted that we record it. This was the first time he had heard the song. *"Odo Akosomoeei"* expressed a striking thought: how fragile life can be and how important it is to cherish every day we have with our loved ones. This was a sobering reality that I knew all too well.

Professor Hyland volunteered to fund the recording expenses at Mr. A.K. Badu's studio in Kumasi. With 13 students from the St. Monica's Training College Choir, I recorded the song. Although I later recorded different versions of "Odo Akosomoeei," this original recording had a distinct clarity to it. It was the first tribute to the memory of a remarkable woman who had such a profound impact on my life. As I walked through the edges of life, I discovered that, indeed, music can soothe pain. Yet, often, the last person to experience this reprieve is the musician.

The close family connections formed early in life don't always strike a chord for us until much later. The ray of sunshine comes when we look back at the memories we formed and come to appreciate the affection that gave us the strength to carry on. In my own world, gripped by grief, I had to keep a family together. I also knew that the daunting task would be to cope with a broken heart and live beyond a heavy cloud. Yet, overwhelming feelings can create a deep well for a song.

As a musician, I still had to travel and continue my musical journey. Some of the memories had become heavier than others. The only semblance of consolation was that perhaps I was here because Nana Nyankopon wanted it this way. Maybe my destiny was outlined in this manner. Perhaps the words from my lips had to come from a place in my heart that was pure and sincere. The world heard my songs, and often the events that unfolded in my life reminded others of their own. My life as Koo Nimo, the musician, had intertwined with millions of lives around the world, so I continued traveling and sharing my music.

A few years later, I met Amma Asibuo, and once again, I learned how unconditional support and genuine love can bind and hold dreams, just as they fasten the hearts of a family together. I had been blessed to fall in love again. I needed her, all of her grace and strength. We soon married and had five children. We were again burdened with grief when we lost our youngest, our kaakyire. I thank God for the good fortune of a great woman whose heart calmed every uncertain moment in my life.

My children brought immense joy to our home. From the start, each of them had unique talents and personalities that set the course for their lives. Whatever talent Nyankopon had bestowed upon them was nurtured in our home. There was no pressing reason for any of them to follow in their father's footsteps, but if the sound of music appealed to their ears, I wanted to be there to help them.

Whenever I think back to not forcing my children to play guitar, I remember so vividly the words of the classical Greek philosopher Plato: "Do not train a child to learn by force or harshness. A child's passion is often best brought forth when nurtured genuinely." Plato also wrote, "Direct them to it by what amuses their minds, so that you may be better able to discover with accuracy the peculiar bent and genius in each."

It seemed children didn't always immediately enjoy my company, perhaps because I studied at every turn while children would rather play. I didn't just listen to music for entertainment. I enjoyed the art and the creative interplay within a song. I had always been captivated by the thought of acquiring knowledge and learning new ideas, but that was understandably not a child's idea of how to spend their leisure time.

In my experience, the nature of my genre of music was such that the diction and lyrics were often too weighty and philosophical for a child to immediately grasp. This reinforced my need to incorporate storytelling into my music style. For audiences around the world, I had to explain music and culture they had never encountered before.

I always had guitars and traditional drums in the home. My children had the chance to explore any musical instrument that satisfied their curiosity. That is an opportunity I wish every child had. Some of my children gradually picked up the guitar and other instruments in their spare time, while others didn't until much later in life. As a father, I find satisfaction in knowing that I didn't pressure my children to become replicas of Koo Nimo. Whether that was a good or bad decision, I may never know. What I do know is that I find great peace in having done what I felt was best at every stage of my children's lives.

One of the most rewarding things has been seeing all of my children embrace the arts and music, in whatever form they chose. I admire their creativity and their deep appreciation for Asante culture and music. I hope that one day, my children and grandchildren will look back and remember a father whose pursuit of life's passions never made him lose sight of what mattered most—his family.

Years after my children had settled in different parts of the world, some became excellent drummers, mastering the fontomfrom, atumpan, and kete. My instinctive urge to teach gave my children a superb understanding of Asante culture and traditional music, while also placing pressure on them to excel. Music provided them with a unique lens through which to understand the world. My father passed on much wisdom over the years, and I hope I did not miss the opportunity to do the same for my children.

In 1998, I met a man from Kumawu during the Papa Festival. He was born in 1898, and despite having lived through a century of life's inevitable ups and downs, he still had as many questions about life as anyone. Perhaps this was a testament to the fact that, in life, we will continue to learn as we grow. It does not matter where one comes from; what makes the most difference is the impact one's life has on the future. We will continue to discover new surprises along our journey.

The old man pulled me aside from the festive crowd. He had heard that I had sung the popular song *"Yaree Ya,"* meaning "the pain of sickness." He, too, had endured life's ups and downs. I asked him how I could grow to his age and still find the courage to embrace the miracle of each day, as he had. He smiled. "Look back at your own life up until today, and make every effort to eliminate everything you've done that you know wasn't your best." Age and honest reflection reveal great wisdom to us all. I could even recall my parents saying the same thing, but without my own life experiences to filter their advice, the meaning didn't resonate until now.

The old man's advice was simpler than I had expected. Much of what we do in life may seem important at the time, but age and time help us uncover the true depth of our actions. I thought to myself, if I make a deliberate effort to change the habits in my life, I may very well live to 100 years. It seemed like a fair proposition, something I could manage. Each of us has the free will to steer our lives along the paths we envision.

In my transition from a young man from Foase to an international figure whose rendition of Ghana's cultural story was to be shared through guitar strings, I've always been profoundly grateful for the people God placed in my life. The places I've been have nurtured me, and the people I've met have encouraged me. Some traits and idiosyncrasies became a part of my character without much effort. I've always pointed out that perhaps my time in the royal palace at an early age instilled a sense of value and an awareness of how influence can inspire generations to come.

There was always joy in living. I learned a great deal from even the most unassuming circumstances. I have walked hand-in-hand with misfortunes and disappointments. As far back as I can remember, I have found it easy to make choices, even the tough ones. I didn't particularly fear making mistakes or suffering their consequences. If it was in my power, I did my best to avoid choices with ambiguous outcomes. Yet, I lived my life to the fullest. I took chances, always aware that even the darkest skies often held rain that could heal and restore. For this simple reason, I didn't want to reach the end of my life and wish I had done things differently.

Kwabena Boa Amponsem, my name came from mighty warriors and men with deep passions for changing history. That passion was also mine. I became a musician whose life's work was to be more than scales and harmony. I was determined to turn desire into something more expressive with words and even more captivating with rhythm. I had found that our minds embrace meaning when it's presented in a manner that aligns with the pace and context we are accustomed to.

For every accolade, I honored the predecessors whose rhythm and lyrics made me fall in love with the art of music. I became a musician identified with Asante culture, a responsibility I carried with great pride.

I became a young artist, but always aware that along with that opportunity came an even greater responsibility to safeguard the culture from which I came. My name and who I had been carried me along shallow shores, and soon it would be my turn to plunge into the deep ends of the ocean. But I would survive.

There is the truth that, regardless of how different our moments may be, there's always the chance of stumbling upon a new, unexplored stage, one I had not yet walked. For a creative artist, this is the strength that ignites hope. In my heart, this vision of the future is far more comforting than dwelling on shortcomings and wondering if my efforts were heading nowhere.

I have learned that the beauty of growing older is the peace that comes with experience. There is a deep appreciation for living life undaunted and with fulfillment. Having sons, daughters, and grandchildren to listen to, and sharing moments I never would have imagined standing under orange trees in Foase, makes life feel as if it has come full circle.

I was born with an opportunity to reach a world my fathers could only dream of. In hindsight, my life's toughest challenges pushed me further. Whenever the fear of failure sought my attention, I reminded myself of the sound of the drum under the village sun—ampon-sem, ampon-sem. I reminded myself that nothing in my life had been a coincidence. Nana Nyankopon's hand guided my feet from the quiet shades of Foase's village to the grandest stages in London and San Francisco.

Life had its ups and downs, but it was faith in God that guided me wherever music took me. Personal disappointment may have stung, but each new day brought fresh opportunities to rebuild what I had lost. If I had the chance to live all over again, I wouldn't change how my life unfolded or how fortunate I was to have done something I loved.

I've been married twice, lost a wife to death, and buried my children. That is a pain no man ever wishes to endure. Life has handed me my fair share of joys and sorrows. Perhaps somewhere in the middle of it all, it gave me the experiences I would one day share with the world through art. My only consolation has always been that the Almighty Nyankopon knows why things happen the way they do.

Through it all, the journey has been fulfilling. I am forever grateful for the family I've had. My children may never fully understand how much of my strength to pursue every dream and passion came from their smiles. While I never set out to make my children relive my life, it was my hope that I would be the best example of a human being for them. They gave me a platform to stand on, and that's something I will never forget. I hope I didn't miss telling them about any pages in the chapters of my life.

Story after story, year after year, I shared with them the places I saw and the people I met. My children have taught me some of the most wonderful lessons, perhaps even in ways that no school or brilliant teacher could have. For most of my life, I played guitar, perhaps more than anything else. I thought that if I could become the best guitarist my children knew, I would have convinced them to give their best to any passion they chose. It was their love that kept my heart close to home, no matter where my songs took me.

It had all been in my name. I had learned to survive by watching my father survive, but the world from which I came had been a strangely perfect journey in its own way. Life had indeed been a process, a learning adventure. When we face our biggest setbacks and wonder whether the sun will rise again, those setbacks may very well become the source of our greatest triumphs. When the guitar's song has ceased, when the audiences are gone, the musician is left alone - if only for a brief moment - to reflect on the words that had filled the skies around him. These are the moments that bring an indescribable peace to my heart.

It has made all the difference in the world to have a constant reminder of all that is most important in life. Family has been my most faithful friend, and I have had the rare opportunity to enjoy this love and support for decades and throughout my music career. For every cheer and every applause, there was the warm embrace of my sons and daughters, who made the sacrifices for a father to pursue his life's ambitions worth every moment. No tune or harmony can bring back the children I've lost or recreate the moments I cannot relive, but I have chosen to believe that it was all part of what made me the man I have become.

Koo Nimo was a child of his village, a voice on a world stage with his own story. The burden brought humility, and no matter where I went, I never strayed too far from home. What brought pain also gave way to hope and an appreciation for life. There has been tragedy, and there has been triumph. There has been death, and there has been life.

As if by some coincidence, the music I created preserved the connection between emotions and moments, carrying the messages passed down by the elders from their fathers and mothers. My story, my ambitions, and even my most gut-wrenching adversities all found their perfect chord. Nothing had been an accident. It never felt out of place.

4

SOUND, SONG AND RHYTHM

Nurturing a Passion with Palm Wine Music

Did I set out to be a folk musician, or did folk music choose me? Perhaps my life's choices and aspirations were more influenced by nature and nurture than pure coincidence. A guitar in a musician's hands is like clay in a potter's, with a world of possibilities open to them as far as their imagination can reach. The songs I was drawn to as a child, and the deep meanings they carried, set my heart on a course that would soon become my own. Maybe I intentionally chose to play this particular genre of music, but the longer I played, the more I discovered that elements of traditional sound had been woven into my very being long before I realized it.

Many music critics I encountered wrote about my *Adadam Agofomma*, also known as the Roots Ensemble (or *Back to the Roots Ensemble*), as the launching pad for my professional music career. Yet, my mind often travels further back than those years, to the days when I sang and entertained small crowds on my own. I had learned many of the lyrics to popular songs from our village, and my love for the guitar began back at Adisadel College.

Close friends like J.K. Barwuah and Kwao Sarfo occasionally joined me for performances. Fred Akuffo later joined the group. Our mutually complementary styles created a unique harmony in our sound. It was a bit nerve-wracking to think that our group could one day become as well-known as the popular bands of the time, but that was a journey we believed would be worth the sacrifice. The natural next step was to make it known that we were a singing group.

As a new band without our own distinct style, we played whatever songs came naturally to us and whatever we enjoyed. We decided to call ourselves *Agoro*, the word for performance or play. One thing we all had in common was a deep passion for music and the desire to use every musical skill we had acquired over the years.

Agoro was simply a group of friends who loved music. That was how we saw ourselves and everything we did. Our dream of what the future could hold had yet to take shape. Our group performed at local events in the village, mostly at funerals and parties where we were invited. We eagerly seized the first opportunity to entertain our community, and playing our music felt more rewarding than any payment could have. But no one paid us, so those early years came with their own challenges.

The excitement and realization that we were doing something we all loved fueled our determination to keep going. Occasionally, when we walked long distances to nearby towns and villages for performances, the event's host would give us a small token of appreciation in the form of money. For *Agoro*, that was satisfying enough. We clung to the hope that if we stuck together and continued honing our craft, our future as a band would be much brighter.

One day, the group was invited to perform at a local funeral, where we met Mr. Sweet. He asked if we could play any *Adadam* music. Mr. Sweet was a robust Fante man who worked at the Kumasi Municipal Assembly. He was asking us to play songs that would appeal to the older generation at the event. They wanted traditional music, but with a modern twist.

Adadam refers to "olden days" music, a style that would be called folk music in other parts of the world. The term often referred to anything from a previous era but was considered by some to be old-fashioned. We knew that many young people wouldn't typically gravitate toward *Adadam* music. We often thought that if not for our exposure to rhythms like adakem, tetia, and konkomma, we might not have fallen so deeply in love with that style. We were drawn to the stories and morals woven into the songs. Still, we wanted to do something different, so our audience wouldn't hear the same sounds over and over. Our goal was to create a new music style, one that projected a unique identity while still being rich with culture and history. This was our chance to highlight indigenous music but with a contemporary twist that could attract a larger audience.

Mr. Sweet's request was simple: entertain his audience and play popular tunes if that was all we could do. I turned to my friend Kwame Gyasi and said, "If we play *Adadam* music and want to be known for that style, maybe we should call ourselves *Agofomma* who play *Adadam*." That would mean "the children from the olden days." The band *Adadam Agofomma* hoped that this event would mark the beginning of our journey toward becoming household names. We made it our mission to accomplish something of lasting value, beyond the ephemeral nature of empty entertainment.

Soon after, on the night of Ghana's independence, we performed at the Kumasi Cenotaph. It was March 6, 1957, and the country was filled with euphoria. The sense of joy was unlike anything the young generation had ever experienced. They took to the streets to celebrate the nation's newfound freedom. The Gold Coast, as Ghana was once called, had been a British colony since 1901. Dr. Kwame Nkrumah and his compatriots had led Ghana to independence from British colonial rule. We all told ourselves that our country had entered a new era, where all our dreams could come true if we believed in ourselves and worked hard, just like our leaders had.

Koo Nimo and his palm wine quintet, now known by many as *Adadam Agofomma*, could not miss the historic occasion. We joined in the celebrations, and I remember playing the song "Nkrumah, Star of Ghana" late into the night. Often, I reflect on the vivid memories of that night in the country's history, and how strangely its impact faded over the following decades.

It was in this atmosphere that we learned about Queen Elizabeth's statement: "The hopes of many, especially in Africa, hang on your endeavors." But for many Ghanaians, nothing resonated as deeply as Nkrumah's words: "The independence of Ghana is meaningless unless it is linked to the total liberation of Africa."

The country's struggle for independence, and its efforts to define its identity and future, had led to this moment. Joy erupted. Seeing Ghana's flag waving on every street corner instead of the British flag was symbolic beyond measure. We all came together to celebrate the right to self-governance. The atmosphere was overwhelming, crowds cheered, and music echoed from every sidewalk. But beneath the jubilation, much work remained to be done. Everyone would be called to contribute, through their vocations, to preserve this hard-won freedom.

We would add our voices to making the struggle worth the price that had been paid. Soon, a new generation of hopeful Ghanaians would emerge as valuable contributors to the nation's future. So much life, sweat, and blood had been poured into securing those happy days, and the next generation bore the responsibility of carrying on the dream. While our band entertained on independence night, that deep sense of duty grew even stronger.

Adadam Agofomma still performed at small local events to build our reputation. We often stayed behind, plucking guitar strings long after the crowd had dispersed. The music never stopped. Whatever contribution I could make to my community and country would come through the music I played. The next step in our group's evolution would be to create our own music. Until then, we had only played guitar, *premprensiwa*, *toa*, *firikyiwa*, and *dawuro*. We had played the top hits of the time, reasoning that these songs were already recognized, and people could easily identify with them. It didn't take much to win applause from a crowd.

The biggest realization, however, which became our defining push, was that if we continued performing music by other artists, we would only be working for them. We could rehearse someone else's song for hours, but it would never truly be ours. If our group wanted to earn genuine respect and remain relevant to our contemporaries, we had to create original music. The challenge then was to create something unique.

From the very beginning, we all committed ourselves without compromise to develop our skills and to be different. It was a gamble, and we were fully aware of the potential pitfalls. Our niche would be to create a distinctive sound, unlike anything people were listening to. The audience needed to see life through our eyes, and our songs had to captivate the listener from start to finish. We were determined to achieve this.

At the time we formed Adadam Agofomma, the goal was not to amass wealth but to find joy and fulfillment in doing something we loved. I always hoped that there would never come a day when the charm of music would fade into a shadow of the past. Much of what became our lyrics could be traced back to the adages I had heard as a young boy.

I had always loved proverbs. The meanings, along with the indirect nature of the words, made a profound impression on me. They provided an artist with what I considered a dynamic platform to craft his own message. To this day, many people in Ghana view proverbs as a form of court language, a type of diction reserved for the cultural elite. This was the language often used in traditional jurisprudence—a sophisticated communication style, reserved for those with the intellect to interpret its deeper meanings.

Proverbs were more than just collections of words; they were expressions of wisdom, often revealing deeper truths. I was captivated by the way these words could be interpreted, and I longed to speak in such a manner myself. Some proverbs were short and clever, their meanings immediately clear upon hearing them. The metaphors were usually straightforward, yet they carried a depth that added a richer layer of understanding to the words.

As a creative artist, performing for audiences from all walks of life, it was essential for my choice of words to transcend both language and geography. What fascinated me most about proverbs was how the subtext of their messages reached beyond any single culture or location. The truths they carried were universal, resonating with people from diverse backgrounds and experiences.

When I moved to live with my sister in the Asante royal courts, everything I saw and learned there became the foundation upon which I would later build my music career. My motivation was genuine, and the rewards were pure. As a young boy in the Asante King's palace, I remember being chosen to hold the umbrella over the head of the Queen Mother, Nana Amma Serwa Nyarko II, when she left for official duties. I kept my eyes and ears open all the time, making sure I didn't miss any opportunity. I was incredibly curious, and my surroundings had become a treasure trove of creative inspiration.

Soon, accompanying the royal family to durbars and festivals became my favorite pastime. A simple task gave me a front-row seat to remarkable cultural performances. The traditional Adowa dance, with its swift footwork and hand gestures used for communication, caught my attention. It opened my mind to the creative depth of Asante culture in ways other children my age never had the chance to experience.

On festive days, especially, all the musicians from the town would come to the palace and take turns performing. There would be horns, orchestras, and bands paying tribute to the royal family and the Asante culture. Many of the songs included proverbs, and without realizing it, I was being immersed in their style. In the court, the use of metaphors in speech conveyed meanings that went beyond what most people were accustomed to. It was a mark of scholarship. The implicit comparisons and witty sayings would eventually make their way into Adadam Agofomma's lyrics.

Every child in Ghana would, at some point, hear the proverb, *"Oba nyansafo ye bu no bɛ, yɛn ka n'asɛm,"* often said by elders to mean that a wise child is the one you tell a proverb to, rather than speaking plainly. In Asante tradition, this saying played a key role in making ideas understandable, and it aligned perfectly with our music. Thus, it was fitting that Adadam's music would be rich with proverbs and adages that added depth and layers to our songs.

In 1966, the group released our first songs, "Owuo ton Adɛa a to Bi," "Nana Yaa Asantewaa," "Odonson," and "Owusu sɛma Ma." These songs offered more than just aesthetic value through metaphors. We preferred this approach as the ideal way to convey our messages, reducing complex storylines into simple words. Our earliest audiences, primarily an older crowd who appreciated the wisdom in proverbs, gave us a cognitive advantage and an added appreciation for our style.

My work with Adadam Agofomma remained a pivotal part of my career and the musician I would later become, nurtured by my friends and band members. For the rest of my career, I would cherish some of my fondest memories from my early performances with the late Dr. Kwame Gyasi, the legendary Oscar More Ofori, Kwao Sarfo, J.K. Barwuah, and Kojo Nyamekye.

In 1953, I returned to my village, Foase, to teach. It was then that I bought my first guitar, a South African-made Gallotone. The Gallotone was a steel-stringed guitar, which was good at building calluses and causing pain to fingertips, if nothing else. Most guitars on the Ghanaian market at the time had been imported from Europe. Ghana also had traditional instruments, one of which was the *seperewa,* sharing many of the traits of the guitar. African guitarists had emerged with sounds that reached far beyond borders, across the continent. Guitarists like the late Sierra Leonean musician Sooliman Ernest "Rogie" Rogers, known by his stage name S.E. Rogie, entertained audiences with unique African sounds.

Professor Mawere Opoku, who later became the Director of Choreography and Dance at the University of Ghana, introduced me to the classical guitar with nylon strings. I will always be thankful for the day he returned from Italy with a classical guitar. He advised me that if I wanted to enjoy practicing, I should use strings that would make the learning process less painful. His hope was that by doing so, I would spend more time practicing and continue to improve my skills.

Despite the variety of guitars that came to Ghana, I never turned away from the nylon strings. I spent countless hours practicing, drawn to the relative comfort of the softer strings compared to the harsher steel ones. It wasn't long before I realized that classical guitar suited my natural abilities and musical inclinations. It harmonized with my baritone voice and my tendency to weave monologues into my music. The nylon strings didn't overpower my words, allowing me to perform with ease, without straining my voice.

What I found remarkable was that Professor Opoku didn't hand the guitar to me as a gift. Instead, he made it available whenever I wanted to practice, which required extra effort on my part. Perhaps he wanted to spark a desire to unlock potential born of determination and self-discipline. Looking back, I realize he understood a fascinating truth about human nature—that we value an object more when it is just beyond our reach.

The passion for music and guitar took me across various places and cities I might never have visited otherwise. I learned songs from legendary musicians like Akwasi Manu, Jacob Sam (alias Kwame Esiar), Ekow Kantah, H.E. Biney, Appiah Agyekum, and Mireku. I took the time to learn their songs and accompany them on my guitar. Gradually, I developed a repertoire that was very different from my peers' but, importantly, one that complemented my voice.

The musician I would become later in life was shaped by long days spent under the scorching sun in Kejetia, the Kumasi lorry park. I had to walk several miles to get to Kejetia Market Square, one of Ghana's largest open-air markets. Despite the heat and dust, the sounds of the market inspired my creativity. Through the noise, I heard the music clearly, each time with new clarity. Sometimes I would sit quietly, wondering what I would hear next.

At the time, there were no buses or taxis to Kejetia from Foase, so I would walk, even in the blistering sun, to the one place in the world where I could hear all types of music. Gradually, Koo Nimo the musician emerged, and I began carving a piece of culture with every song.

Throughout my early years in music, nothing intrigued me more than how I developed a photographic memory. Being able to take mental snapshots and recall them with perfect accuracy made it easy for me to play popular songs I had just heard in Kejetia. I would sing them while walking to school. I often joked, "When it comes to music, I had my Ordinary-Level education at Kejetia, my Advanced-Level education at Kumasi's central market, and my university education in the Asantehene's palace."

Koo Nimo, the creative artist, wanted to tell stories through music. I wanted, more than anything, to share the thoughts and experiences of those around me. For my life with a guitar, I embraced Plato's words: "Music gives soul to the universe, wings to the mind, flight to the imagination, and charm to life." As an art form, its creative boundaries were limitless, and it was profoundly effective in expressing emotions that were otherwise difficult to articulate.

I saw the joy in people's eyes when I performed. That priceless reaction reaffirmed the path I had chosen for the rest of my life. The satisfaction never faded, even after decades of making music. The strangest thing about music is how even a baby, who knows nothing about the world it has entered, can pay attention to it and enjoy it. It must be a powerful medium of communication.

Music from a sincere heart, born from a life where I had little control over whose lives I touched, connected with audiences in ways that words alone could never do. Many years ago, I sang in the church choir and listened to the popular works of George F. Handel and Johann Sebastian Bach, but none of those gave me the pure joy I felt from making my own music from the things I saw around me.

Throughout my career, I often thought about how my genuine passion for music had been nurtured from humble beginnings by my grandmother Nana Tutuwaa Mansah. Whenever we visited her village, we found that she had enough of everything the family needed. She went out of her way to instill pride in us, encouraging us to be a reflection of the family, whose worth was not tied to material possessions but to a much richer human heart. I was raised to care about people.

Because of this, from a young age, whenever I heard of tragic events, my heart would sink. There was little Koo Nimo could do with his guitar, but I often hoped that my song would bring comfort and a smile to someone's heart. That was the inspiration that guided my long walks from performances at places like the Hotel de

Kingsway. Even when the venues were miles away, I was filled with enthusiasm.

My upbringing was simple. Even before I went to live in the Ashanti royal palace, I wasn't pressured by the desire for material possessions. This became an asset because I didn't sing just for money. Whenever I entertained, people laughed and cheered, and that alone gave me immense joy.

I remember how, occasionally, people would stop my group on the street and give us gifts. No matter how small, our true satisfaction came from the fact that we had shared our music as an art form, and the audiences walked away with smiles on their faces. Interestingly, such memories remind me of Brigadier Twum Barima, who served in the Ghana Army at the time. He would often stop his car along the side of the road to listen to us play, no matter where he was headed.

In Kumasi and throughout Ghana, highlife music dominated the airwaves and social events. Historians trace the origins of highlife to the 1800s, when Ghana was still known as the Gold Coast, under British colonial rule. Local instruments like the apentemma, firikyiwa, and donno all played important roles in creating an authentic sound. The Asante people, known for their inventiveness, had a particularly prolific sound style.

Other popular traditional instruments included the three-pronged bass sanza, called the premprensiwa, similar to a rhumba box used in Jamaica. Many learned to play the ntorowa, a hollow gourd rattle woven with beads and seeds. The nnawuta, two iron bells, provided rhythmic patterns, while the dawuro, a banana-shaped metal bell, and the donno, a squeeze drum, added to the sound's richness.

In 1954, I went to Accra to complete my courses at the Medical Research Institute. Even though I had little to do in the evenings, being a young guitarist eager to showcase my talent, I had the chance to sit in on rehearsals with popular bands like Gyasi's Band, Onyina's Band, and Kakaiku's Band. It was entertaining to watch them play, and I learned a great deal by observing how they managed their bands and the work behind the scenes that made their performances possible.

This was where I met Isaac Evans Maison, known as I.E. I later played with his band before returning to Kumasi to join Antobre's Band. Fred Akuffo and Ansong sang alto and treble, while Yaw Gyawu played the conga, Kwasi Kramo played the bongo, and Boakye played the maracas.

Long before I studied the intricate physics of sound, I took for granted the extraordinary creativity of earlier musicians who deciphered its elements simply by listening closely. This inspired a new generation to add their own variations to music. African rhythm, combined with traditional guitar, influenced a larger society and culture, much like jazz did in other parts of the world.

Until it found its place in the mainstream, highlife was a genre played for the upper classes. In most societies where social classes were distinguished, the commoners couldn't attend private events, where the wealthy could afford to hire entertainers. The story grew that the village people could hear the sounds but could only peek through windows. They would say, *"These people are living the high life."* Seeing people dance to a particular kind of music, seemingly enjoying life, was enough to make others think they were living the *high life.*

Over the years, highlife music has evolved. Artists have found ways to infuse other musical styles into it, attempting to add their own flair. I am fortunate to have lived through the decades that witnessed this creative transformation of the traditional highlife music that dominated the 1950s and 1960s. While the music may never be what it once was, the classic styles born of sheer brilliance and originality set the stage for people like me.

Stories abound about how early foreigners who came to Ghana sought entertainment from local musicians. The musicians invited to play debated whether to perform their own style of music or stick to the jazz and blues the foreigners were accustomed to hearing. They chose to play the music they knew. This was the era that would give birth to local legends and breathtaking performances from musicians like Kwabena Onyina, E.T. Mensah, and their contemporaries in highlife.

As mesmerizing as highlife had been at the outset, in the parts of the country where I grew up, it was palm wine music that ruled the day. *Sadwa ase nwom* - the Asante-Twi translation - described a palm wine music style named after the wine made from naturally fermented oil palm sap. That was the common man's drink. People would often gather in quiet areas of towns and villages while waiting for the *Obetwani,* the palm wine tapper, to bring his pot. The popular meeting point was under the big shade of tree branches. The people who sat here were unpretentious, and the men who came with their guitars had to speak their language. The songs reflected life through the eyes of the common man.

Palm wine music was born with an authenticity that neither the guitarist nor the audience could alter. Smiles and tears took turns on the faces of the crowd. While the men took long sips from their calabashes, they listened intently to every word, and the meaning in the songs influenced every moment of their lives. Gradually, that connection with people who shared the same hopes and fears as I did became a real joy for me.

I think back to January 1961, when I was invited to perform at a music award event in Accra. Some of my songs were considered, alongside works by other notable musicians of the time, in the highlife music category. Professor Mawere Opoku objected, arguing that my songs were much different from highlife and that palm wine music should be in a separate category. The *Sadwa ase* style of music came from the Akan words "Nsa" (drink) and "ɛdwaase" (gathering). This was the first time a style that had won the audience's applause was to stand on its own. Gradually, something that had started with a few musicians sitting leisurely under trees, playing guitars, would be introduced into Ghana's mainstream music.

For as long as I could remember, my bands performed in small entertainment venues, before people who genuinely appreciated what we did. Audiences listened intently, some sang along. It wasn't until I went to Britain in 1984, at the Commonwealth Festival in London's Holland Park, that I discovered how much the distinctive sound of palm wine music had become our differentiator. Even for international artists familiar with highlife music, this was something new, deeply infused with intricate patterns and progressions.

The palm wine guitar style was characterized by thumb-and-finger picking, with a series of complex chords assembled into simple melodies. Perhaps it was this interlocking style that made the learning curve steeper than it might have been. It differed from bossa nova or choro, which had more complex chords combined into more intricate melodies. In our minds, we were convinced that the focus of palm wine music was to eliminate complexity and make the end result simple so everyone could enjoy it.

In my own way, I gradually developed my skills to take my craft as far as possible, playing music to the best of my ability. I didn't compare myself with other guitarists. There was always an opportunity to learn from others and exchange ideas with my contemporaries. Even as my career began to evolve on an international stage, I was still, in my heart, the same young boy from a small village in Ghana. My humble determination was always to dig into my past for a traditional sound, which I had now shaped in the style of Odonson.

As my music career took shape, my hope was that someone, someday, would listen to a sound, a song, or a rhythm, and think of Koo Nimo. I consciously decided not to merely imitate other works but to find my own path. The people I wanted to reach with my music were from Kumasi and Accra, Wenchi and Takoradi, Sunyani and Foase. Soon, my audience expanded to include people from Mali, Uganda, Nigeria, Senegal, South Africa, and Burkina Faso - Africans sharing my culture, traditions, and language through art, some of which was strikingly similar to their own. A world was opening to me, one that would take my music to huge auditoriums in America, Europe, and Australia.

The people who listened to my music wanted nothing more than to identify with my lyrics and stories. I had brought Asante culture to them through music, and they wanted to understand every word. They were farmers and doctors, teachers and students, painters and craftsmen. They came from all walks of life, but the common thread they shared was Koo Nimo and his guitar. If I had seen myself only as an entertainer, I would have only entertained. But by seeing music as a powerful medium to connect minds and cross boundaries in ways nothing else could, every performance earned its worth.

I had become a musician with no formal training, so I learned to play the guitar the same way a few people I knew did. We watched others, practiced every day, and kept an ear attuned to the guitar strings to pick up even the softest sounds. This had been my training — many years spent listening to harmonies and chords. The only difference for me was finding out what I could do differently to create my unique sound.

I once met Jacqueline Smith Bonneau, the jazz pianist and niece of the legendary Thelonious Monk. The encounter was particularly fulfilling because I have often said that my music career was heavily influenced by Monk's talent. Even after his death, his group, Sphere, continued their remarkable creative journey, entertaining audiences. Jacqueline gave me a copy of 27 handwritten compositions. Later, in 1981, I flew to New York to be part of a documentary film, *Thelonious Monk: Straight, No Chaser*.

Produced by Clint Eastwood and Bruce Ricker, the film told the story of the jazz legend's life and how he connected with audiences in ways many musicians could only dream of. It was deeply inspiring to contribute to the legacy of a genius who had once inspired me to dive deeper into my craft and pursue my own career.

Creating new harmonies from simple patterns was a fulfilling exercise for me. Chords that became part of my repertoire included flatted fifths, diminished sevenths, and suspended fourths, as well as major sevenths and sixth chords in second inversions. The key difference was a fundamental technique following simple logic. In my own way, I thought about a guitar chord in a way an eight-year-old could understand. If a child could grasp the logic, as complex as it initially appeared, I could find a clever way to make that sound easy to incorporate into our music.

The influences on me as a young musician were gradually shaping my voice. My interest in internationally celebrated artists had evolved by then. Over the years, I had listened to a great deal of jazz music, from Duke Ellington, Wes Montgomery, Charlie Parker, John Coltrane, and Count Basie, to works by Antonio Carlos Jobim, Laurindo Almeida, and Thelonious Monk. I had discovered how jazz music had its early roots in African American communities, which retained African rhythms and influences such as polyrhythms and improvisation. I was drawn to the variety in artistic presentation, its audacious sophistication, and its simplicity.

Just like the mentors I've had, both near and far, connecting with audiences was essential to me early in my career. Every time I performed *"Abrokyire Abrabo,"* I shared a story from 1962, when I studied in England. The cold winter snow blanketed every inch of the city, and the rain didn't help. London was incredibly cold. I joked about "that terrible winter. It was so cold that the elephants in the London Zoos had to drink champagne just to move."

Having lived in a warm climate all my life, the sudden cold breeze, likely one of the coldest winters I would ever experience, came with many memories. The elephant joke always evoked laughter, but more importantly, it highlighted the shared experiences that we all bring to this journey of life. On one such occasion in England, 300 parliamentarians burst into laughter throughout the performance.

At other times, I recalled sayings from my boyhood, such as "Chop money was the perpendicular bisector of marriage." Jokes and aphorisms have an uncanny ability to connect with an audience. The humor never overshadowed the message, and I found that even when people didn't remember the tunes, they remembered what made them laugh.

Chop money was a slang term used in Ghana to describe the money a husband leaves on the table for his wife and children's upkeep. When the *chop money* didn't appear, the marriage often hit a rough patch.

From the winding paths in Foase, I never could have imagined my guitar reaching the stages I would perform on throughout my career. What set me, Koo Nimo the musician, apart was my African identity. My attire could speak volumes and cross language barriers before I even sang a note. It helped that I would always be associated with the people I represented and the culture from which I emerged. This was the very dream of my forefathers, and what their own fathers had strongly encouraged. It was carefully woven through my music and the Adinkra cloth I wore.

For all my life, I have been an African who found value in discovering a world of beliefs, customs, and knowledge accumulated over time. If there was one thing I knew how to do, it was to be an African. Whenever I saw a British or American musician perform, they wore traditional outfits, often a black suit and tie or an elegant dress. It only made sense, then, that whenever I performed, I would dress in a way that not only made me feel comfortable but also represented who I am.

The presentation of the music became just as important to me as the songs themselves. In 1976, I was invited to an event at the

Smithsonian in Washington, D.C., in the United States. My uncle, who was Akroponghene at the time, gave me *danta* to wear with my cloth. We also wore our traditional *kyaw-kyaw* or *ahenema* sandals.

The exhibition of culture was always incredibly significant to me because we did not have the luxury of forgetting that for many people around the world, *Adadam Agofomma* was their only window into Ghana's culture. There were times we performed without wristwatches or eyeglasses, as neither accessory was associated with African culture. This attention to detail started when performing for traditional elders, where custom required musicians to remove such accessories. Eventually, it became a habit.

Whenever I've discussed odd cultural contexts in music, I've often compared them to a person drinking beer from a traditional *calabash* or a woman dancing *adowa* or *kete* in high heels. Some elements of life are odd together, and these two combinations were certainly among them. People who've tried these combinations say that the palm wine never tasted the same from a wine glass. It may have been a figment of their imagination, but some things simply do not fit together. As a musician from Ghana, I wanted all of our performances to be authentic, and that meant that even the seemingly insignificant appearances had their own value.

In 1980, I accepted an invitation as a visiting Senior Lecturer at the University of Cape Coast in Ghana. I taught traditional music, including the six-string harp-lute *seperewa* instrument. I found teaching to be one of the most transformative professions, as a person's mind and ability to capture information evolved every time knowledge was imparted. I had learned much before then, but I never stopped. The truth is, we can all learn from anyone and anywhere.

As I had convinced myself, I taught my students that traditional style music needed a well-matched traditional style, and I remember how the young minds unveiled perspectives I had overlooked through the years. I thought that being able to tell our story and sing our songs from our place of origin was the only way the world would see our culture and admire its uniqueness and authenticity.

The musician in me nurtured a passion I didn't even fully understand until I experienced some of my most exciting moments in life. More importantly, it was through reflecting on those moments that everything came full circle for me. At the end of the day, the true sound, rhythm, and song have to come from a place where the artist seeks to share new dimensions and information with anyone who listens. The people who will come long after we're gone will have to look back at everything we did and hopefully find some value in the words and songs we left behind.

Ghana has a traditional Sankofa symbol, which depicts a bird looking backward with an egg in her beak. One leg points forward into the future, but the bird looks behind to where it came from. The symbol represents a culture's regard for both its future and the precious moments of its past.

Koo Nimo, the creative artist, had to look ahead to a future where his palm wine guitar music would find an audience in every corner of the world. But equally important was a reminder of what his ancestors had dreamed of. A decade on a creative journey had not been a blur; the experiences had been a light that shone brighter with each string and every sound.

I met with Professor Mawere Opoku to discuss my burning question about the deeper significance of Sankofa. We spoke for hours about who our forefathers were and what they would have wanted us to guard through the generations. The value of the past is not only in the memories we find in history books but in unlocking an enduring legacy that shapes our present view of ourselves. This memory should instill a humble pride in what the Creator endowed in our ancestors, to be passed down to future generations.

Sankofa is a symbol that, no matter how far I traveled from home or how many smiles my songs elicited, remained permanently etched in my mind, guiding every step I took. Professor Mawere Opoku explained, "Any aspect of culture that does not select from the good practices of the past to replenish the present and cast a shadow into the future cannot stand the test of time."

Regardless of who sat in the audience, I always wanted to be the best Koo Nimo I could be. Looking back, I believe it helped immensely to have surrounded myself with people who held me to high standards. I remember an event where I was asked to entertain a Japanese delegation and government at the State House in Accra. Professor Mawere Opoku invited me to Accra to rehearse for four hours a day over four days, even though the entire concert was to last only 15 minutes. We were so engrossed in perfecting our performance that we could not rehearse enough. The rigorous practice paid off with the excitement from the audience. After a few more events with such a focus on precision and enthusiasm, it became easier to strive for excellence.

There was also a performance at the Alliance Française in Kumasi, where the audience gave our group a standing ovation. The same diligence and commitment to performing our very best had ripple effects on everyone in the group. We played guitar, *fontonfrom*, *adowa*, and *Adwubi kete*. My adopted son Noah traveled from Australia to participate, and Nana Yeboah from the Ayigya palace danced in a way no one had ever seen before. The pairing of Nana Yeboah's traditional dances and Noah's outstanding drumming gave the audience at the Alliance Française a show they would never forget. Years later, I still think fondly of that memory - the joy on the faces of the crowd enjoying our African music, played with such mastery and flair.

Like many artists I admired growing up, I knew that the only way to continue improving was through dedication and sacrifice. In 1988, I shared the stage at the Guitar Summit at the Lincoln Center - Broadway, New York City. I performed with one of Latin America's most celebrated cuatro players, Puerto Rico's Yomo Toro, who had recorded over 150 albums over six decades. Many called him the Jimi Hendrix of Cuatro.

Toro, for his part, sought to preserve the traditional Puerto Rican folk music known as *Jibaro*. Perhaps his influence made me even more confident in working to preserve my culture. For every new door that opened to me, the weight of its significance for Asante culture and the Ghanaian people was on my shoulders. The success of those memorable performances was not just in the joy of performing but also in knowing the difference I was making in my own society and sharing my culture's story on a world stage. It was refreshing to think about the opportunity I had to safeguard everything our forefathers handed down to us.

Between 1962 and 1965, I spent time at Len Williams' Guitar Center in London. This gave us the chance to infuse our experiences into every string and chord. Len Williams had emigrated from Australia to London in the late 1930s and became one of the most respected jazz guitarists of his time. He eventually focused on classical style and established the London Guitar Centre, where young guitarists like me could learn.

Through my previous encounters with Ivor Mairants, I met the late American guitarist Barney Kessel, known as one of the greatest jazz guitarists of the 20th century, particularly for his vast knowledge of chords, inversions, and chord-based melodies.

I came to Len Williams' Guitar Center to learn classical guitar. My first teacher, Janet Buckenham, left a lifelong impression on me - not just for her music instruction but also for her patience and kindness. When I was about to leave for Ghana, Janet's team asked me if there was anything I needed to continue practicing. I requested one copy of everything I had learned, both as a way to continue improving and as a teaching resource.

In 1964, on Janet's advice, I bought a classical guitar from Danish guitar maker Harold Peterson, and later, another from German guitar maker Oscar Teller. One of my fondest memories from London was when Janet referred me to another excellent teacher, Stella Mackenzie, whose office was near Dillon's bookshop in Central London. She taught music theory, specifically for classical guitarists, and introduced me to Jack Duarte. From every one of these talented people, I learned new concepts that seamlessly fused with my own style.

In one of my early visits, Jack asked me to play anything I knew. I chose to play a traditional Ghanaian tune. Jack had never heard anything like it before. He was speechless for a moment, then said, "This is you. This is your talent." His words took me back to Professor Duncanson's comment decades earlier when I was still a teenager at Adisadel College. Jack's blue eyes lit up, and a huge smile spread across his face. I played the *Sadwa ase* style while humming along, occasionally explaining the lyrics. Jack's encouraging advice was a powerful affirmation, and we remained lifelong friends.

When something that had once been a hobby became an incredible platform to reach the world, anyone in my position would pause to reflect and feel grateful for the opportunities life had given. The hours I spent arranging grocery boxes in London supermarkets for five shillings an hour gave me a window into the world of many others. It wasn't much, but sometimes life has moments where we have to make the best of whatever little we have. My mornings had once started with running errands on cold days for a Hungarian Jewish teacher, Mr. Berkovitz, who taught music theory. I will forever be grateful to him for allowing me to work in exchange for his lessons.

Later in my career, I discovered something interesting about myself: more than making music, I wanted to communicate. I never could have imagined that the most fulfilling element of writing music would be how it inspired and challenged people. The true drive had always been the act of sharing a thought, and here I was, at the zenith of a young career, ready to soar beyond my wildest dreams.

One of the most fun moments was telling jokes between songs. It began during my days teaching ethics and etiquette at the University of Science and Technology. I brought elements of culture from the classroom to the music stage, and soon, audiences were scribbling my words on paper before I even plucked a guitar string. Once, I told the girls in the crowd, "Whenever you decide to fall in love, leave a small portion in the northwestern corner of your heart for yourself, because humanity is weak." Their experiences varied, yet they all knew what I meant. It was one thing to elicit laughter, but when people listened to life's lessons with a smile, that is what any artist would dream of.

My career unfolded into beautiful fragments, leaving memories wherever I performed. I recall meeting Joe Latham, who came to Ghana in 1968 to teach chemistry. After becoming a close friend, Joe was the one who genuinely sought to make sure my music traveled beyond the shores of Ghana. By the end of 1968, twelve of my songs had been published in English. Joe often spoke about how the lyrics and meanings behind the songs added a new dimension to his perception of the world.

Dr. Joe Latham became a teacher to me in ways he probably never imagined. He would respond to my weekly letters, and one day, when I asked him for his thoughts, he quoted George Bernard Shaw: "A miracle, my friend, is an event that creates faith." Maybe God leaves us the ability to choose our paths and commit to dreams on purpose, allowing us to find our own faith.

Joe believed that some events create faith, and others are created by faith. However random the universe may seem, nothing was more compelling to Dr. Latham than how a person's faith triggers actions and challenges us to act. Until his untimely death in 1991, I never missed a chance to share his immense contributions to my life, which have become the foundation of the legacy I aim to leave behind.

In Dr. Latham's opinion, the strangest thing about music was how it allowed us to communicate with people from all walks of life, even when they barely understood the words. That miracle lives in those moments. With his encouragement, we set out to translate my songs into English. Two decades later, twenty-one songs had English versions ready for international audiences. *Ashanti Ballads* was produced in Lancashire, England.

How Koo Nimo, a boy from Foase, a village deep in Ghana's Ashanti region, became a teacher inspiring young people who would never know the life he lived, must be a miracle. How the rhythms became a language, and how each string spoke in ways an artist could never have predicted, must be a miracle. How Koo Nimo found his way into world-class institutions like Harvard, Yale, the University of Washington, and the University of Michigan, and took a moment to wave back at an applauding crowd at New York's Lincoln Center, must also be a miracle.

My friend, Dr. Latham, would have said, "It was the faith in your culture and the stewardship of what your forefathers handed down to you that made it possible."

5

LOUDER THAN WORDS

A CAREER IN MUSIC, ASSOCIATIONS AND RECOGNITIONS

I sat on stage at the Great Hall in Kumasi. That evening, I was set to perform songs with the acoustic guitar, *dawuro, nnawuta,* and *premprensiwa*. I had embraced the next phase of my career, but nothing could have prepared me for the surprise awaiting me on the auditorium benches. The evening was as quiet as any other. The young students were supposed to be seated shortly and enjoy an evening of music with guitarist Agya Koo Nimo. The audience trickled into the auditorium. I sat back, watching as people walked out upon discovering I was the one to perform.

No one knew Koo Nimo. No one cared to hear what I had to say. Still, the show proceeded as planned. I was desperate for the night to pass quickly so I could walk away from my first disappointment as a musician. Chord after chord, the students grew increasingly disinterested. We continued playing. They began walking out, one after another. We had struck the wrong chord. There is perhaps nothing more heartbreaking for a musician than to witness such overt dislike from an audience. It pierces like a dull sword. This was the second time I had encountered disgruntled, sullen audiences.

The first time I faced such rejection was at the Center for National Culture. My friend Kofi Twumasi and I were performing a rendition of popular Latin chords. These were the classic styles many guitarists had learned, and we imagined the audience in Kumasi would fall in love with them as well. But nothing could have been farther from the truth. Audiences anywhere else might have given us a standing ovation, but we weren't just anywhere—we were in Kumasi. This audience booed. They were unforgiving. From the corner of my eye, I saw them walk out, one after the other. I should have trusted the lessons I learned from my experience at the Great Hall.

At the Center for National Culture, disappointment struck again. The dissonant chords with unfamiliar progressions were not what the audience had come to hear. The silence deepened our embarrassment. So, I did what I should have done at the Great Hall. This time, I stopped the performance. With the little courage I could muster, I pleaded with the audience to listen. A few had stayed in their seats, perhaps out of patience or sympathy, offering us the semblance of an audience. They probably wondered what more I could possibly add to the already gloomy evening.

"Thank you," I said. All I could do was thank them for the lesson in understanding an audience's taste for every performance. This is something I would never forget for the rest of my career. I should have known that audiences listen to entertainers and different kinds of music for reasons known only to them. They have expectations, and it is the artist's job to uncover them. The disappointment helped

me greatly, and I probably would not have learned this any other way. But beyond the frustration, there was a silver lining in the awareness that not everyone in an audience would appreciate my work.

I had never fully contemplated the idea that, no matter how hard I try, there would always be someone who walks away. As a creative artist, how you react to these circumstances can shape the rest of your career if you channel your energy positively. Every time I spoke with my friend Dr. Ntiforo, who was with me during the Great Hall performance, I was especially grateful for the courage to persevere in the face of adversity. I had learned that at any low point in my career, I needed to hold on to the last ray of sunlight and not give up on myself, even when some of the audience gave up on me.

Accolades and awards have never been my driving force in music. Perhaps that's why my heart never sank too deeply in disappointment, nor did it soar too high in celebration. In the end, the pain and joy in each of those moments gradually shaped me, slowly chiseling away at the parts of my career that needed to make space for the person I was striving to become.

My heart was immersed in music and culture, and both found a home on my guitar frets in a perfect interplay. They taught me lessons I couldn't have learned in any other way. Life has a way of rewarding us when we do something we genuinely care about, but the applause is seldom what keeps the songs alive in a musician's heart.

In the late 1930s, a palm-wine guitarist named Peasah first played *Owuo te se Nnoboa,* and Gyasi sang the same song a few years later. They were contemporaries of legends like Akwasi Manu and Mireku, all celebrated for their Sadwa Ase guitar style. I wrote a new version of the song in 1982. The word *nnoboa* has its roots in the villages, where one farmer could not clear a vast farm alone. As a result, a sense of community was born, where the men supported each other and worked together to accomplish once-overwhelming tasks.

My inspiration for the lyrics was probably not too different from Peasah's and Gyasi's, but I hoped to create a rendition that wove messages about community and relationships into it. The popular saying in our community was that "death is everyone's business." When our neighbor grieved, we grieved with them and offered condolences from a deep sense of belonging. For those of us who grew up in a village where belonging gave us a richer understanding of humanity's value, death was not a distant rumor. Just like *nnoboa*, Koo Nimo, the musician, was embarking on a journey he did not have to travel alone.

Musicians, like farmers, also knew *nnoboa*. We had to work together, playing in bands and lending helping hands where we could. When we sat under the palm trees to play music, we were a family, and this did not change when the stage became brighter and the audience came from near and far.

Recognition from Ghana's music industry came as a product of my work, and I learned to take the time to appreciate it fully. Each time an award acknowledged the sacrifices I'd made to climb a little higher, I was keenly aware of the responsibility to stretch my ambition even further. Maybe I wanted to express to the world a true appreciation for even the faintest applause. Even more, my story might uplift another person whose ambition resembles mine and whose resolve will someday lead them to a life with music.

Sometimes, we stumble upon opportunities at the most unexpected times. These were the moments when we had to remember what our talents mean to our community and anyone else listening. When a particular guitar's tune wasn't what I had in mind, a strum would produce a completely different sound, purely by luck. I had come to accept the fact that being at the forefront of palm-wine guitar music meant carrying a mantle to run as far as I could with the weight of culture on my shoulders. Hopefully, the unexpected moments would work in my favor.

Back in Foase, I had not become a musician to be a celebrated figure in my corner of the world. My name did not have to be on the lips of audiences around the world to convince me I had done my best. As a musician, I was living my life the best way I knew how, realizing that a person's leadership character only emerges when the years gone by shape their deepest insights.

In the late 1970s, Mr. Faisal Helwani asked my late friend Kofi Ani Johnson to visit me in Kumasi. This was a time in Ghana when there was very little strategic organization in the music industry. Musicians performed as solo artists or in bands across the country, and many more were looking to belong to a creative group to protect their work. Mr. Helwani had seen this trend firsthand and was determined to help bridge the gap.

Many artists lacked advocates or a vibrant musicians' union to create new opportunities for them. The music landscape was slowly taking shape, but it was still modeled on ideas from other countries. Some pioneers believed it would take a great deal of work to define our own path. In Ghana, musicians played their music and entertained crowds like any other artists. The challenge was creating a framework that would protect them in case of personal accidents, support their careers when record sales were insufficient, or during legal battles for intellectual rights. These were issues that every musician knew could derail their dreams, but no single song could alleviate the concern. Mr. Helwani's efforts were critical and timely.

This is why he encouraged me to get actively involved in the musicians' union. Our predecessors had dedicated much of their careers hoping for change, but the social landscape was shifting rapidly. New ideas were essential to build a framework for safeguarding artistic value and intellectual rights. At the time, writing music often led to piracy, with little concern for protecting intellectual property.

Both Jerry Hansen and Eddie Quansah had served as presidents of the group and made strides in the interests of creative artists. They had done their best with the resources available, but much more needed to be done. The loopholes grew faster than the practical solutions. At the heart of it all was the need to educate artists to fully appreciate the importance of a musician's union and contribute in any way they could. The challenges for musicians demanded someone to help carve a new path for the union. Kofi Ani Johnson assured me that I would not carry the torch alone.

I traveled to Accra to help the group begin this important work and breathe new life into the Musicians' Union of Ghana. It was an exciting prospect, though undeniably daunting. I had little knowledge or experience with copyright laws, but I had gained insight into other business operations that many musicians were unfamiliar with.

Back in Kumasi, I spent most of my Sundays at the Kumasi Cultural Center helping musicians understand their rights and the nuances of business contracts related to copyright law. My work with the union was to help musicians redraw mental frameworks to benefit from the cooperative. I had to give them a reason to stand in unison, just as different musical parts contribute to one melody. I needed all the help I could get.

Much of what I learned came from Mr. Mason, who had studied copyright overseas. He taught me about composers' and arrangers' rights, and music royalties. Mr. Anim Addo, who worked at the copyright office in Accra, helped shape the solid foundation of Ghana's copyright laws for creative works. We faced what we thought were challenges at the time, including music piracy, but in hindsight, it wasn't as widespread as it would later become.

Music piracy and the disregard for intellectual property rights had long plagued the music industry. Communication among musicians was scarce, especially for those in smaller towns and villages beyond major urban centers like Accra, Kumasi, and Koforidua. While record companies and musician unions struggled to find solutions for ensuring fair compensation for creative work, some individuals managed to illegally reproduce records. This issue was far from new, and musicians in Ghana were engaged in a relentless battle to protect their art and livelihood.

In 1979, I was appointed president of the Musicians' Union of Ghana (MUSIGA). I served in that position with Art Benin, Victor Patterson, Jedu Blay Ambuley as vice president, and Nana Ampadu as secretary. We hoped to usher in a new era of representation for Ghanaian musicians and enable them to protect their creative rights. Many distinguished musicians, including King Bruce, E.T. Mensah, and Kwao Mensah, also served on the executive committee.

If music was to remain a profitable enterprise for those who dedicated their hard work to it, while still providing the artistic fulfillment that drew people to music, we had to decide on a clear path forward. In a country where it was very easy for individuals to reproduce any creative work without legal repercussions, this was not going to be easy. We knew it would require bold steps and carefully planned initiatives.

Our challenges went beyond just financial struggles. MUSIGA faced a formidable task: convincing fellow musicians to come together for a common cause and form a unified platform for advocacy and access to resources. We emphasized that if we could stand together, musicians would gain a supportive network of creative individuals who understood their fears, dreams, and struggles.

A major step in that direction came when the famous British musician Mick Fleetwood and attorney Michael Shapiro visited Ghana in 1981. Fleetwood, best known as the drummer for Fleetwood Mac and inducted into the Rock and Roll Hall of Fame in 1998, was in Ghana as part of a collaboration with African musicians whose style, though different, was unusually complementary to their own. MUSIGA helped set the stage for what would become a truly memorable musical masterpiece. Fleetwood's management paid 100,000 US dollars as seed money to the office of the Minister of Culture, Nana Prempeh, and Fleetwood joined forces with other International artists to record the album *The Vision*.

Many artists soon traveled from the United States to Accra for the recording sessions. At the time, the celebrated John Lennon had just died, and Fleetwood asked us to create a song in his honor. With guitarist Kofi Twumasi, we mixed *kete ababan* to add our unique sound, vocals, and polyrhythmic percussion to the songs. The result was a piece of work that could only emerge from cross-cultural collaboration, which was rare at the time.

Charting a path for Ghanaian musicians was gradually taking its toll, but it had become rewarding. We discovered how much Ghanaian music had found its way beyond our shores and continued to offer audiences a window into highlife and palm wine guitar music. Three years later, I was reappointed president of MUSIGA for a second term. We had staff members as copyright administrators to liaise with government officials to help enforce copyright laws. After years of hard work laying the groundwork for a coordinated effort in the music community, its value had become evident. This was the first time many musicians received the royalties they were due.

In 1989, I was sent as part of a delegation to Mali for a conference with other international music groups. The organizers sought to use music as a platform for nation-building across African countries. The late 1980s were a time of political and social instability in parts of Africa, and uprisings often had a ripple effect on neighboring countries. To reverse this trend, Africans needed to engage in broader dialogue and seize every opportunity to foster peace. Musicians could use our platform to share messages of unity and hope.

In Ghana, there had been developments within MUSIGA, and differences of opinion were brewing. Shortly after returning from Bamako, Mali, I had to step away from my position in a union that was now choosing a new direction. Jewel Ackah became the president.

I had a great deal of unfinished work from those years, so I returned to Kumasi.

Though I was unaware of the unfortunate developments that followed, I accepted the group's decision. I did not regret the time and effort I had spent working with some of the most energetic and selfless visionaries I met at MUSIGA. The only thing I was concerned about was that my reputation would not be inadvertently tarnished. The comforting truth was that I had led the group honestly and with all the integrity in my heart. If there was anything worth salvaging, I wanted to walk away with a clean conscience, knowing that Koo Nimo had given his best effort to his peers.

Looking back, one of the earliest accomplishments of my tenure at MUSIGA was the emphasis on training and educating musicians in Ghana. There was no way to predict what future generations of musicians would become. We could only hope that the value of dedicating oneself to rigorous training as an innovator and true artist would not be lost. We often visited government officials at the Castle in Osu, Accra, to push for opportunities that would help musicians develop their talents. The MUSIGA agenda sought to provide creative resources for musicians. As I left my position, my only wish was that all the work we had done would not unravel. My prayer was that the strides we made, despite the colorful challenges we faced, would not vanish into thin air.

Where one chapter ended, another began. Life beyond MUSIGA did not become less hectic, as I spent most of my days working with the Copyright Society of Ghana (COSGA). Dr. Ephraim Amu, at nearly 100 years of age, was to be the chairman of the association, but he did not have the strength to manage its daily operations. He wrote to the government officials with the name of his recommended replacement. In 1985, I was appointed interim chairman in his absence.

Unlike MUSIGA, COSGA's primary focus was on copyright protection and addressing infringements. One of our first tasks was to work with the Ghanaian classic *Yaa Amponsa*. The musicians H.E. Biney, Kwame "Sam" Esiar, and Ekow Kantah, who had begun as the Kumasi Trio in 1928, had passed away, but they had recorded twenty-four songs, including this popular hit. COSGA played a major role in ensuring that any use of an artist's song earned the appropriate credit and compensation. *Yaa Amponsa* demanded such credit.

American musician and singer-songwriter Paul Simon wanted to use *Yaa Amponsa* in his latest production, *Rhythm of the Saints*. He wrote to seek permission through the Copyright Society of Ghana. These were the years when Paul Simon, known for his work with Simon & Garfunkel, was making waves in the music world. Incorporating the *Yaa Amponsa* tune into Simon's recording would highlight how music can transcend language and culture, building bridges across oceans and worlds. That was Paul Simon's hope. Cameroonian-born Vincent Nguni played guitar on *Yaa Amponsa*.

No sooner had COSGA become the industry's primary advocate for intellectual and creative rights than the group negotiated a sum of 38,000 US dollars as the first royalty payment to the Government of Ghana. I always thought this was a significant validation for the group, demonstrating the worth of our work. In turn, the government established the Ghana Folklore Board to oversee this new entity and protect the rights of Ghanaian musicians. As chairman of COSGA, my immediate priority was to facilitate the enforcement of copyright provisions.

When I was invited to serve on the National Folklore Board of Trustees, I had just turned 50. I was still finding my way through the new challenges and experiences that came with the role. It felt like a tremendous opportunity to continue contributing to the preservation of the cultural sounds we believed were vital to safeguard for future generations.

Twenty-five years after *Yaa Amponsa* was first heard, the song found its way into Paul Simon's timeless and classic recordings. The original composer remained unknown. The closest person to the original creator, who would be owed financial compensation, was Sam, but he had passed away in 1951. Under Ghana's copyright laws and the Berne Convention for the Protection of Literary and Artistic Works, the rights to a work are transferred to the nation 25 years after the creator's death. This was the basis for founding the National Folklore Board.

There were not many awkward moments, as one might expect from a group writing the rules as it went, but we gave every task our best. Many more songs' posterity would depend on our efforts, but for a group with limited resources, opportunities were not always kind. In truth, Ghanaian music had thrived long before my contemporaries took to the stage, but we saw every performance as a small yet unique addition to a gradually evolving genre. For what we were able to achieve for creative artists in Ghana, no award could fully express the gratitude and joy that even the memory of those years brought to us.

We remained grateful for any award we received along the way for the music we loved.

We were immensely indebted to people like lawyers Amegatcher, Larkai, Willie Amarfio, Nana Prempeh, and Nana Bosumprah, who dedicated much time thinking through the legal architecture and loopholes that could have become pitfalls for the association. Beyond their work, they were conscious of the impact every contract could have on the music landscape. Any success in this endeavor would go a long way in promoting Ghanaian music both at home and abroad. Institutions like hospitals and schools were exempt from making royalty payments, as we reasoned their goal was not to profit from our creative work.

COSGA had to lead the fight to ensure musicians received their fair share of every royalty. This was particularly challenging in our society, as the legal framework had not been properly defined. Equally important was our responsibility to ensure musicians were not forced to sign legally binding contracts that put them at a creative disadvantage. I often look back on these years as the formative phase of Ghana's music copyright system and the gradual transformation of our music from entertainment and art to a marketable product.

The satisfaction from long hours of work came from the results we saw in the lives of musicians who spent years refining their craft but had little knowledge of the commercial pitfalls in the industry. A few years into my leadership at COSGA, Ghana hosted an international music conference, where I was honored alongside Professor Nketia and John Collins. The memory of this event has stayed fresh in my mind, perhaps because of the stories and images of people we touched with our work. Every challenge we overcame was a ladder for musicians to stand on and reach for their own dreams.

I was selected as an Honorary Life Member of the International Association for the Study of Popular Music. Encouraged by this recognition, I found it refreshing to see the government playing its part in ensuring laws were enforced, though much work remained. My work in the association was a thrilling experience, like a man running through a dense fog in the middle of a desert only to stumble upon a creek.

Despite the lingering fog, there was a quiet sense of hope that our work was making a difference. Though much remained uncertain, we clung to what we knew, and that became our source of strength and reason to smile, even in the face of countless challenges. We had reached a moment in COSGA's journey where we could pause, look back, and finally take a breath.

In Kumasi, I met a good friend, Kwaku Kwarteng, a musician who had never received a royalty payment in his career. I encouraged him to visit the COSGA office in Accra, but he lacked the money for travel. We arranged for funds to be sent to him in his hometown.

For some musicians who lived farther from Accra, convincing them of COSGA's value was as difficult as convincing them to travel long distances. We successfully assisted Kwaku in earning royalties and the credit due to him. There were other talented musicians like Kwaku who needed an advocate, and their livelihood could depend on it, but they lacked awareness of what to do next.

Despite my workload, my heart never strayed too far from my passion for learning more about the guitar. The lasting impression was the message my audience took away from my music. This was the richest experience of all. Every performance connected me with people from different walks of life, each of whom found a common thread in a thought or tune. There was nothing more inspiring than singing a song that all of them would interpret uniquely and appreciate palm wine music even more.

One of the most humbling recognitions of my career came in 1991 when I received the Asanteman Award from Asantehene Nana Opoku Ware II. This recognition meant a great deal to me, especially because it came from the leader of the Asante people. I imagined it would mean the world to those who stood by my side, contributing their talents and unwavering spirits to our painstaking endeavor.

Much of the person I have become is due to the culture and Asante truths I grew up around. The musician I am today and the way the world knows me emerged from Asante traditions and philosophy. I have had the privilege of sharing the Asante story as best as I could, offering a glimpse into our world. The honor from Asantehene was humbling.

A few years later, Otumfuo Osei Tutu II honored me with another Asanteman Award. I had been in Malta at the time, so I visited the Manhyia Royal Palace soon after arriving in Kumasi. For my career's work, I've always appreciated the recognition from those whose opinions I valued greatly. It was always an opportunity to grow, and every honor served as encouragement to carry on.

The satisfaction of having achieved something meaningful was amplified when it came from your own people. These were some of the most unbelievable experiences of my life because I had imagined that any acclaim would come toward the end of my career, or even life, when the messages in my songs would have come full circle. To have been blessed with such recognition was more than words could express.

Koo Nimo, the artist, had gained popularity beyond the shores of Ghana. I attributed that to my work with international organizations and involvement in incredible music festivals worldwide. I often encountered people who knew more about my songs than I expected.

Throughout my career, I was occasionally surprised by how quickly my image appeared in magazines and publications around the world. Perhaps the lyrics meant more to people than I realized. Maybe the lantern of thought had been sparked by the strings of a guitarist from a distant village and continued to burn. I made every effort to use my experiences in song, just as I did with everything I discovered over time. My passion had been refined through the years, and the only pride I had was in the threads of my kente cloth.

As I engaged with global audiences, I soon learned that researchers of African cultural music and Asante traditions had found a musician they believed embodied the African story told from the Asante perspective. Perhaps my small contribution and introspection helped shed light on the way of life. It was immensely satisfying to know that the imagery of my traditional appearance was speaking volumes about the Asante culture in ways I hadn't had the opportunity to show.

I didn't set out to become a celebrated figure wherever I went. Every deep-seated passion I had at the start of my career was coming to fruition, one performance at a time. Whether I was a headline in a United Nations publication, mentioned in a BBC News segment, or celebrated by my closest friends, it didn't matter. I was driven by a dream to tell stories through music, and there was extraordinary peace in seeing my dreams come to life. My love for the guitar had become the faithful linchpin to any height I set my eyes on.

Eventually, I came to terms with the fact that being a public figure meant living under a bright spotlight for the rest of my life. Whatever opportunities my talent created for me, I also had the responsibility to present Ghana and Africa on the world stage to the best of my ability. I was determined to protect the zeal and pure enthusiasm that had once motivated me to hone my craft under the hot sun of Kejetia Market and along the dusty roads in Foase.

In 1991, I received the Flag Star Award from the Entertainment Critics and Reviewers Association of Ghana (ECRAG). This came shortly after completing one of the most prolific projects of my career. "Osabarima," which translates to "A Great Warrior," was composed by Gaddiel Acquaah and became the title track of my 1990 album. Soon after, my good friend Kwabena Fosu Mensah sent me several newspaper articles written about the song. It was intriguing to discover how the world perceived the album, but even more rewarding was seeing the project come to fruition.

The lyrics of "Osabarima" resonated differently with different people. It was as if our individual lives were running parallel to one another, and the only thing that cut across them was the song. I played the song to honor all the people we had lost along the way, those who had inspired the creative talents we had worked so hard to develop despite the challenges we had faced. I did my best to focus on what lay ahead. Despite the overwhelmingly positive reviews for the record, I didn't want its meaning to get lost in the whirlwind of praise.

A few years later, I received the Konkoma Award for my contribution to Ghanaian music. People often noted how my preference for traditional musical instruments and singing in my native Asante Twi language had defined my style. This was no accident. As an Akan, my roots run deep in history and culture. I could no more claim another culture as my own than I could take another person's mother as mine. This realization guided the rest of my career, and I sang about who I was and what I knew.

I used traditional musical instruments and worked diligently to create a sound rooted in tradition, with my native language being the most comfortable medium for self-expression. This approach gave me an extraordinary confidence in being my authentic self. For every contribution I made to society, the only thing that sustained me was the belief that the strings of a guitar mirrored a part of life we all know too well. The sounds may vary, louder or sharper, but together, the chords create something words alone cannot fully express. Perhaps this is what I could pass on to the next generation, along with a message of hope. Hope is contagious.

As a young musician, I saw how my passion for music made a difference in the lives of many aspiring artists. Though our journeys may have differed, we were all driven by the same zeal for creativity. I often told my contemporaries that at every stage of life, we may never fully understand how many people we have touched with our work, nor how our greatest moments often come from the chances we take.

Researchers have noted our tendency to emulate the motivations and attitudes of those around us, and how this gradually influences our own performances. I understood this truth early in my career, which made me especially mindful of the messages I was sending through my songs, and how they could impact other artists. My work with both MUSIGA and COSGA reflected this awareness; it was why our resolve was never deterred by our sometimes grim reality. If any young musicians found inspiration in me, I hoped my life and music would help guide them on their own journeys.

A few years ago, I had an interview with some prominent highlife musicians, and they mentioned Koo Nimo as a major influence on their careers. Much of the appreciation for my work has come from my peers. A new generation of musicians was discovering that their rhythm and sounds had roots in the same traditional elements that inspired many remarkable artists before them. These were people who had worked hard to find a platform to showcase their talent and originality.

I also had the privilege of meeting Kojo Antwi, one of Ghana's prominent musicians, at the University Guest House in Accra. He sat next to me and watched me play guitar for a while. It was clear from the genuine excitement in his eyes as he watched me pluck string after string. It has been heartwarming to see how he has since become one of the most successful African musicians of his generation.

It is especially reassuring to know that some of the people we meet along the way carry forward treasured messages through their own music, in their own way, despite differences in genre. Society's rapidly changing landscape often suggests that we're too busy to pay attention to the experiences unfolding around us. I caution others not to be too quick to walk past what is truly part of their nature and culture in search of something they can never be a part of.

During my years at MUSIGA, I hoped young musicians would remain grounded in cultural influences, using them as a foundation to tell timeless stories through song. When the day comes to reflect on the impact of my songs, I hope their true value will be seen in the unshakable desire they've sparked in the people I've encountered along the way.

George Darko, another excellent musician, was one of the first I met early in his career. I often recall with joy that George was my first official guitar student. His lessons were easy and fun, thanks to his humility and eagerness to learn, qualities I rarely saw in young musicians. He was excellent from the start. George went on to make a name for himself as an outstanding Ghanaian highlife musician, achieving stardom with what became known as Burgher highlife. In his celebrated hit *"Akoo ti Brofo"* ("A parrot can also speak the English language"), I saw traces of the same ingenuity that had marked many remarkable artists decades earlier.

I could never have predicted that my life would be shaped by such humble gratitude for every honor I received. I often thought of the people whose lives I studied intently, whose passion for hard work gave me something to aspire to. While many of the people we admire may appear in books and come from distant lands, I was fortunate to have my own culture as the guiding stars showing the way.

It was my hope that through any creative work, my fellow musicians would recognize the influences that traveled back to the quiet villages. The long nights spent advocating for musicianship in Ghana would soon be seen in young people confidently pursuing their own creative passions, inspired by people like Koo Nimo, who lived his life to the fullest.

In my work with musicians' associations in Ghana, I've had the honor of lending a helping hand to other Ghanaian musicians like Mike Ofori, whom I first met at the St. Andrews Training College in Mampong; George Ankuma Mensah, known by his stage name George Spratz; and William Afreh, also known as Paa Willie. Paa Joe, who played for the band Butterfly and later in Jewel Ackah's group, was a refreshing talent to work with. The classical guitarist Eugene Oppong Kyekyeku, who closely watched my guitar playing, never put his instrument down. It was a pleasure to watch him excel, embracing the beauty of the guitar's melody from the start.

Applause and awards reminded me that people were listening, and for that simple reason, the heart of my music had found a joy I could never have imagined. In 1997, as Ghana celebrated the 40th anniversary of its independence from Britain, I was awarded a Medal of Honor by President Jerry John Rawlings, as one of the country's distinguished citizens. I was humbled by this recognition. My only wish was that I had inspired people to identify the ways in which they could make a difference in the world.

At COSGA, someone once asked why I had never used my public persona to take part in politics or engage in the social discourse of the time. The association and the people we served were meant to remain non-partisan. This was crucial, as politics could have tainted the independence of the group. Our focus had to remain solely on advancing musicians' rights, regardless of our political, social, or cultural differences.

Throughout my career, I did not actively indulge in politics or use my music to influence the political climate, which was still evolving. While I had opinions on controversial events, I remained mindful of expressing genuine feelings through my music. The artist in me was always aware that a metaphor could inadvertently be interpreted as a political statement or propaganda, but that was beyond my control.

I reminded myself that I was, first and foremost, a musician. If I had something to say, I understood my responsibility to remain an objective reporter of events and perspectives. I have been fortunate to have lived through some of the most challenging, politically charged periods in society and still contribute to progress with an uplifting form of music. Just as one would send words in an envelope, I scattered thought-provoking ideas throughout my songs, without becoming a political tool.

I wrote a song, "A Dog in a Manger Policy," about the moral courage of a person who walks away from political office when they have ceased to add value to their country. Inspired by events in the 1960s, as many African countries emerged from colonial rule, it reflected the hopes of reshaping nations and the future that lay in the hands of public officeholders. While some leaders made remarkable changes, others overstayed their welcome, leading to uprisings and demands for change as citizens grew frustrated with leaders who seemed to abandon the people. The song was a broad observation of a continent in search of a post-independence identity.

Over time, Ghana, like many other African nations, found its voice on the world stage. I always encourage musicians to continue telling their stories, sharing observations from all walks of life. Decades after my tenure as the president of MUSIGA, if I have any advice for the next generation of artists, it is this: Unions must continue to educate their members in all aspects of life, not only music, but in life skills and business knowledge that are critical to success. I believe that if a group takes care of its members, it will endure, carving a place for posterity. For musician unions like MUSIGA, it is essential to encourage musicians to serve as the voice of their communities and to prioritize each other's well-being. The pursuit of excellence begins with valuing the creative contributions we make to society, an irreplaceable role that cannot be overstated.

I have been blessed by the high points of my career, which now lend meaning to the low points in ways I could never have imagined. Some moments have been like moving pictures of what honor truly looks like. On September 28, 2014, I had the privilege of performing with the National Symphony Orchestra as part of the 20th-anniversary celebration of the National Theatre of Ghana. It was an unforgettable event, showcasing some of my popular songs.

On stage with me were the Ghana Police Band, Tema Youth Choir, and my Adadam Aggofomma group. Dr. Pascal Zabana Kongo, a brilliant musical teacher, had shown great interest in my work and wanted to present my songs in an unusual arrangement with violins, cellos, violas, trumpets, and trombones. Dr. Kongo arranged eight of my songs, including "Naa Densua," "Osabarima," and "Otuo Akyeampon," with a passionate precision that preserved the essence of the original compositions. Songs I had once performed in the palm wine style were now being reintroduced to a new generation, with added flair and captivating arrangements.

What made it particularly intriguing was how Dr. Kongo's French musical orientation, being from French-speaking Zaire, brought a different perspective to the arrangements, something many of the Ghanaian musicians were not accustomed to. Some members of the orchestra suggested changes, but Dr. Kongo, though shy, responded firmly, "Play the song exactly as I have arranged it." The performances were breathtakingly beautiful. Dr. Kongo passed away a few weeks after the event, but it was an honor to see my life's work open a new chapter, and his admiration for my music was incredibly rewarding.

The foundations of MUSIGA were laid to ensure future generations would not face the same uncertainty we once did. The ripple effect of my dedication to the craft would touch hearts I may never meet. That, perhaps, is the essence of a legacy - an enduring legacy worth more than any accolade or applause. And they would be louder than words ever could ever say.

6

ONYINA

The best years with guitarist Kwabena Onyina

The best of friends are seldom the ones a person knows for most of his life. Only a few people get the chance to find someone to grow along with and are lucky enough to have them as a safe haven for their deepest fears and wildest ambitions. Occasionally, we bump into kindred spirits along life's journey, and they end up giving us the wings we most desperately need to soar. Such people are those whom God places in our lives. They find self-sacrificing reasons to help us smile when we need it most.

Kwabena Onyina was two years my senior, and long before his fans crowned him King, he was my closest friend. I first heard his music while in Accra, captivated by his boldness to experiment with new styles. His distinctive finger movements and fearless approach to music left a lasting impression on me. I could see that his innovation would be the foundation of a deep friendship, one where we could challenge and inspire each other, learning from our shared passion for music and life.

When I left Korle Bu Teaching Hospital in Accra after my Clinical Pathology program, I returned to Kumasi and decided to look for Onyina. I found him through a mutual friend, T.D.B. Agyekum. I had listened to Onyina's songs on the radio but knew little about the man behind the music. I had been particularly fascinated by his use of rare diminished chords and unique harmonies that added depth and richness to any sound.

In 1964, we quickly became friends. In a world where our talents sparked genuine curiosity in each other, I could not have had a better person as both my closest critic and my most loyal fan. Onyina never formally trained to read music but had developed a flawless ear for sound and learned to play his unique harmonies. Much of our friendship blossomed during our Sunday afternoon trips, where we played guitar at nearby schools.

Beyond the music, it was during such ordinary days that I was fortunate enough to discover a friend's heart. One Sunday, I couldn't join him because I had injured my calf muscle in an accident earlier that week and had to be admitted to the hospital for several days. Onyina came to visit me, and we spent the afternoon trading stories.

As I lay in bed, it dawned on me that despite his newfound success, not everyone knew the pure talent that was Onyina. I was standing next to a once-in-a-lifetime musical genius whose impact on music in Ghana was unlike anything I had seen. A legendary musician was among us, and we were all going to miss the chance to delve into his mind and know the man behind the rhythm. As a musician, he displayed his skill with such finesse and a mesmerizing ease that it was beautiful in every way.

Many years later, Onyina's reflection on the portrait of his life, shared with me while sitting in my hospital room, became the version of his story I hold most dear. In that moment, I saw not just the musician, but the man who had shaped so much of our journey together. I have always hoped that his story will continue to inspire and resonate with a new generation, fostering an appreciation for his life and the lasting impact of his work. His legacy, rich with creativity and courage, is one that deserves to be celebrated for years to come.

In the hierarchy of innovators in Ghanaian guitar music, I have always spoken of Kwabena Onyina as one of the most prolific and remarkable artists of his generation. He is one person whose influence on Ghanaian music will never fade with time. His excellence was likely rooted in his uncanny appreciation for life's inherent predisposition to change. In all the years I knew Onyina, he was always willing to do things differently and, in his own small way, to give creative excellence, even when no one asked for it. As I recall, much of my own success was nurtured in Onyina's company. That is a gift my friend left behind long after his time on earth was done.

Kwabena never stopped refining his skills. Whatever he lacked in formal music training, his passion for the guitar's unique place in music made up for it. For a musician who probably had enough talent to excel without much effort, Onyina found that he could never learn enough. He intently observed the finger-picking styles of some established guitar greats and kept his ear glued to the most elusive sounds of the guitar's strings. He continued to study his craft into his later years, hoping that the next generation would have a higher standard to live up to. The bar would only be high if he, Onyina, was determined to raise it with his skill. Onyina inspired newcomers to the music scene, many of whom would later become household names, to create even more admirable work.

I remember how E.K. Nyame, a Ghanaian guitar legend, had made his mark and built on the foundation laid by another brilliant guitarist of his era, the celebrated Appiah Agyekum. For his part, Agyekum had gained huge appeal in southern Ghana, throughout Accra, Volta, and the Akuapem area. It was against that backdrop that Onyina quickly carved out a name for himself in the Ashanti region. Playing guitar and making music was born for Onyina out of a decision to excel in a craft he was genuinely drawn to and to move forward with passion.

While his personal life had its ups and downs, the comfort and creative satisfaction he derived from the guitar came from the fact that, despite life's events, Onyina had complete control over the outcome of the sounds. It was his infectious attitude that left remarkable traces for a generation of musicians who saw a great example and wanted to emulate it. When I first wrote a few words about him years ago, I described him as "leaving his footprints on the sands of time and as a real professional who is truly excellent in his accomplishments." Years later, I still find this to be the most accurate picture of Kwabena Onyina.

Onyina's music was an honest reflection of himself. One chord after another, he trained himself to master every sound from the guitar. Life, as he knew it, was full of distractions, and most people spent time thinking and worrying about what they had no control over. It is easy to find ourselves lost in our own shortcomings, rather than taking deliberate steps to excel in the opportunities available to us in the moment. Onyina was particularly purposeful, vibrant, and down-to-earth in everything he was part of. What made the strongest impression on me was the fact that the standards he set in the art of guitar playing remain unsurpassed in Ghana, long after he played his last tune.

It was early in our friendship that I learned Kwabena Onyina was also born on March 5, 1932, in Agona Ashanti. If fate had a way of pairing two hearts and minds whose vision for life sat on the same side of time, this was it. We shared a love for the guitar and melodies, and thanks to being born on a Tuesday we even shared a name. Our childhood stories were similar, both of us having grown up in small villages, and we shared an awareness of what we had to do to live our dreams.

Onyina's father, Opanin Kwabena Mensah, had been a driver by profession and only played the guitar as a hobby. This is where Kwabena Onyina first saw his interest in the guitar take center stage in his heart. His mother, Ama Konadu, was a trader in textiles. Onyina was named after his grandfather, Nana Kwabena Onyina, who, at the time of Onyina's youth, was married to his grandmother, Nana Abena Aboagyewaa. Later in life, he recalled how all of them had been instrumental in his development, offering unique insights that helped shape his own.

In some peculiar ways, both of our childhoods and formative years were quite similar. Onyina was the only son of his mother at the time, as his sister had died at an early age. In his family's home in Ashanti New Town, Onyina had three sisters from his stepmother, Adwoa Ababrese, Yaa Gore, and Agnes Asuako. Both of our fathers played musical instruments, so we were both exposed to acoustic guitar music from an early age. Coincidentally, we both idolized some of the great musicians of the time, including Charlie Byrd and Charlie Parker, so we would spend many hours recreating the popular songs and replaying the chords as best as we could.

Onyina started his schooling in 1936 at the Salvation Army Complex Missionary School. Such schools, often started and run by missionaries, taught local children reading, writing, and mathematics. They also often formed brass bands and taught students to read music, exposing boys like Onyina to this environment from an early age. I recall years ago when we traded nostalgic moments, and he would describe all that he had learned in the tiny school building near the house of the late Kofi Dagarti.

Long before many of his peers and the world knew the depth of his dedication, Onyina would often pick up his father's guitar and practice in solitude, away from the spotlight. His curiosity guided him along every fret, each note a new discovery about his own talent. The more he uncovered, the deeper his connection to the instrument grew. The belief that geniuses are often shaped in the quiet shadows, nurtured by the sweat of relentless effort, was undoubtedly true in Onyina's early years.

Unfortunately, the unattractive reputation that guitarists had earned in the local community made Onyina keep his talent to himself. Musicians were often found drunk at parties and living carefree life-styles, which left much to be desired. As a result, many fathers did not encourage their children to learn the guitar as much as they nudged them to play other instruments. Onyina's mother sang in the Agona Seventh-Day Adventist choir, alongside his grandmother, who was a composer. A pure craving for music easily spilled onto Onyina. The passion for music had been passed down to him, but the commitment to excel was something he had to nurture every step of the way.

Onyina's mother passed away not long after he had started primary school. Just before the family could recover from the dev-astating loss, he also lost his father in 1945. For Kwabena Onyina, formal education, as he knew it, ended abruptly, and life shifted into an entirely different realm. The unassuming quiet days quickly turned into a life-changing phase, and a boy had to soon become a man. Kwabena's uncle, Opanin Kofi Obeng, an ex-serviceman who had returned from India in 1945, decided to look after his nephew. He took the young orphan to Koforidua in 1946.

Living under the roof of a man who was now a shoemaker, it was no surprise that shoemaking was the profession his uncle chose for him. Nothing about leather or threads gave him the same elation that the guitar gave him. Onyina worked as an apprentice for Opanin Yaw Poku, a local shoemaker. Throughout our many conversations, I never thought to ask him, but I can only imagine the burden of having to suppress his creative appetite to follow his uncle's request.

Life had taken a turn he was unprepared for, and gradually, it would take its toll. He later recounted many days of being depressed and lonely because of the loss of both parents. This experience even found its way into many of his songs. Songs like *"Ma yɛ ankonam, me ni obiara,"* which means "I have become an orphan, I don't have anyone," offered glimpses into the heart of a young man whose reality had taken unimaginable turns. He later wrote the song *"Me nim sɛ sei na ewiase bɛyɛ a n'anka mɛka me na yɛm,"* which translated from Twi means, "If I knew life would end this way, I would have stayed in my mother's womb," capturing his feelings at the time.

Often, when Onyina and I reflected on how our lives had unfolded, he said his saving grace might have been living near a Methodist Chapel, where he would often hear church music from a distance. Onyina also often spoke about a tailor, whose name he later forgot, who exposed him to music. The man was an accomplished accordion player, and Onyina would sometimes follow him deep into the night to his house, as he played his accordion along quiet village paths. His mind was made up: he would live his life around music.

Onyina had an uncanny ability to hear and decipher sounds in ways that were different from most people. The man told him stories about the accordion, but for Onyina, every note on the instrument made him think about how that same note could sound on the guitar. The accordion, invented in Europe in the 1800s, had gained popularity in some music genres. The instrument's loud sound, in an era where few owned amplifiers, helped musicians entertain audiences without much audio help.

The tunes made a lasting impression on Kwabena Onyina. Whenever the accordion's bellows would fill with air to force sounds out of holes with small reeds over them, it was as if Onyina's heartbeat had synced with every rhythm. The accordion captivated many musicians because one hand always played the harmony, while the other played individual keys simultaneously. Onyina wanted to mimic this unusual harmony on his guitar.

An artist like Kwabena Onyina was never satisfied with just knowing enough to maintain a career. He was curious enough to keep exploring everything he could about the guitar. Often alone in his quiet world, he saw the opportunity to pick up unique styles, despite having no formal music training. Just as a sponge soaks up water, Onyina soaked up knowledge at any chance. In my humble opinion, this is what made Onyina stand out among his contemporaries.

Perhaps one person who had the greatest influence on Kwabena Onyina was Mr. Kwame Boafo, a footballer and guitarist from Koforidua. As a boy, Onyina had seen his father play guitar and developed an interest, but fascination didn't immediately translate into a desire to nurture a musical talent. Music piqued his interest, but Onyina didn't learn about the guitar from his father before he passed.

It was Mr. Boafo who taught Kwabena Onyina to play the guitar. Onyina spent many hours listening to the complex harmonies of international music groups like the Andrew Sisters, Bing Crosby, the Mills Brothers, and Glenn Miller's Band.

The Glenn Miller Orchestra, as it became known, was the most popular and sought-after big band in the world at the time. It was formed in 1938. Far away, they never could have imagined how a young man was enthralled by their creative works or how they helped him forge his own. An artistic and exceptionally curious Onyina listened attentively. After hours of immersion in his mind's adventure, Onyina finally found his space and voice with the guitar.

Knowing Kwabena Onyina reaffirmed for me the notion that curiosity is often a key trait of genius. Seldom do you come across, if any exist at all, a remarkable and creative person without an inherent curiosity to uncover something. This is likely because curiosity forces the human mind to stay alert, rather than drifting along with the passing of time. For an artist, it is this curiosity that compels one to wonder about the possible. It is the constant pursuit of novel ideas that often transforms the simplest words into magnificent lyrics and an ordinary sound into a musical masterpiece.

For a guitarist, strumming guitar chords may evoke a thought that leads to another chord, and before you know it, a pattern has evolved into a melody. Kwabena Onyina took his lessons seriously, allowing his mind to delve into new possibilities in music. A few months after his newfound obsession with the guitar, Onyina was on his way to building a career as one of the most absorbing and revered musicians of his generation. The year was 1948.

The guitar, unlike the piano, could be easily carried everywhere and became his greatest companion. The young Onyina would practice late into the night, even while lying in bed. In quiet moments of solitude, he would often reflect on the loss of his parents and the tragic events of his childhood, but playing his guitar provided a much-needed escape. The songs did not numb the pain for Onyina; he often spoke of how certain pivotal events in his life always felt as though they happened yesterday, as the sting never fully dissipated even with the passing of years. It did not come as a surprise when he lost interest in the shoemaking profession.

In 1950, his apprenticeship in shoemaking ended. This new chapter meant he could take his guitar even more seriously. Onyina became an itinerant musician, entertaining friends and playing at functions in Koforidua and nearby towns. The life of a traveling musician had its benefits, but it also came with occasional setbacks.

One of the important figures Onyina often entertained was the former Omanhene of New Juaben, Nana Adarkwa Yiadom, the uncle of Omanhene Daasebre Nana Kwaku Boateng. The time spent with the royal family and other esteemed personalities gave Onyina his first real validation, affirming that his talent was not only special but deserving of public recognition. These encounters played a pivotal role in shaping his confidence, as the respect and acknowledgment he received from such influential figures marked the beginning of his journey toward greater visibility.

Soon after, Onyina met Kwasi Wiredu, a philosophy student from Ashanti New Town who attended the University of Ghana in Legon. Later, Professor Wiredu became a lecturer at the University of Florida in Tampa. This encounter had a transformative influence on Onyina's life. Kwasi introduced him to the music of great contemporary guitarists like Barney Kessel, Wes Montgomery, and Tal Farlow. Soon, he provided Onyina with works by Laurindo Almeida, Kenny Burrell, Charlie Christian, Charlie Byrd, and Andrés Segovia, among others.

Perhaps the most unexpected, yet remarkable aspect of this friendship was their shared interest in music that was not widely popular among their peers. They would study the music of these legendary artists for hours. Kwasi Wiredu had a profound impact on Onyina, and every resource he found enriched Onyina's technique. Onyina recalls how his friend hunted for books and classical guitar records to expose him to even more styles.

As a young musician, Onyina's life was filled with trying moments. In 1949, he was arrested twice for disturbing the public peace with his guitar at night. He was arraigned in the Koforidua Magistrate Court, where he pleaded guilty. He was fined one pound and one shilling on both occasions, but none of this discouraged him from playing music anywhere, at any time.

Friends came to his rescue and paid the fines. I believe such moments inspired Onyina to push further and challenge himself even more. He may have found comfort in expressing his gratitude to his many friends in Koforidua by becoming a creative perfectionist. Many who knew him later in life would have celebrated his successes even more had they seen the taxing moments under the quiet stars that refined his resolve and shaped him into the accomplished player he would become.

In 1951, Kwabena Onyina organized his first trio in Koforidua. For many - and certainly for Onyina - music was the epitome of a collaborative endeavor. Many sounds came together to create meaning and connections between instruments, forming a unique musical personality. Gyamfi, a typist and tutor at a commercial institute, teamed up with alto singer Sarpong and Kwabena Onyina to form the Cooler's Band.

It did not take long for Onyina to realize that the atmosphere in Koforidua was not conducive to pursuing a music career, so he decided to move to Kumasi. There, he added a young Nigerian guitarist, Bandele, and Kwame Ampong to sing treble. Afro Boateng also joined as an alto singer, while Kwabena himself sang tenor. Attakora, later known as Nana Attakora Manu, a mechanic at the Kumasi Magazine engineering complex, joined the band as a conga player. In the early years, Kwame Appiah took on management duties and was tasked with finding performances for the Cooler's Band across the country.

Kwabena Onyina's remarkable sense of rhythm and natural understanding of harmony guided his use of chords in a way that often displayed a deeper comprehension of the connections between guitar strings. Those who watched him closely were in awe of his skill. His style and seamless blend of solo work and accompaniment eliminated the need for a second guitarist. Bandele transitioned to double bass and soon became the bedrock of the Cooler's Band.

Gradually, a group formed for the sheer joy of playing music for entertainment became a household name. A new voice emerged in the highlife scene, with a signature style. The defining moment for the band probably came when renowned singer Agyekum T.D.B. from nearby Akim Wenchi, who had been working with Kwame Gyasi, left his band to join Onyina's. He found a home with the Cooler's Band in a way that showcased his own talent. Soon, Onyina's band had taken center stage in Ghana.

With Great Britain's colonial rule as the sociopolitical backdrop, Ghana's music scene was flooded with brass bands and police bands. The British government and officials often sponsored these to entertain foreign personnel in Ghana. Highlife groups and solo artists added their own flair, keeping partygoers dancing through the night. Musicians like Kwabena Onyina played guitar and entertained audiences, many of whom were visiting Ghana for the first time and had few encounters with highlife music.

At the height of the band's local success, they had a golden opportunity to sign a record deal with an international recording company. This would usher in a new era, even more fascinating than Onyina had anticipated earlier in his career. They met Mr. Daniel Kyei, a photographer, trumpeter, guitarist, and businessman from Ntonso Ashanti, who later became chairman of the Kumasi Council. Mr. Kyei took over as band manager. In 1953, Cooler's Band rebranded as Onyina's Guitar Band.

Onyina introduced dissonant sounds into his highlife guitar style through the use of diminished chords. Most students of music theory distinguish between consonance, a stable harmony or interval, and dissonance, which is often seen as unstable or transitional. One interpretation of dissonance is that it arises from beats resulting from simultaneous tones or their upper overtones of slightly differing frequencies. For many, dissonance would simply be a combination of notes that could even sound unpleasant. This was not an issue for Onyina. He added his own flair and transformed dissonance into a rich and captivating sound.

Agyekum responded to this by using chromatic notes in his singing, involving modulations. Onyina's distinctive style required other band members to adjust their skills to complement his own. This approach was soon embraced by the two alto singers Welbeck from Akim Oda and Yaw Broni from Akim Aseni, both in the Eastern region, who had just joined the band.

Throughout his quest for excellence, Onyina was careful not to lose touch with the reality gradually defining his career. I recall an evening in 1957 when a woman in Kumasi was admitted to the local Okomfo Anokye Hospital after she had bled profusely. She needed blood donations to survive. I approached Onyina about the situation, and it did not take much convincing to have him eager to help save a life. For Onyina, life was not just about music and fame.

Onyina believed that no act was insignificant in a life where the true value of a random act of kindness was unknown. He came to the hospital ready to donate blood. As it turned out, the woman did not need our blood after all, but at least she had seen a world where people shared in each other's pain and cared for one another. To me, the incident showed a level of concern for a perfect stranger's desperate moment. I knew from that moment that Onyina was someone I could always count on as a friend.

In 1961, a national guitar band competition was held in Cape Coast, Ghana's Central Region. After many incredible performances and showcases of talent, Onyina's band won the event's finale. Some of the band's unforgettable songs included "Wiase Nsemadooso," "The Many Challenges of Life," "Odo-Ye-Wu," "Love Can Feel like Death," "Lumumba" (a tribute to Patrice Lumumba), "Nantiyie" ("Wishing You Well in Your Travels"), and "Ohiaasoma Wo" ("When Poverty Sends You Searching"). All of Onyina's songs quickly became crowd favorites. Another song that won the hearts of many beyond Ghana's shores was the widely popular "The Destiny of Africa."

It was on this stage that Kwabena Onyina became King Onyina. A young man who had spent much of his life in the shadows of popular musicians had carved a name for himself. The late Dr. Ephriam Amu, a veteran Ghanaian musician, was one of the judges for the event. Along with Professor Atta Annan Mensah, a professor of ethnomusicology in Cape Coast, they witnessed the unveiling of a new chapter in highlife music, to audiences larger than Onyina had probably ever imagined. These were the days when he wished his parents had lived long enough to see what his life had become.

Two years later, President Nkrumah invited Onyina, along with some of the most influential artists of the time, Kwame Gyasi, E.K. Nyame, the great comedian Lord Bob Cole, and Kaakaiku, to accompany him on a tour through Mali, Tunisia, Poland, and the Soviet Union. This high honor made Onyina realize that his role as a cultural ambassador to places where the highlife genre and Asante culture were probably unknown had officially begun. In some performances, Joss Aikins, the leader of the Broadway Band from Takoradi in Ghana's Western Region, played alongside Onyina. The audiences, coming from all corners of the world, always left captivated by a fresh style with Onyina at the center.

In 1964, the Decca Recording Company in Britain invited Onyina to London. Decca Records, which had started in the late 1920s, had become, by the mid-20th century, one of the largest record companies in the world. While in London, Onyina performed at a concert at Battersea Town Hall, with the Black Star Band backing him. This would become one of his most memorable performances, with a supporting cast of fellow guitarist and celebrated Ghanaian composer Ebo Taylor, singer Joss Aikins, and saxophonist Teddy Osei from Osibisa Band. Onyina's overwhelming success added a new dimension to his popularity.

Recognition of this nature earned him a seat as a member of the Performing Rights Society of Great Britain in 1964. For people like Onyina, worldwide success did not stray his heart from his humble beginnings, and he was always gracious to the people he met along the way. The memory of long days in the shoemaking shop stayed with him.

Despite all his accomplishments, Onyina believed that national unity and a noble devotion to one's community were the true marks of selflessness. He wrote the song *"Lumumba,"* which was later transcribed in Kumasi with a crystal pickup to a cassette in Onyina's private collection. Events that moved a country and its people across Africa deeply touched Onyina's heart.

Patrice Émery Lumumba, Congo's first democratically elected Prime Minister until his abduction and assassination in January 1961, was a key figure in Pan-African nationalism. His influence resonated throughout the African continent and impressed many across the world. After helping win independence from Belgium in June 1960, it was only twelve weeks before his government was overthrown in a brutal coup. The legacy of such a nationalist leader had a profound impact on Onyina.

In 1972, Onyina organized a new band called The Sweet Melodians. The group featured emerging musician Lady Talata, organist Francis, lead vocalist Otis Asamoah, and several others. For many Ghanaian artists, the challenge was keeping a music group together for an extended period, and this undoubtedly helped the band develop continuity in both performances and personal relationships. Yet, the artists naturally sought their own opportunities for stardom. Onyina's band faced this challenge repeatedly.

Back in Koforidua, Onyina fell in love with a beautiful lady, Biama from Begoro. They married in 1960 and had four children, but tragically, three of them died shortly after birth. The only surviving son, Kwabena Ampofo, passed away three months after their divorce. After Onyina's marriage to Yaa Pabi from Mpankrono, near Kumasi, and later to Madam Mercy Annor from Adumanu, he still sought a lasting connection with love. He longed for companionship with someone whose hopes and ideals he shared, and, just as importantly, who had a passion for music.

In 1961, Onyina met Madam Agnes Owusu, known to many as Amma Pokuaa or Aggie, from Antoa, a small town near Kumasi. The immediate spark in their relationship grew from Aggie's deep love for Onyina's music. With all the uncommon diction and lyrics in

Onyina's songs, Aggie had to be incredibly passionate about his music to sing all of his songs from memory. There was love in the eyes of a man swept off his feet by a woman whose charm and grace were as striking as her beauty. Aggie loved music, and her heart was filled with melody that spilled out at every chance. The calmness of her smile gave a glimpse into her beautiful world, where Onyina was king.

Aggie's ability to recall Onyina's songs with such precision impressed him greatly. The two shared a remarkable bond that was instrumental in their lifelong union and brought joy to everyone around them. Aggie would become a recording star in the band's later years. This enthusiasm carried the couple through life's challenges, and after having eight children with Aggie, Onyina was always grateful for the blessing of such a companion in his life.

Kwabena Onyina, the guitarist, was installed as Barima Kwame Onyina, Chief of the Oyoko Abusua in Agona Ashanti, in November 1984. The people from his hometown of Juaben in the Ashanti region, who had migrated to Agona over the years, saw their native son become a household name, someone who did not let notoriety erase the footprints he had left along the many paths he had traveled. In his later years, Onyina spent much of his time in his Kwadaso Estate home with his wife and children, as well as in Agona, Ashanti, where he served as the chief of the Oyoko clan.

Onyina's popularity spread far beyond his birthplace, throughout Africa and Europe. Yet, he always reminded himself of the deepest passions that had drawn him to music and the opportunity to inspire the world through it. Cheers from large audiences were not the ultimate validation of a song's worth. For Onyina, if his message had added value to someone's life and told the story as honestly as he could, his work was complete.

The creativity and ingenuity in Onyina's music will always remain unforgettable in the annals of Ghanaian and African musical history. Onyina remained an inspiration to musicians of various temperaments and styles, pointing to the universality of one man's musical accomplishments. Some of his closest friends, including Mr. VOD Twum Barimah from Kibi, Langford Kofi Amoako, and Mr. Ampomah, the pharmacist, often spoke about Onyina with deep emotion. They paid tribute to a man who lived with the confidence that if we do our best in life, we walk away with nothing left to prove and nothing to regret. Onyina's children expressed their gratitude to their father in unique ways and were fortunate to witness his remarkable contribution to highlife music. Kwame Sefa, Ama Konadu, Kofi Obeng, Maame Serwaa, George Kwame Onyina, Raphael Onyina, Nana Aboagye, Kofi Agyemang, and Akosua Boatemaa became his world. They had a front-row seat to the life of a legend, and I was most fortunate to call him my friend.

Onyina saw a bit of himself in his nephew, Pat Thomas, and endlessly praised his talent and determination to excel. Thomas later became one of Ghana's leading musicians, someone Onyina greatly influenced throughout his music career. In his later years, Onyina recognized that a new generation of musicians would rise to entertain audiences with some of the styles he had created. For a musician, your life's work tells not only how you lived but also why you lived. People like Onyina belong to a masterclass of talented guitarists whose influence on highlife music lives on.

Many years later, my mind would often drift back to the exhilarating performances shared with Kwabena Onyina, a friendship and bond, woven together by the strings of our guitars, as inspiring as anyone could hope for. Whether playing songs at a funeral in Akim Kyebi or at a glamorous award ceremony at Ghana's National Theater, the authenticity of Kwabena Onyina's talent was always evident, displayed with both flair and grace. Each performance, whether humble or grand, reflected the depth of his passion and the true spirit of his music, leaving an indelible mark on everyone fortunate enough to witness it.

I think back to a quiet afternoon when I lay on a hospital bed, listening to Onyina retrace his life's journey. I listened and wished he could tell every young and aspiring musician that "Talent is not enough. It is God's gift and ought to be developed." A strange truth about life is that if talent opens a door for a person, it won't hold it open forever. The task then falls on the person's shoulders to work hard to keep the opportunity in their grasp. If anyone knew how much determination could drive a person beyond their talent, it was Onyina. He went on to add, *"Practice your instrument seriously and remember, there is no one just like you. Be yourself, and achieve the best in whatever you are meant to do in the service of your God and maker."*

We all see genius as an exceptional natural capacity for intellect demonstrated through creative and original work, and that was exactly how Kwabena Onyina's music and his talent left an indelible mark on Ghanaian music. Pan-African leader Marcus Garvey said it best: "God and nature first made us what we are, and then out of our own created genius, we make ourselves what we want to be."

I had been fortunate to share in the life, work, and journey of a friend. These were some of my best years as a musician and a man, having a friend and brother whose imagination and brilliance pushed me along my own journey. The world knew Onyina from a distance and imagined what inspired his talent and zeal. I sat with him long enough to be amazed by his pure skill.

Onyina passed away in 2010 at the age of 78, leaving behind a legacy that continues to resonate with me. For the friend I will always hold dear, from whom I learned so much about music and life, I can only hope that I've contributed in some small way to the many threads of his finely woven legacy. His influence remains a part of me, and as I continue my journey, I carry a piece of him with me, forever grateful for the lessons he imparted. I hope I have added one more strand to many parts of his finely woven legacy.

7

TETE WO BI KA, TETE WO BI KYERE

THE VALUE OF TRADITIONS AND PRESERVING CULTURE

In 1984, I attended the Commonwealth Festival in England. I introduced palm wine guitar to an audience, some of whom had previously heard of highlife music. They loved the sound and listened intently. The grins on their faces hinted that they had never heard this type of Ghanaian music before. The style accentuated a culture's distinctive musical forms and traditions, with delicate guitar chord progressions.

While in England, I used my stage performances to explain the mindset behind palm wine guitar music and the inspiration behind the fingerpicking style, which aimed to make every string and chord stand out as clearly as possible. It was as intriguing to me as it was to the music lovers who spent their evenings nodding to the rhythm. Coincidentally, in 1983, the British Broadcasting Corporation appointed Dennis Marks to produce and direct the documentary *Repercussions*.

Repercussions was a film about West African popular music, produced for British television. At the time, the world was still discovering the varying musical styles across the African continent, and the film added another voice to the dialogue. One of the key personalities in the success of the film was Professor John Miller Chernoff. Other musicians, like Nana Kwame Ampadu, Smart Nkansah, Sonny Ade, and other prominent musicians from British West Africa, were also featured.

The BBC sought to go beyond the surface of the lyrics, aiming to uncover the history and stories behind the songs. The world wanted to understand more than just the music, it wanted to know how we lived, why we chose the tunes we did, and how our worldviews shaped the melodies and rhythms we shared. The art of our music was not just an expression of sound, but a reflection of our lives, our struggles, and our dreams.

To give the visitors a firsthand experience of where the music got its name, I took them to a small forest a few miles away from Kumasi. There, we saw farmers working around a line of palm trees, waiting to be fermented. The farmers made a local palm wine drink from the naturally fermented sap of the palm tree.

We sat on wooden benches in the quiet woods, where the calm winds whispered through the green leaves of the surrounding trees, almost as if they were singing along. I played my guitar and spoke at length about the Asante culture, with a deep sense of solemnity and reverence for how its influence had shaped my life and career. My past had taught me everything I knew, and through our music, the lessons of our ancestors would continue to live on. It was a powerful reminder that the threads of our heritage are woven into everything we do, and through music, we keep those connections alive.

In the later months of 1985, *Repercussions* aired several times on British television. This marked the introduction of a new style of West African music to an international audience. Its sound, like falling rain, patiently dripped drop by drop, soon flooding the listener's heart with a masterpiece of culture. The long journey of a culture, one that began long before we were part of it, carried wisdom that could not be transferred in any other way. When our fathers and mothers pulled us aside to remind us of who we were, their hope was that our lives would shine even brighter than they had ever dreamed, and that our voices would soar higher than their wildest aspirations.

There is perhaps nothing more fascinating than reaching a place of discovery about the foundations of a society's life and the events that define its existence. Who we are as a people, and every strand of our life's social development is rooted in the lives of those who came before us. In my own world, I found the guidance of my footsteps through theirs, a priceless gift bestowed through folktales, proverbs, and songs.

My grandmother, Tutuwaa, told me a lot about the Denkyira people. My mother sang about our history and our journey, quietly hoping that I would never forget who I am and where I have come from. Our fathers lived in what became history for me, and certainly for generations to come. Their songs became our songs, and their dreams and pursuits, though the years have quickly passed, have become ours too.

What I know is that, for much of any society's evolution, interpretations of tradition are often given a negative connotation. Our past often bears a dull scar on its value, perhaps because we never lived in that time and are thus quick to abandon everything that arose from those moments. Maybe, in our haste to belong to an oncoming future, we inadvertently convince ourselves to leave behind the greatest parts of our lives, only to later ignore their value. Maybe, for some of us, no one took the time to tell us who we were or where we came from. For others, the elders in whose light we found our own steps, told us that *tete wo bi ka*" and *tete wo bi kyere*."

In Asante, the word *tete* describes the past. It often signifies something left behind, or that which belongs to a moment of lesser importance than the present. The Asante embrace the truth that the moment is gone, but the life within it lives on. As I traveled around the world, it almost felt as though there was an innate pressure to abandon our old selves and morph into who we imagined ourselves to be. But if life has taught us any invaluable lesson worth hanging onto, it is that we cannot change who we are, nor can we change our *tete*.

Tradition has often defined those traits of civilization and social life that we would like to move past. Others see them as unwanted remnants of the past, old, even strange. Consequently, the word *traditionalist*, at least in some circles, describes a person stuck in a time long gone, someone unwilling to look forward to the present. As a creative artist, however, I learned that our music and our art echo the words of our past and the lives of our forefathers. It was as though our biggest leap into a new day was firmly rooted in our yesterday.

"Tete Wo Bi Ka, Tete Wo Bi Kyere" was originally written by Dr. Ephraim Amu, a Ghanaian composer and musicologist. When I first listened to the lyrics, I couldn't help but ponder the deeper meaning that gave birth to what would become a classic song in Ghana's musical legacy. Whether or not a person knew where we had come from, the fact remains that all of our lives are tied to a moment before now, the impact of which lives on beyond what our eyes can see.

If indeed *tete wo bi ka* - the past has something to say - what does the past really want to tell us? Will its voice be loud enough, and will the words pierce deep enough to reach a heart filled with the hurrying winds of life that blow ceaselessly? Our forefathers had probably left a long trail of thoughts and words for future generations in the hope that we would be curious and conscious enough to gain some value from them.

As a young boy, I found myself completely captivated by the transition of customs and beliefs from one generation to another, along with everything that stirred passionate thoughts and helped develop social ideology. I learned about how the Akan people spoke about *amamre* and *amanee* - the former meaning customs, and the latter meaning challenges. History wasn't filled only with glorious moments, festive celebrations, and cheerful days. The dark and gloomy moments were ours too, and they had something to say.

The not-so-pleasant occurrences in our history didn't make those events any less significant. Rather, the story of a people is woven into its culture and speaks loudly with an authenticity that could not have been achieved in any other way. No sophistication or intellectual exposition could change the trails of our past. I had come to realize that I had inherited a great tradition.

The stories surrounded me from birth, their essence enveloping me even as a young boy. I grew up with a deep curiosity to understand more about my heritage, eager to uncover everything my parents and family had passed down. Their strength became a source of quiet pride, grounding me in humility, while their shortcomings illuminated the path I would take. It was through their triumphs and struggles that I found the resolve to carry on, carrying their legacy forward with each step I took.

Growing up in Foase, a village rich in culture in Ghana's Ashanti region, when I did something my father disapproved of, he would remind me that our people are expected to do better. Our people were expected to excel, let integrity be their closest aide, and hold themselves to a high standard in everything they did. It's fascinating to think back and hear the voices of old men in Foase urging me never to forget the stories of triumph, sacrifice, and faith that passed through the years. I was also reminded to share those stories with my children and their children. My admiration for *tete* - the history in whose remembrance we found our strength - grew out of an awareness of many truths I may never read in books, but which would guide my steps along the way.

As an Akan, whenever I wrote songs, they were about people I knew and those I had heard about. There were great people like Kumawuhene Nana Otuo Akyeampon, renowned for his daring vision and courage in leading his people despite incredible odds. They fought for a future generation so that we would not lose our way.

There were leaders like Tweneboa Kodua of Kumawu, Ejisuhene Diko Pim, Adwumakaasekesehene Asenso Kofo, and Ashanti Mamponghene Boahen Anantuo, all of whom gave their lives for their people and for a future they could only imagine. I wrote songs about Nana Yaa Asantewaa, who is honored in our history for leading a battle against the British imperialists, and about Okomfo Anokye, who served as a great advisor to Nana Osei Tutu.

In any tribute to these prominent figures, my unpretentious goal was to sing in honor of their lives and legacies. I retold their stories so that their great work and hopes would not be lost like chaff in the wind. As a creative artist, I was constantly reminded that the golden moments ought to be retold and relived, to be a part of a story that cannot be erased by time or the fragility of memory. My music's core message was *tete wo bi ka*.

Some of my most formative years as a boy were spent in the royal courts. I paid attention to even the seemingly insignificant events and allowed my curiosity to feed on every sound, every word, and every song. The drums and trumpets were loud with stories. The colorful cloths and elegant adornments bore imagery about how the Asante people had come to be a nation. This is where I first understood our history through the eyes of courageous men and women who shaped the destiny of their people.

The royal courts taught me a great deal, from the quiet hallways to the open compounds where the elders sat on idle days. Occasionally, when chiefs from other towns would meet in the palace, their spokesmen, Nananom Akyeame, would convey the chiefs' messages. As was the custom, the chiefs never spoke in public. I marveled at the eloquence of the spokesmen, who were expertly trained in local customs and heritage. I wanted to learn what these men knew. Their unusual diction would now be described as figures of speech, but it was the mastery and confidence in their voices that made their words pierce my mind.

The elders recalled what their fathers had told them about *tete*. I listened, I learned, and I asked more questions. The Twi language was always filled with idioms and inferences that added another layer of meaning to the most routine interactions. I carefully wove each idea into the songs I later wrote.

The words from Robert P. Downes' 1902 book, *The Art of Noble Living*, "An oak tree cannot develop its native majesty in a flower pot", reflect on the limitations that life's circumstances can place on us. This idea resonates deeply with the Asante people. The more we step out into the world, despite the unfamiliarity of the terrain, the more opportunities we encounter to stretch beyond the confines of our immediate surroundings. Like the oak tree, we find our true strength when we get the freedom to grow and face the vastness of life's challenges. It is in these moments of growth and exploration that we discover our potential and purpose. The meaning resonates with the Asante people.

Our past becomes our roots deep in the earth, in search of a majesty that is brought forth in the lives of generations to come. The *odum* tree, the Akan name for the oak tree, despite its daunting stature, first appears as a tiny plant in a pot. The plant cannot become a tree while trapped in the small pot, but its early life in the pot was crucial to its growth. Someday, the little roots will have to find a home in the earth, and only then can the tree reach its full potential.

For people who grew up in traditional Asante households or environments deeply immersed in culture, such growth was no happenstance. We were like little seeds given the soil to grow into trees. Humble as they were, some creative artists made a very conscious effort to invoke the wisdom of our ancestors' poetry and gave credit to those from whom we inherited this wisdom. The past has something to say, and indeed, it spoke through us.

Audiences have always come from their own worlds to listen to mine, drawn in by the stories I have to tell. From my Adinkra symbols and Kente cloths to my Ahenemma, my appearance has always been a reflection of the rich heritage I carry. The Kente threads from Asante Bonwire, in particular, have woven more than just fabric, they've added a depth and color to my songs that words alone could never capture. My history is a story I've always shared with pride, for it is not just my own but a testament to the generations that have shaped me. Each time I stand before an audience, I carry the weight of that legacy, woven into every note and every word.

I spent some time with Dr. Ephraim Amu, who will undoubtedly be remembered as one of Ghana's and Africa's most remarkable music composers. When I first met Dr. Amu, it was around the period of Ghana's independence from Great Britain, in 1957. The country's national pride had risen to the forefront, and the songs of those years ushered the country into its hopeful era of freedom. Among his distinguished compositions was "Yen Ara Asase Ni," which translates to "This is Our Native Land."

The song became one of the nation's enduring hymns, and to this day, it still evokes the same dream of a beautiful country as it did in the 1960s. Our forefathers' lives remind us of the high price and sacrifices paid for our freedom and dignity. In my work with Dr. Amu, I saw how a genuine desire to convey Ghana's most important messages inspired his passion and how it latched onto every word he spoke. He was convinced by what history sought to teach us and did not want to lose the opportunity to pass it on.

I had been invited to perform his song "Ohemma Mo, Ose Mo" at the Ghana Broadcasting Corporation in Kumasi. As was the norm at the time, whenever an artist was to perform a song by another composer, the two artists would rehearse the song together. I always thought of this practice as partly for the artist to earn the composer's blessing and also for the composer to offer artistic advice.

Through the years, I have come to appreciate such exchanges even more, recognizing their value not just in connecting with others, but in honoring the true essence of the music. It was always important to me to perform each song as it was intended to be sung, preserving its original spirit. In this pursuit, I found an invaluable opportunity to learn from one of the greatest musical minds of my lifetime, Dr. Ephraim Amu. His teachings not only deepened my understanding of music but also shaped my approach to honoring tradition while finding my own voice within it.

During our time together, what made a great impression on me was his uncomplicated outlook on life and equally captivating passion for nature's excellence. This was a man who would compromise neither his skill nor his intuition, but most importantly, never let a fleeting second pass without using his talent to shine a light on his country's history. Dr. Amu was a lecturer at the University of Science and Technology. He would often talk about how impressed and encouraged he was, knowing that there were still young African musicians who did not shy away from the chance to challenge their own ingenuity and create songs that would outlive them. In a way, the intent of the composer always rests at the heart of the sound. It didn't take much to see how ardently Dr. Amu supported culture.

I remember how sometimes he would only drink water from a calabash. His affinity for and appreciation of tradition and culture was incredible. We talked about what history had taught him and how he believed the work he was doing would shape a country's future far beyond what he could imagine. Over the years, I have been asked if Dr. Amu's influence sparked my preference for traditional Asante attire during my performances.

Coincidentally, my reason for always wearing Adinkra or Kente cloth was simple: it was the only cultural attire that complemented my music style. The person on stage spoke just as loudly as the guitar's strings. There was no way of knowing which seemingly insignificant part of my appearance would have the most impact on a crowd. The distinctive patterns and symbols in the traditional cloth always told a story of their own. The artistic details on the sandals, *ahenemma*, told a discerning audience about the person behind the music.

These symbols were how my culture had lived on through the years. Dr. Ephraim Amu was almost 100 years old when we sat to talk about how he bore a responsibility greater than himself and lived the optimism our forefathers carried with them. He enjoyed the song "Owuo Ton Ade a To Bi," which translated to "Buy when death sells." This is the inevitable bargain, the one we all buy in the end. But if we have lived our lives well and left a good legacy for generations to follow, it is worth it.

Many years later, I would replay the words to Dr. Amu's favorite songs. I always found it particularly intriguing how the smile in the eyes of a legendary composer nodding to the lyrics never faded from my memory. Anytime I have had the chance to talk about my long conversations with Dr. Amu, if I have any regret, it would be that I had not known him earlier in my life. His work and discipline inspired me greatly. He talked a lot about his own journey, almost as if to give me a glimpse into his world through his eyes. The wisdom handed to him through the generations before him gave me a chance to learn invaluable lessons that shaped the rest of my life. That may very well be why he wrote *tete wo bi ka, tete wo bi kyere*.

My music career was finding its place on Ghana's entertainment scene, at a turning point in the country's social life. This was a time when it seemed to me that Ghana, and indeed Africa as a whole, was dipping its toes into the deeper waters of international music but was unsure of what would become of its identity. The events unfolding around us - independence and leadership changes, had an enormous impact on what would become of the nations. It was not turbulent; it was just uncertain.

In the 1960s, as African countries pushed away from colonialism, it seemed as though parts of Africa were on the verge of losing their identity. What I have always concerned myself with was preserving the unique attributes in every culture and the value they bring to civilization as a whole. The different genres of African music gradually absorbed other styles, all pointing to the emergence of a new era of cross-cultural music. Years after I have sung my last songs, my hope will be that a future generation will look into the past and find songs like "Odonson," "Otuo Akyeampon," and "Akora Dua Kube."

In Ghana, highlife music had become immensely popular, but we knew that style would not always remain the same. In many cases, Africans had immersed themselves in Western influences, and this was evident in the sound we produced. We were gradually altering our lives and heritage into becoming a shadow of our fathers' dreams. If we turned away from what brought us to this moment, how much longer could we hold on to what our past had to say?

Hard as we tried to deny it, we had to confront this reality and begin the meticulous effort to reattach parts of our lives that had peeled away with time. While a core part of who we were remained, our culture often traded the representations of .our identity for something we inadvertently learned from the outside world. As creative artists, our hope was that there would always be an African whose tradition and father's songs gave him gentle pride. I used my guitar and my talent as best I could. Musicians had a distinctive platform to remind us that indeed the past has something to say and certainly has something to teach. *Tete wo bi ka, tete wo bi kyere.*

The richest part of our life and every moment we experience lies in our awareness of where we have been. It is this understanding that shapes what we do with our lives in the present. This consciousness becomes our guiding light, illuminating the path through tunnels of uncertainty as we move forward into an unknown future. By reflecting on our past, we find the strength and clarity to navigate the challenges ahead, ensuring that each step we take is purposeful and rooted in the lessons we have learned.

Throughout Ghana and around the world, I have been fortunate to serve as an ambassador for the traditions that have shaped the rich tapestry of Asante culture. I've stood on the stages of some of the world's most prestigious venues, humbled by the opportunity to explain the deeper meaning behind our words, songs, proverbs, and rituals. Each moment was a privilege, as I shared with others the wisdom and history that have been passed down through generations, connecting people from diverse backgrounds to the heart of our culture.

To paraphrase Professor Mawere Opoku's words, it is my prayer that our culture will be inspired by our past to fulfill a present need and impact all we endeavor to achieve for our future. For that to happen, the stories ought to be continually told, and the sweat from our forefathers' journeys ought to leave a lasting trail for generations to come. The rhythm of our own lives should not displace the deep crevices of a culture's evolution and how it inspired the lives of the people gone before us.

Much of the music I made had many elements of my culture intricately woven through its lyrics. It certainly was more by design than coincidence. This had been largely due to my firsthand experience with the Asante culture, Asante language, and the value of our customs in ways that are almost impossible to express in conversation. Words do their best to shed light on the meaning of what our past seeks to tell us. As a musician, I am grateful for the opportunity to amplify the words with a tune that gave the listener another avenue to comprehend what could have otherwise gone by the wayside.

I have listened to many keen observers of my work in different parts of the world tell of the natural influences of Akan traditional sounds like *adowa* and *kete* in my music. What brought me great joy was the realization that whatever I had lived through had tremendous value, and it was worth sharing. More than anything, I always wanted to make music that enlightened audiences, just as much as it entertained.

Openness to the world around me, a curiosity to discover, and the humility to explore have brought me immense intellectual growth. During the long days spent with village elders, my goal was simple: in my own small way, I sought to delve into our roots and understand the depths of where we had come from. It was through their stories, wisdom, and experiences that I was able to connect the dots of our history, uncovering lessons that continue to guide me today.

With every new song I wrote, I found that there was much to uncover, but it was worth peeling the pieces off one moment at a time. There were elders in Kumasi who had been delighted to lend their wisdom and knowledge, and now their voices would be heard around the world. They treasured the traditions and had lived long enough to grasp their powerful effect on society.

Much of what I know today, I have gathered over many decades in genuine dialogue and learning. As I came to find out, this is the only way a heritage transitions from generation to generation and hopefully carries along the rich virtues by which our forefathers lived. Our tradition taught me a great deal, and for my work as a creative artist, it became the proverbial stepping-stones across a swampy terrain of life.

I think back to Nana Kwaku Firi from Buabeng-Fiama, in the Brong Ahafo region, the man who taught me to play the *seperewa*. He was an old man who gratefully clung to the rich memories of his past as best as his fragile memory would allow. He remembered the people and vividly recalled the places. Local elders like him had lived through decades of sociocultural changes and had listened to their fathers and mothers share what their grandfathers had learned. There was pure excitement radiating in his eyes when he talked about *Nkane tete*, a time past.

In African villages, these stories brought fathers and sons together and gave mothers and daughters a chance to forge resilient bonds. With history's wisdom as their most invaluable guideposts, the elders in society had been the best people to offer counsel. And they did. They taught me about life, long before mine unfolded with a guitar in my hand. Even then, I saw my role as an ambassador for their raspy voices, and that maybe, someday, I too would get the chance to tell the world about our customs. If indeed music was to be the central part of my life, I would be only a channel for a people who had lived before my time, and my guitar would be their voice as the world paused long enough to listen.

It is what I learned early in my life that made me decide to travel to remote villages and spend hours with especially the elderly. Many of them had all the time in the world and all the knowledge that experience could hand down. They would often reminisce, quietly, and try to remember everything as quickly as its faint traces came to mind. I took notes and listened intently. Even then, I knew that the old men in our societies had so much to give, and without the tremendous opportunity to pass on their knowledge, these important stories about our beliefs and philosophy would be lost forever.

Tradition, for many people around the world, was easily perceived as something beautiful in a time gone by, but now considered archaic and seemingly unimportant. I heard some people say it was the unseen but unwelcome guest that paralyzes a person from moving another step. Perhaps because of my vantage point, I saw it differently. I have always been especially grateful for the kindness of my own memory, that through the years, I can still remember much of my life in great detail. The images did not fade despite life's adversities, nor did my joy give me false hope in a world where nothing was promised. What is even more intriguing, in an almost surreal way, is how I have become the old man I traveled many miles to see in years gone by.

My hair is now grey with age, my hands are tired with time, and the only strength I have is in a heart that is eternally grateful for the insight I discovered through *tete*. *Tete wo bi ka, tete wo bi kyere.* As is true in every aspect of life, the practical worth of a seed in the ground may be judged by how much fruit it bears. The patience in the dark soils of the earth springs forth a new life to tell an extraordinary story. The inspiration in its leaves is measured by how far its branches extend to touch a world it did not even know existed.

I have fate to thank for taking me to places where the beauty of our past was tangible, rather than an abstract value. Tradition was often seen as what was wrong in society, what hindered flourishing success and forward thinking. But I remember the words of my father, Opanin Kwame Amponsah, that "Until an awakening to reality opens a person's heart to appreciate *tete*, it is almost impossible to persuade him of how every inch of his life is rooted in a history he knows nothing of."

Whenever I went to perform on stage, and regardless of the grandeur of the auditoriums, I did not lose sight of my role in sharing my tradition, having become the ambassador of my ancestors to a world they could not have fathomed. The path and pain of our ancestors will not be in vain if the meaning of their every stride is handed down so that future generations do not repeat the same missteps they had to endure. Our past does not only define our future, it illuminates even the darkest paths.

The knowledge of a society's evolution is not without its tearful moments. For Africans, one of history's best-documented and painful tragedies was the transatlantic slave trade. It took place across the

Atlantic Ocean in the years leading up to the 19th century. Men and women from different regions along the African coast were forcibly dragged from among their families and communities into what history called the New World.

It is one of life's nearly impossible moments to imagine, a journey that makes one cringe at the mere thought of those dark and unnerving days. The Africans who lived through the horror would tell their children all that their journey had entailed. I can only imagine the cold nights on the distant seas, where even the thought of death's cruel sting would turn into a desperate wish. But those who survived the ordeal carried their songs, wrapped in uncertainty and tucked into their hearts. Hope for a future kept their blood warm and served as company for fragile hearts. The traditions of their land did not fly away from them, for it was those cherished cultures that reminded them of who they were.

In the 1980s, my music took me to parts of the world where people had learned to hold on to the vestiges of their ancestors' songs. They clung to whatever remained of a culture stripped away by years of pain. During an interview a few years ago, I shared my observations on how the men and women who had been taken as slaves and transported to America and the Antilles carried many components of their cultural heritage with them. In the midst of unimaginable horror, those gloomy days still brought a little ray of sunshine through the rhythms left within them.

In some plantations, their instruments were forbidden, as the noise and sound were as foreign to their captors as aliens from outer space would be to us today. The places changed, and so did the people - plantation after plantation, cotton field after cotton field - but the music never did. Despite the pain and the struggle to survive the brutal lives they were subjected to, the men and women who left Africa's shores in chains managed to sing the songs their ancestors sang and tell the stories their fathers and mothers had told them.

Their instruments became whatever they could lay their hands on, much like we did in Foase and in many villages across Africa. Music scholars point out how calypso, the music genre popularized by Afro-Caribbeans in Trinidad and Tobago, sounded similar to other music they had heard from somewhere in Africa. The same is true for Brazil's samba, which retained its fast-paced rhythms and the excitement they evoke. There has never been any doubt in my mind that *"tete wo bi ka, tete wo bi kyere."*

As I discovered, it is incredibly important for every generation not only to understand the traditions handed down to them but also to find in them the blueprint for leaving their own mark. There was always comfort in knowing how much of our past holds our present together. This is the refreshing sentiment that heritage provides: life with roots. We can walk alongside the depths of our culture and find our story.

In the 1988 documentary *Crossing Over*, I spent time with Trinidadian Calypsonian Lancelot Layne during his visit to Ghana. He had come to a place he called the land of his ancestors to explore the similarities we so often ignored but which kept our spirits intertwined. I received a call from the Ghana Arts Council in response to a UNESCO project in Trinidad and Tobago. Through my Ghanaian lens, the project aimed to identify the similarities and differences between the calypso and highlife genres. Both styles of music have always shared much in common, dating back to British influence during the colonial era.

As an artist, I found that internationally collaborative projects like *Crossing Over* offered valuable teaching moments. Unlike some of the countries in which I had performed, the culture in Trinidad and Tobago was completely foreign to me. The musicians there had long conversations about the life stories we shared, even though our lands were many miles apart. We learned a great deal from each other through the experience. *Crossing Over* won the 1989 Best Video

Documentary award in Trinidad and Tobago and another award in 1990 in Martinique.

In Trinidad and Tobago, I performed with many remarkable artists who were well-recognized and respected internationally. Their encounters added depth to my understanding of the world. The legendary Aldwyn Roberts, better known by his stage name Lord Kitchener, was an internationally famous calypso musician with whom I shared the stage. He had written songs like "Africa I Want to Come Home," "Jump in Line" (1946), and later "Mama Dis Is Mas" (1964), all of which earned him great commercial success. For Roberts, however, it was his wit and graceful melodies that made him one of Trinidad's most beloved calypso songwriters.

Just as Lord Kitchener talked about how his own story and culture had been pivotal to his learning and musical journey, another accomplished entertainer, Lord Pretender, also recalled how earlier musicians in the Caribbean had influenced his career immensely. Lord Pretender, whose real name was Aldric Farrell, was an impressive calypso vocalist. He was also widely revered as the master of *extempo*, a lyrically improvised form of calypso music. Not many musicians possessed the rare talent of leaving words that stuck in the minds of audiences over time, at least not as naturally as Lord Pretender did.

With both of these men, I spoke at length about the cultural influences in calypso and highlife. We discussed the rhythms, the finger movements, and even more about how their music had evolved while still preserving the value of their ancestors' work. It was my encounter with one of Trinidad and Tobago's best jazz guitarists, Fitzroy Coleman, that forever imprinted the value of gracious respect for our *tete* in my mind. He taught me everything I could learn about the guitar in our short time together, and he did so with the panache of a true maestro.

While in Trinidad and Tobago, I recorded the Ghanaian classic "Yaa Amponsa" with Len "Boogsie" Sharpe, one of the greatest steel drum players in the Caribbean. Sharpe had neither attended music school nor could he read music, yet he never missed a beat, leaving audiences longing for more after every performance. What was profound in this encounter was the unapologetic confidence that emanated from the stories handed down through the years. The musicians I met in the Caribbean knew that for all the work they had done and would do in the future, they had greatly benefited from the sparkle of their forefathers' limelight to bring their dreams to life.

Throughout my time on the UNESCO project, I watched and learned as the musicians taught and spoke about life through the sounds of their instruments. The towns echoed with the words of their forefathers everywhere I turned. I visited cocoa farms and watched farmers go through their normal days, basking in the beauty of nature and the scorching sun. The breeze that surrounded them as they stood underneath the trees reminded me of farmers in Foase.

I was also part of the Ghanaian delegation to the International Conference for Guitar in Martinique in 1988 and again in 1990. Some of the world's leading jazz guitarists attended the event, making it both an inspirational and enjoyable experience. Musicians like Stanley Jordan and Joe Pass made the trip a splendid memory. Later in the festivities, an unforgettable performance with guitarist Boo Hinkson from St. Lucia made the night in Martinique one of the highlights of my music career. Many years after the trip, I vividly remember working with the great classical guitarist Gilbert Addy, as though it were yesterday.

In all these world travels, one thing remained true: the world was not only interested in being entertained by an African artist, but also curious about where I had come from. What made our songs different? What was our story? What was our history? The thought sank in for me that to abandon the rich traditions that came before me would be to discard the most central part of who I truly was. It is worth our time to set aside the preoccupation with the present, look back occasionally to retrace our fathers' steps, and learn from their courage and hope. Hence the adage, "A person cannot know where they are heading without knowing where they began."

Many years ago, I was invited to perform at a royal funeral in Kumawu, a small town in the Sekyere Afram Plains in Ghana's Ashanti region. It was around the time I had been on a quest to learn all I could and attune my creative energy to understand the subtle differences in the subcultures of the Ashanti groups. I traveled to see Nana Apraku, a man who understood the most mundane events as mirror images and continuations of something greater. In his understanding of life and nature, nothing was happenstance. He had lived through a culture that had become the constructive imagination of what our forefathers dreamed of. After a few days in Kumawu, I wrote the words to what eventually became a tribute song to Nana Tweneboa Kodua.

The depth of Nana Apraku's insight was just what I needed as a bridge to the knowledge of the Asante culture in a way no one had shared with me before. The significance of the moment could only be captured with music that told a powerful story with almost spellbinding yet soothing words.

Tweneboa Kodua Birempɔn, Kodua Tweneboa
Katakyie a ofua tuo ne afena bɛko
Kodua hwɛo, Okyere hwɛo
Mereto wokwa, abutu wo kwa, akyerɛ kwa
Wona wonkɔto a tona tona
Waye dufɔkyeɛ sɛsɛnkosɛnko sɛne akwantimfi
Yehuri tra woa yasi amenam
Yefa wase a, wabɔ yɛn ane fɔ.

Yekwati woa ya yera
Yede akuma si womu a wagye amene

Adofo Piesie Twaamim Birempɔn kɔkɔɔ a
Ne din ne ne honam sɛ
Otiburukusu a ɔso ayeɛ ne nnemmire nam
Kumawu Adofo Akwasi Koramoa Birempɔn.
Tweneboa Kodua Daasebrɛ
Mmerɛnkɛnsono ani ampam
Otipin mu werɛmpɛ ampen a odi oko mu akoten

Tweneboa Kodua Gyan Nkansa a ofiri Kumawu o
Nanaee hwɛdeɛ mahunu.
Hwedee ma hunne
Otuo Akyeampon ee
Nanaee meyɛdɛn ni Wafɛfoɔ mmarima akɔ agyina abeyi wo obarima
Werɛmpie mu Asiedu Katabaako a wone.
Wafefoɔ kye adee wofa srɛ
Obiribiti a ehu nni ne tiri mu
Bisa Amoakwa ne Gyan a wobisa wɔn.

Adekyeɛ mu nsɛm
Otipasare a ne tirim awɔse apa Kwao- ɔhye - akwa a ɔhyee atɛni
Akoson Gyaami a ɔhyee abɔfoɔ nnan
Boama Asiama Akuamoa Aduana Atwea ne Abrade,
Agyeman
Barima Otuo Akyeampɔn se ɔma wo
Dammirifua due due!

Later that year, I traveled to Wenchi in the Brong-Ahafo region, where I met Nana Appiah, who advised that we visit Nana Kwaku Boansi. He welcomed us warmly and explained a great deal about how the intuition of our forefathers had guided a people to spread their wings and soar. Nana Boansi spoke with such conviction that we left with a renewed love for our history. It was refreshing to realize that our work, as musicians, held a significant role in both our communities and in a world far away.

Many years earlier, I had read the classic work *Confronting Silence*, a collection of writings by the Japanese composer Toru Takemitsu. Published in 1995, a year before his untimely death, the book reflected his thoughts on nature, which profoundly influenced his compositions, as well as his struggle to reconcile Western music with Eastern aesthetics and philosophy. The color of his world was changing quickly, perhaps from what he believed his ancestors had given him, and he did not want to let go of it. Toru Takemitsu's words stayed with me for many years, even inspiring some of the lyrics I wrote in the late 1990s.

When I had the opportunity to meet Japanese authors, they were curious as to why a young African man would be so deeply interested in a book that was likely unknown to many of his peers. Yet, it was a work of philosophy whose meaning resonated across many cultures, including mine. What I found most inspiring about Takemitsu was his curiosity to learn from the traditions he revered in his past. "I think of time as circular and continuity as a constantly changing state," he wrote. Our fathers' footsteps will live again when the time comes around, carried forward by whatever we preserve in our culture.

If a man could become a living embodiment of his own imagination, I realized that I was gradually becoming a woven layer of the cultures I encountered. The reassuring voices whispered to my heart that whatever talent our creator had given me should be used to share our world with people who would otherwise never know about us. Perhaps the beauty of life is that the older we get, the better we are able to identify those things that matter for future generations and to embrace their significance in the life we live today.

I also sought modern musical techniques for my own intellectual satisfaction. I had convinced myself that the guitar's potential was limitless and that my songs could draw upon the interpretation of any connection with culture. Throughout my music career, expressing culture in its pure form remained incredibly important to me. Ultimately, if Koo Nimo, the musician, had one goal, it would be to preserve traditional music and share it on a world stage.

Just as I had chosen to play a particular genre of music because of the quiet appeal in its style, I wanted the messages of our history to resonate with audiences. The *sadwa ase* style was the perfect storyteller, perhaps because of its calmness, which prompted listeners to reflect on the words. In some parts of the world, a similar sound - folk music - is still synonymous with world music. While this genre may not have gained mass popularity, its diction is genuine, and its originality endures.

The genre became a seamless overlap between the man I was and my passion for music. As an artist, I firmly believed that I would be doing myself a great disservice if I lost my identity and spent the rest of my life emulating others. If I ended up being the very best at repeating someone else's work, I would still have crowds cheering, but the question in my heart would be: If the generation after me did the same, what would remain of the culture that once shone brightly in our hearts? What would become of the pride that once gave us a voice and a song?

At times, I wondered if I could have reached more people with my message over the last several decades if I had sung in a different way. I will never know, but that doesn't diminish the satisfaction. There was perhaps nothing more absorbing and reassuring than replaying songs I had written over the years, only to uncover a refreshing new dimension I had never experienced before. The mirror of life reflects the legacy of my forefathers and the history that was their life's work, and I feel fortunate to have gained so much wisdom. If I had to do it all over again, I wouldn't change a thing.

A journalist once called me an intellectual philanthropist. I assumed that meant someone who freely passes on knowledge and experiences. For the creative artist and student of culture that I became, the satisfaction of sharing the Asante culture was second only to the joy of learning about it. In turn, I give every credit and tribute to the men and women whose words have carried me along the way.

The elders, *Nananom Mpaninfo,* who gazed into the horizon and imagined a day when our life's work would become the pride of our children's hearts, found the strength to continue in that direction. It was these elders in my community who reminded me of who I truly was. I felt proud and could not fail them. This was my feeling every day as I watched the sages rub their white beards and calmly drink their palm wine while talking about a life that had been a daunting undertaking. Yet they trusted the uncertain paths, with faith that *tete wo bi kyere* - they would always find their way back home.

Even if we are vaguely aware of this truth, the way we live through the seemingly mundane moments of life determines how we triumph over the fault lines in the world around us. How we treat ourselves and guard our destiny is rooted in the precious stories told to us through the years. How we build our communities and celebrate our maker begins with an unmistakable imprint of our past that lasts through our lives today. My ancestors lived in an oral society and passed on messages and history through speech, stories, and songs. The towering achievements of ancient times were a crucial part of our culture, woven carefully through *Anansesem* and *Anwonsem.*

Tete wo bi ka, tete wo bi kyere, our past has much to say and teach. Our duty is to listen. No matter how quickly times change in the music world, none of our struggles and labor will not have been in vain. Long before there were cassette players, compact disc players, or even more sophisticated instruments made possible by advances in technology, I remember listening to music on a vintage wind-up gramophone. Though much of the music was for entertainment, it was still imbued with moments that struck a familiar chord in my mind.

The music came from years past, but it still held the power to sing of truth, joy, and hope. It still taught audiences about our lives and our world. I hoped that one day, my songs would resonate with the same deep meaning in the ears and hearts of audiences around the world. This was my hope: that my work would echo the prayers of my father, long before now.

Tete wo bi kyere - an irrefutable truth that the past has something to teach. Standing here at the end of my career as a musician, I see everything in life slowly weaving through our days, beckoning us to stand tall and leave a mark for the next generation.

8

PIECES OF A WORLD IN SCALES

A Global Ambassador of Highlife and Culture

The more of the world I saw, the more I longed for home. Every place had its own story and song. My career had launched me into an incredible exchange, with my world at the center of a cultural journey.

The remarkable journey I could never have imagined took me to places I never thought I would go, countries where highlife music, and at times even Ghana itself, were little known. This country, tucked away on Africa's western shore, was not a name that came up in their daily lives, and certainly, the music I brought with me was not something they would have ordinarily encountered. Yet, it was through a series of chance events that highlife and palm wine guitar found their way to these audiences.

With every step, I could only hope to leave a mark through the strum of my guitar. The people I met along the way offered me glimpses into their lives, often much different from the images I had once imagined. For those whose curiosity about highlife music resonated with the rhythm of my songs, the smiles on their faces never seemed to fade. It was in those moments that music bridged the gap between worlds.

Koo Nimo the musician was to give the world a window into a culture with each chord and melody. I told them of where I had come from, and of the customs deeply ingrained in my heart. It made me who I was. My past experiences had crafted a home in my heart, and wherever life took me, there was a stark reminder that every song and every word had within it a message to be shared.

Being able to return to the places where I nurtured my music career and relive some of my most fascinating memories was always breathtaking. I used to take those memories for granted, but I learned to cherish them when I saw the value the rest of the world placed on such things. My lifelong dreams would come true, and the world would get the chance to see them through the rhythm of my guitar's strings.

If I have been able to impact an audience around me, and leave a lasting impression on people throughout Africa and the world, there is no greater joy for me than that. I could never forget how some of the unassuming dialogue and words along the way turned into lyrics with captivating brilliance once they found their place in a song. Beyond the music and beyond the strings, what became my greatest accomplishment was that no matter how far I went from home, I did not entertain an urge to change who I was and what I stood for.

I recall an event in America that probably marked the beginning of our traditional music taking on international appeal. It was in

1976 when my group, Adadam Agofomma, was invited to represent Ghana at the Festival of American Folklife. It was the institution's 200th anniversary. The festival had been organized by the Smithsonian Institution in Washington, D.C. From the mid-19th century, the Smithsonian had been not only one of the world's largest museums but also a prominent American institution, an advocate for global knowledge, and a platform for building global connections through culture. We had not performed on such an international stage before then, but there was a sense of calm and ease, even with the crowd staring at us.

After a hugely successful performance, we had struck a connection with audiences who knew very little about our music style. They clapped, cheered, nodded, and smiled. Whenever I stopped to interpret the Asante Twi words into English, the audiences would smile even more. Before we took our turn on stage, my only worry had been how well the audience would appreciate our lyrics. The language was unfamiliar, but they quickly discovered how the music style was inherently not too different from what they were accustomed to.

A friend once remarked that for an international artist, the measure of an excellent presentation is often wrapped in an invitation for an encore. The audience in Washington, D.C. left the auditorium with great reviews of our music style and asked where we were performing next. We were also thrilled at the reception and wanted the audiences to want more. It was a feeling that you had given your best effort, and more importantly, knowing your words had found their way into the hearts of the people who heard you. As we traveled to different countries, any such appreciation reminded us that music has the inherent ability to nurture deep communication between people, even in the absence of shared language.

The next few years took us across African countries, performing in some of the celebrated venues on the continent. We collaborated with local musicians, and with every performance, we were on our way to building what would soon become our signature style. Eight years after our performance at the Smithsonian, an exciting opportunity landed on our doorstep. Adadam Agofomma received an invitation to participate in the African Music Village in London, organized by the Commonwealth Institute. The event gave center stage to performers from around the world. This was an excellent exhibition for us, and an opportunity we had to seize.

All the performances were scheduled to take place in London's Holland Park, a popular public park in the Royal Borough of Kensington and Chelsea. We had heard of Holland Park before, and how it had, through the years, attracted both artists from all corners of the world and individuals seeking an audience for their own causes. If there was one thing we knew for certain, it would be that our audience would be very unpredictable. This could be a good thing, but nerve-racking nonetheless. All we could concern ourselves with was giving exceptional performances and not worrying about the crowd's applause.

I found that London had surprisingly diverse communities. Immigrants from all over the world had made their home there. There were many people in London speaking languages like Bengali, Urdu, Punjabi, Arabic, Turkish, Yoruba, French, and Gujarati. Our songs would be in Twi, from the Akan tribe in Ghana. I thought to myself that such ethnic diversity was sure to give our performance a mixed audience, with unique expectations and music lenses through which they would view ours. We discussed this among the group, and we agreed that such audiences unearthed a new challenge, as well as great excitement.

During Adadam Agofomma's rehearsals, the organizers of the African Music Village received an unexpected telegram from the Ugandan band saying they could not attend. Since every group had their assigned time slot, a last-minute change in the lineup could significantly affect the turnout and reception.

We arrived in London ahead of schedule, fully aware that any unanticipated event could jeopardize our big opportunity. We were determined to do everything we could to ensure we were there on time. When the Ugandan band unexpectedly didn't show up, the organizers had little time to adjust the schedule. They came to the facility where our group was rehearsing and asked if we would step in and give a double performance to fill the gap. It was an unexpected request, but at that moment, we knew we had to rise to the challenge.

While the organizers apologized for the inconvenience, we found it to be a welcome blessing to have an extended performance. We were up for the task. Now we had no alternative but to entertain a crowd, but about whom we knew little. But perhaps their anticipation for a different sound would result in a better reception than we imagined, and that would very well turn out to be one of the most exhilarating moments for a musician thrust into the international limelight.

Any other group could have been given the opportunity to perform on such a stage, but the organizers chose us, and we were ready for the challenge. We had found ourselves in a rare moment of good fortune, one that many artists dream of, a chance for an encore performance on a world stage. The organizers were counting on us to deliver a performance that would captivate the crowd, and we were determined not to disappoint. As we played song after song, the energy in the room grew, and the audience's smiles transformed into enthusiastic applause.

Soon they were on their feet dancing to the highlife tune. Others just listened intently, but with their glowing faces, they loudly expressed their appreciation better than they could if they spoke a word. The African Music Village turned out to be one of the most incredible performances of our young band's career. We stood on a world stage, told our stories in our language to people who had come from a diverse cultural landscape, and won their hearts.

My memory often travels back to one particular rehearsal. Since we had been slated for a double performance, we had stayed up late into the night planning our music selections and woke up at dawn to continue our preparation. We did our best to lessen the noise, but soon the quiet skies of London were filled with reverberations and echoes of African traditional instruments.

The residents of London's affluent Kensington neighborhood were unaccustomed to the loud sounds of African drums echoing early in the morning. Before long, the complaints started to trickle in. Not wanting to overstay the warm welcome we had received, we quickly adjusted our rehearsal style, opting for quieter sessions to be more considerate of our surroundings.

In the summer of 1988, I performed at Alice Tully Hall, in the prestigious Lincoln Center for the Performing Arts in New York City. The 1,096-seat chamber music hall had welcomed some of the world's most prominent musicians and singers since it opened in 1969. It was an honor for me to sit on this stage and play "Akora Dua Kube" and "Yaa Amponsa." After my performance, I was approached by Mr. Jed Wheeler for an encore. Although the scheduling did not give time for the audience to stay much longer, once again, I was moved by the reception of Ghana's traditional music on a world stage. For them, it sounded like jazz music fused with a hint of blues and folk music genres. When I walked off the stage to shake hands and thank people for coming, they thanked me for coming to share the Asante culture with them.

Later, in 1989, the United Nations Children's Education Fund (UNICEF) sponsored a Conference of Artists and Intellectuals in Bamako, the capital city of Mali. This initiative was part of an effort to create a platform to help in child survival. At the event, I performed a song about the six communicable diseases that were alarmingly sweeping through the African continent - polio, tuberculosis, diphtheria, measles, tetanus, and whooping cough. The conference was an avenue for educating the general public, but just as important, the music would be a vessel of hope.

Musicians from different countries performed together, and we left with remarkable admiration for one another. Music had brought us together in Mali, and each one of us left behind a piece of his culture. Music has played a significant role in societies and reinforced social patterns and behaviors. In parts of the world, it has connected the people to ideologies and encouraged them to stand in unison for causes that one voice could not impact on its own. For UNICEF, international events like these were a remarkable platform to engage a diverse group of people across Africa's heterogeneous landscape.

Through the years, I found that most African music genres expressed a profound philosophy, with religious and social messages strung together in a way no other medium could have made possible. The style had often evolved but kept its original appeal and power of persuasion. In a small way, men and women with instruments added their voices to affect lives across Africa. The results were overwhelming, and the impact was lasting. I have always looked back and been eternally grateful for having been part of such happenings.

A few years into my international travels, the 8th International Conference on Guitar was held in Martinique, in the French Caribbean Islands. The conference brought together some of the emerging musicians of my generation, as well as renowned artists of the time. A meeting of guitar minds in such an environment meant that all of us learned a great deal about each other and our music. The nights were often filled with endless guitar renditions of classic songs. We laughed and exchanged stories about what we all did alike or differently.

These were the kinds of events that introduced musicians like me to an incredible network of talented individuals who carried with them unique styles from their own cultures. I met celebrated artists like Chet Atkins, Sharon Isbin, Manuel Barruesco, Marcel Dadi, Leo Brower, Joe Pass, Stanley Jordan, and Laurindo Almeida. The trip to Martinique was a very humbling but instructional experience, and one from which many others walked away discovering something new about palm wine music.

Every little accomplishment, it turned out, had ushered me into a larger world where millions of people still wanted to hear the songs we cherished back in the Ashanti villages. I had become an international musician, but I was still Koo Nimo from the village in Foase, tucked away outside one of Ghana's big metropolitan areas. Our music constructed our interpretation of life itself. I met many other musicians who, despite their attraction to other genres, always received my music with genuine warmth.

Through God's infinite wisdom, my fortune led me to spend several decades of my life at the Kwame Nkrumah University of Science and Technology. I had never once enrolled as a student, but now I could not help but think that whatever I needed to learn in a university, I might have learned during this period. The task for the rest of my life was to let the winding roads I traveled in different countries and cities leave a trail of hard work and passion for life. When the next generation discovers my work, may the music urge them to reach out to the world and share the Ashanti story.

Later in my career, when the University of Science and Technology in Kumasi awarded me an Honorary Degree, a part of me could not shake off an overwhelming sense of humility. Universities train young men and women to pursue vocations that help them fulfill their own passions and contribute to society. In the years that I worked at the university, that same challenge had become my internal guide, and for everything I did, I hoped it would be as fulfilling to me as it would be to the people who watched me. I was awarded a Doctor of Letters, Honoris Causa, and was deeply grateful for this honor. The date was July 25, 1992, long after I had walked the hallways as a lab technician.

The university had a profound impact on my development and appreciation of the intricate relationships of things around me - events and people - just as I saw in the laboratory where I worked. My gratitude rests in the fact that I cherished every waking moment and embraced every encounter at the university. As it turned out, in many places around the world, it was as though where my words ended, the guitar's strings took over. When Koo Nimo was long gone, the music would stay behind. My life and journey had become my footprints.

Over the years, people asked if I could have had the same outlook on Asante culture and traditions if my life's circumstances had led me in a different direction. Would I have cared to understand all I could about my heritage and uncover its richness? What if I had been born into a different world, one in which the absence of some of life's luxuries did not force children to innovate? What would I have become? What if I had attended a prestigious university and received formal music training under the tutelage of celebrated creative artists? Would my songs still leave behind a piercing aftertaste of a unique African culture? Those were the probing questions - interesting to think about - but the answers to which I will never know. All I have become is because of what I am most familiar with.

Whatever gift I had been given and whatever chance I got to display it, I made sure it counted. What if I had attended a prestigious university and received formal music training under the tutelage of celebrated creative artists? Maybe my style and lyrics would have been different if I had sat in the seats at universities. I do not think I will ever know the true answers.

Around the world, I met great mentors and incredibly supportive musicians, all of whom added a little more to my creative thought process. If I was to become anything like an ambassador of my culture to the world, these encounters were incredibly invaluable. As intriguing as the thought of a future may have been, I always made a conscious effort to embrace every present moment life gave me and did so without any reservations. I did not blame fate and destiny for what I did not have. It is only by seeing the world through my own eyes that my lessons and legacy have become my own.

If my fortune had been any different, whether or not I would have learned more or less is something I will never know with any degree of certainty. Whether or not I would have been able to make a different impact on my generation is something I cannot fully fathom, but I cannot barter the hands life has dealt me. My foot had set on whatever soil it was destined for. I smile at the thought of having had my world-class university education in places like Kejetia market and the Asantehene's court, Manhyia, Kumasi. They sharpened my tenacity in ways I could never have imagined, so when I ended up in places far from home, I had something to say and a piece of my culture to leave behind.

As best as I can recall, life in Kejetia was busy, aggressive, and not the ideal environment for the faint of heart. Yet amidst the beautiful chaos, it also had an unusual serenity and a strange tranquility at sunset. It prepared an artist for a world in which life would travel at its own pace, where none of us would have any control. The guitar's tune had to be louder, and each fret had to tell a story of its own.

The sounds of early morning footsteps and sleepy yawns from the traders filled the market air with their own music. The chatter from the crowds of shoppers, the horns from the lorries, and the taxi driver's yells all fused into a fascinating harmony. If only I had known that someday I would be telling the world what I had seen and heard, I would have stood in the middle of the crowd a bit longer and tried my hardest to catch every sound as quickly as it filled the air. In retrospect, one of my highest gratifications was how the world around me added a little sparkle to my musician's heart.

Sitting on a stage in Seattle, Washington, I wondered what my song would have been if my heart had never ached, and if I had not lived through some of the sorrow and pain of life. What would I have to sing about if I had not met legendary musicians and teachers who imparted some of what they had learned through their years? What if I had not lived my childhood in Foase? What if I had not lost my parents and had not spent most of my early years in the Ashanti royal courts? Maybe I still would have ended up with the same experiences, but maybe Nana Nyankopon would have set me on another pathway. What would have become of Koo Nimo if the guitar's strings had not given a young boy such a sense of joy?

Whatever good may have come from a different life, only the Creator knows. It may have colored my life's lenses differently and maybe given me a reason to discover another gift, and another world. Anytime I look back at my life, I am confident that there is nothing that eluded me because of the way things turned out. As with anything in life, it also made a difference that I have had great help in making my voice louder and my rhythms interesting.

As it turned out, fortunately, wherever there was an academic gap, the lessons from elders and the community filled it with rich knowledge of history and philosophy. All my incredible encounters became turning points that would shape my young mind. I discovered how a learning attitude steers a person into places others would easily walk by. Wisdom is not a virtue you find in a university. You can learn a lot in university lecture halls, but even though that was not my life's path, it never stopped me from learning.

The challenges also did not stop me from walking into libraries and reading classics by Robert Louis Stevenson and Charles Dickens, among others. This desire was encouraged and refined by men like Professors W.E. Abraham and Kwasi Wiredu. At Adisadel College, they created a Reading Club and gave many curious minds an opportunity to blossom. My love for reading did not end within the walls of the meeting rooms. Knowledge was not confined to any one place.

Between 1969 and 1970, I traveled to Britain on study leave. In my part of the world, a study leave is usually a period of authorized absence granted to students prior to their examinations. My time at the Manchester School of Music gave me the rare opportunity to learn a great deal about harmony and classical guitar. The University of Salford is still known for its reputation for band management. The students came from diverse cultural backgrounds and were offered courses across a range of musical spheres. There was also an excellent opportunity to engage with other musicians.

Life in Salford had a profound impact on many artists' techniques. I was no different. As a creative artist with a curiosity to explore, there was always something to learn, discover, and convey. There have certainly been more audiences than I thought I would meet when I began my career. Guitar strings have kept me company, even on quiet days away from home, helping tell a story about my culture and people.

What talent I had helped carve out a career in some of the largest university auditoriums in the world. I got the chance to teach all I knew to students who were also nurturing their own inspirations. I loved being able to share stories with young minds who were seeking small windows into a distant world, like the one from which I had come.

I remind myself that whatever I am doing in the present moment is worthy, and that all the experiences I have had, whether in the royal courts or under the sun in the market centers, were never in vain. The extraordinary life lessons I learned in the village of Foase became the foundation of who I am today, shaping the critical years of my life in ways I couldn't fully grasp at the time. These lessons have since become the stories on which my own journey rests, and the legacy I carry with me, wherever I go.

Years ago, I was performing at the University of Alberta in Edmonton, Canada, when an entertaining evening turned into an introspective episode. I saw people from all over the world listen to my stories about culture and Ghana. People heard how our worlds were very much alike and realized music's profound ability to weave our seemingly detached worlds into one. These were the surprising connections that prevented my voice from fading in the midst of an audience whose worldview could not have been much farther from my own. The guitar's sound spoke softly, string after string.

Music had become the language that transcended color and race. It transcended age and home, too. To stand tall in these majestic auditoriums, on a stage with complete strangers eager to hear your words, was always humbling and a reminder for me of why I chose this path. I could not have imagined how the vivid memory of my past would survive the years and give me the words to sing. It meant taking a plunge into the deep end of life's ocean and hoping to swim calmly to shore.

My words had to do more than entertain; they had to enlighten and spark a beautiful curiosity about life in Africa. I realized I was meant to be more than just an entertainer; I was meant to be a musician—one who could speak through melodies and rhythms. I was meant to be more than a lyricist; I was meant to be a teacher, sharing not only music but the lessons life had taught me. Whatever life had in store for me, there stood a boy from the village of Foase, lecturing some of the brightest minds of our time, imparting wisdom in a way that transcended borders and expectations.

I stood in front of crowds in prominent institutions like Harvard University, Yale University, and Melbourne University. The questions in the minds of captivated audiences were still the same. With my guitar in hand at the University of Michigan in Ann Arbor and at the University of Seattle in Washington, I found that what seemed like a string of coincidences transformed into an enduring legacy. People had come from different backgrounds to experience music that took them on a journey into Africa's heart. The music became the very storylines that illuminated the rich Asante culture to an audience who did not know much about the world from which I had come.

One of my favorite institutions to visit and perform at was Macalester College in Saint Paul, Minnesota. I had made friends in Saint Paul through the years, like Mr. Sowa Mensah, who was the director of the cultural group, and Dr. Akosua Addo, an ethnomusicologist. The familiar faces in the crowd made it feel almost like a home away from home. The international statesman Mr. Kofi Annan had graduated from Macalester in 1961, so some of the students and faculty at the institution knew of Ghana before I set foot there.

Some were curious to find out how the little-known history and culture of Ghana had influenced one of the most prominent figures in modern society. Others came to learn about international sounds and guitar patterns that were completely foreign to them. It all made the encounter much richer than just a musical presentation.

When I was back in Ghana working at the University of Science and Technology, I had opportunities to learn from some of the greatest minds of the time. If I could share even a fraction of what these men and women taught me, I would have brought our experience and our philosophy one step further than where I stood. I had learned that a person's impact on life is more than the fruits of a profession or trade. It is born out of whatever an individual deems important enough to be remembered by. That becomes his legacy, and no matter where life takes him, that will be the footprint he leaves behind.

Whenever I had the chance to be part of a university research team, I took advantage of it to add a voice that would otherwise not be heard. On those trips, we met many people from very different backgrounds, each with their own versions of life. In my humble opinion, there was always an opportunity to improve upon our current station in life, and every experience, especially those involving other cultures, became that avenue. The challenge was to acknowledge that every person we encountered was an unfinished story, and that encounter could impact us beyond what we had initially imagined.

This is how we discovered that the wisdom to live our lives with a sense of purpose is not restricted to university auditoriums. As I traveled to different countries, the literary works I had read years before painted a picture that came to life when I stepped foot in those places. I had read about the societies, the cultures, and even some of the prominent characters. I had always been fascinated by biographies. The idea of quietly retracing the steps of influential people and conducting a comparative study of their characters was intriguing. From their lives and experiences, I learned. There were unique stories in every life, and a person who appreciates the wisdom in others' experiences would find a goldmine of knowledge in any life account.

Over the years, the thought that vividly stayed in my mind whenever I traveled beyond the shores of Ghana was that many people would come to see the Ashanti, Ghana, and even the African continent through their encounter with me. This had an enormous impact on my discipline and pursuit of excellence. I might not get another opportunity to retell a story if I could not find the words for it in that moment. Koo Nimo would always get another chance to play guitar on stage, but perhaps a person in the audience might never get another chance to hear about our culture and highlife music. It is this realization that perhaps urged me to work harder. My timing had to be precise.

At every concert, my performance had to be impeccable. My knowledge of the culture had to be authentic. Most important of all, my commitment to my guitar's strings - letting rhythm and song flow through freely - had to be resolute. I would look back at my career and appreciate how a person like Koo Nimo, with music trapped in his heart, did all he could to let the world enjoy palm wine guitar music.

I think someone asked me many years ago what life must have been like working as a laboratory technician. How did I cope and survive another minute when the ingenuity of music notes in my head would not cease to play? When you love something, it becomes an obsession. Gradually, in everything you do, you see your passion through it. The time away doesn't erase the joy it brings; in fact, it adds another dimension of inventiveness. I never turned away from the sound of music, and that was what fueled my passion whenever I looked into the audience waiting to hear our songs.

In an almost inexplicable way, whatever I found myself doing in any moment bore a strange resemblance to plucking the guitar's strings. This is what I told audiences in San Francisco and Sydney, Australia. In one of my reflections, I shared how everything in life, it seems, could be a series of notes and beats, all in perfect harmony. I always thank God for how destiny found me in the quiet days in Foase.

One of humanity's greatest legacies is the art of storytelling, but I would not have had any stories to tell if I had not walked alongside some of the most talented and inspirational guitarists. Even as the tips of my fingers struggled to press another guitar fret, the painful moments added a certain depth to my life that I did not recognize at the time. If there is any truth in how our lives eventually come full circle, it is for me to find a way to construct my observations and lessons every day. This is what we share and how we connect with others.

By 1998, I had collaborated with professors in Ethnomusicology at the University of Washington in Seattle and at the University of Michigan in Ann Arbor. I had been invited to be an Artist-in-Residence to teach Palm Wine Guitar Music, as well as a course in Asante Court Music and Dance. The study of music in its cultural context gave me a rare opportunity to explore even more deeply the two things I had immersed my life's work in music and culture.

The interdisciplinary appreciation for folklore, cultural studies, and anthropology made ethnomusicology both fulfilling and enlightening for me. Beyond that, it was a rare chance for me to write a new page about the culture I had known and to explain dance and song to a new generation who listened to music with a different kind of keenness.

Music is a social process, where understanding its distinct elements depends heavily on what it means to the society where it originated. Just as the Ashanti language was different from those of other tribes and people, so was the music. Meanings are consequently ascribed to songs from a unique cultural outlook. My lyrics had been the brainchild of some of the fascinating events in my life, but the true credit falls at the feet of the legendary performers whose style and skill opened doors for me and showed how there was more to music than the part of the world theirs was able to fill.

Back in Ghana, I lectured at the University of Cape Coast and worked as Chief Laboratory Technician in the Biochemistry Department at the University of Science and Technology. Wherever I went, and in whatever I did, there was no more pressing thought than this: there are no wasted moments in a man's life except those he allows. The random observations of biochemistry became riveting creative impressions and starting points for writing songs. Just like finding the right lyrics for a song, even moments that seem random have an inherent guiding star. I didn't think it would be so, but that is how seemingly unrelated experiences deepened some of life's mysteries.

My most gratifying moments have come from the knowledge I have shared over the years. Just as I had some of the greatest guitar teachers in England and America, I have also had the privilege of revealing highlife and palm wine guitar chords and music theory to a world I didn't know existed when I first set out. Passing on what our ancestors had given us to future generations has been a humbling task for me. I didn't embark on a music career with the thought of leaving a legacy that would carry on long after my life's work was done. I had been blessed with the opportunity to share with the world all that had been given to me through the years.

For every person who encouraged me to keep the music alive in my heart, I felt an uplifting sense of fulfillment, knowing I had come to a moment where I saw my life's work tied to the music I loved and to the hearts of the audiences I met along the way. The Ashanti story will carry on, and if Koo Nimo's songs have left even one indelible mark in the mind of someone, somewhere, the journey has been worth all the sacrifices.

One reality that consistently kept me grounded was the undeniable truth that I was not the first to walk this path. There had been others who came before me, whose efforts and sacrifices paved the way for me to stand on the stage and share my gifts. I never took that privilege for granted. It was a humbling reminder that I was merely a continuation of a much larger story, one that had been unfolding for generations before my own.

Performing was always a source of immense joy, not because of the attention it drew to me, but because of the deeper purpose it carried. The opportunity to share my culture and our music with a global audience was an experience I cherished, but it was never meant to become a source of arrogance or pride. The stage, to me, was not just a platform for self-expression; it was a place where the voices of those who had gone before me were echoed, where their dreams lived on.

My work, regardless of how creative or innovative it may have seemed at any given moment, was always framed within a larger context. It was a stepping stone, a bridge that connected the past with the future. I understood that whatever I created and shared would not only serve as a reflection of my own journey but would also lay the groundwork for the generations to come.

As time passed, I began receiving a string of invitations to perform in cities across the globe, stepping onto stages before audiences who knew very little about the world from which I had come. It was an eye-opening experience, seeing how the world was both vast and interconnected, how music and culture could transcend borders and touch hearts regardless of distance. While I had the opportunity to entertain, I also had a responsibility to educate and showcase the beauty of my culture in all its richness and complexity. My work was about offering a window into a world that might otherwise remain hidden and doing so with respect and humility.

I was humbled enough to recognize that my art had the power to do more than just entertain, it could also connect and inspire. It was a reminder that the stage was never just about the performers; it was about the message they carried with them, the stories they told, and the culture they shared. I was not just sharing my music; I was sharing a part of the world I came from, hoping that it would inspire others to look beyond their own experiences and see the beauty in what we all share as human beings.

It is my hope that the lasting impression of Koo Nimo's songs has brought my home to the world's doorsteps and that I've taken a little bit of theirs with me. My footprints along distant shores may wash away with time, while others may be covered with the dust of years, but I have done my best on every stage. My prayer has always been that every accomplishment along the way, in every part of the world, would leave a small mark. The individuals who will carry on with a myriad of music genres may someday look back and find the people who inspired the familiar faces they now know.

And some may even be strangers, like Koo Nimo and his guitar.

9

WHY WE SING

THE LIFE BENEATH THE LYRICS AND THE SONG

The palm wine tapper stirs his pot slowly, a soft hum escaping his lips as he moves in rhythm with the afternoon's heat. The warmth of the day settles around him, and the village seems to pause in its usual quiet dance. Beneath the wide shade of the tree, the men of Foase, both young and old, gather, as they have done countless afternoons before. There's a comforting familiarity in their presence, a sense of belonging that echoes in the air. The tapper smiles, his face lighting up as he takes the first sip of Nsafufuo, savoring its rich taste. One by one, the young men take their turn, each with a calabash in hand, passing the ritual along with unspoken understanding.

Every sip deepens the bond among them, a quiet communion that links their triumphs and sorrows, unspoken yet deeply felt. Musicians gather beneath the tree, their guitars weaving melodies that blend with the rhythm of life itself. The music carries not just notes, but reflections born from their own journeys, their struggles, and joys.

Storytellers, with their voices seasoned by time, share the lessons of their lives, offering the wisdom passed down through generations. Familiar proverbs slip effortlessly from their lips, like an old friend returning home. Traditional songs rise up, flowing naturally from the heart of the village. And we sing.

After decades of creating music and performing around the world, time and dreams had merged into a gentle stream of tunes from my guitar chords. I remember the palm wine tappers back in Foase and the villagers who sat under the big trees, all with their stories written on their faces. Like them, everything I had learned about life gave me the words to say.

My words and my songs often bore a striking resemblance to those of others in the crowd. Every string of my guitar made my voice even louder. The way my life had turned out would not only live in the back roads of my memory because when I sang, the people heard their own lives in the words. The connection was profound. I was fortunate to have the chance to share it through music.

Music had guided my every turn and my way into the future. The same songs I had played to entertain millions around the world had been the pulse of my own life's work. Maybe the reasons why we sing are just as basic as the reasons why we breathe. Music is life. When our experiences are filled with pain and joy, songs convey our deepest sentiments like green leaves calmly waving in the forest winds.

We sing when we are hopeful and looking forward to seeing our dreams come alive. We sing, also, when a heavy heart has no other way to relieve the weight of a day. Maybe much of our life is knit together in such a way that only music unravels a part of us that even words cannot fully express. And maybe that is why we sing.

I remember how I felt the first time I heard one of my songs on the radio. I smiled. I had made my first recording, the highlife tune "Go Inside," back in 1955 with I.E. Mason's band. Even though I was working at the University of Science and Technology at the time, I still devoted much of each day to my passion as a creative artist. My instinctive reaction upon hearing my song on the radio was elation, followed by a little laughter. For some strange reason, it didn't feel surreal. I had worked hard for my music to reach more people than those I met when I sang at funerals or in spur-of-the-moment concerts around the town. This was a turning point in my career. I laughed out loud with gentle pride.

I smiled, slowly turning up the volume. There was a part of me that had expected my life to turn out this way. Every day, with the guitar's strings stuck to my fingers, I had lived with the expectation that someday my dreams as a creative artist would come true. One day, I would also get the chance to entertain people with all the same passion I had nurtured as a boy. Now, my song would find its way to ears from afar and near.

There was a pure satisfaction that came from hearing my voice on the radio. Aside from being a musician, there was always joy in hearing how the strings transformed my words for the listener. For many years, I had practiced through the day and often deep into the night. I lived in anticipation of the day when a larger crowd would hear some of what I imagined in the quiet of the night. My voice through the radio sounded like a man living in the moment where imagination and ingenuity collided, and it felt like I was truly finding my own way. But in that instant, just when I felt accomplished, having done the best I thought I could, another sentiment crept into my mind: my journey had only just begun. I was to spend the rest of my music career finding out why I sang.

I had discovered that our forefathers left much of their legacy through songs. I learned much of what I knew about life's virtues through music, and it had become the only way I knew to leave a thought behind. I had become a musician, with my words finding an even more perfect pitch to entertain. With a feeling that never faded, even after many decades, a part of me always listened to every string through the radio as if to discover if a strange sound had crept into my songs. My eyes would be closed, as in a trance, humming along with every note.

Music, I soon found, unveils the artist's heart. It paints the words with color. What if people knew more about me than I would have liked? What if I said something I didn't intend to? I paid even closer attention to my own words. What if life, through my eyes, was too dim or too bright to be true for a listener? Even with all the questions, nothing subdued the fulfillment that came along with a song's impression on an audience. These are the emotions creative artists walk through and live with. It is at the crossroads of these feelings that an artist is invited to create music. That is why we sing.

I wrote the song "Yaree Ya, Ohia Ye Ya, Adesua Ye Ya" in the 1970s. It soon became one of the most popular songs of my career. The Twi words translate to mean "Sickness, poverty, and gaining knowledge are difficult tasks, or even painful." Sickness and poverty, especially, came with an unusually hefty price. They sometimes came along with misery. In my eyes, misery was always the unexpected companion, and the pain it brought left its scar too. So were poverty and sickness, both of which brought such discomfort, and no person, tribe, or country was immune. Circumstances may differ from place to place, but the pain in a person's heart feels the same everywhere.

In "Yaree Ya," although the words were all in the Twi language, the meaning was truly universal. Its popularity was born out of relational simplicity, a thread that connected people from all walks of life. The song was simple and true. Even if for a brief moment, there were some of life's misfortunes that indeed cut across social and cultural differences. I was not too surprised that the song resonated with people across Ghana.

Surprisingly, the most intriguing responses came from people I hadn't even imagined when I wrote the song. Audiences from Europe, America, and even Australia connected to something deeper than just the rhythm, they found meaning in the melodies and words that transcended distance and culture. It is in those moments that an artist takes a step back and sees the world through a different lens, a world shaped and inspired by the very song they created. And in those moments, we understand why we sing, not just for ourselves, but for the way music can bring people together, wherever they may be. That is why we sang.

Over the years, I saw people trudge through the muddy trails of adversity. I saw the faces of melancholy and gloom, and felt their sting. Irrespective of whatever direction life leads us, misfortune has a way of making even the awakening to the morning sun a painful experience. Even when we have done our best to avoid all the surprises in life, somehow we are never prepared enough for all the pitfalls. In this song, I used an example about borrowing money. It turns the borrower into a beggar, and poverty sends him on a journey he would rather avoid.

Again, when sickness or disease has left a person desperate for strength, the simple things in life, once taken for granted, become the most cherished things. When we sat underneath the branches in the middle of Foase and Kumasi's woods, these were the moments we sang about. Sickness took away my parents when I was too young to understand. There is nothing that fills the void in the heart of a young boy who loses a mother and father, his young life altered by the death of people he had always adored. This was my story.

The emptiness brought forth a song to comfort my grieving heart. So when I sang, the words were not foreign to me. When sickness took the lives of loved ones and left a family in tears, the songs gave us all a moment to lift our heads. For every adversity, there were millions more with unique versions of their own, but perhaps a tone, a chord, or a rhythm was all it would take to bring relief to a face in the crowd. This is why we sing.

I had the good fortune of growing up in Foase, a small village with a personality as rich and vibrant as its people. Every time I returned as an adult, I saw the same struggles, of poverty, and disease, unchanged by time or distance. Despite the different places I'd visited around the world, those struggles echoed the same, no matter the continent or the language spoken. The color of discomfort might have shifted, but the weight it carried on the soul was the same. The faces may have changed, the settings varied, but the pain of a grieving heart remained constant, untouched by the years or the miles between. It was a reminder that no matter where we are, we are all connected by the shared experience of suffering and the enduring resilience of the human spirit.

Similarly, knowledge rarely comes without sacrifice, especially for the young boys and girls who walk long distances under the scorching sun and pouring rain. I had once walked in those shoes, feeling the weight of each step as I made my way to school. As rewarding as education is, the reality of spending long days and nights immersed in the pages of books is far from glamorous. It is not the kind of work that offers instant joy or recognition, but rather a quiet, steady commitment. The reward comes later, when the lessons learned begin to shape your world, but the journey itself often requires more endurance than excitement.

Learning bore within it a fulfillment we hoped for, but every time I walked the dusty paths as a young boy, I would wish that someday the knowledge would give my life a richer appreciation of what tomorrow held in store. That was my hope. Fortunately, for the children who spent their mornings on the winding paths in the middle of a quiet village, it was the rewards in the end that made every footstep and every blister worthwhile. That is why we sing.

In 1984, my group was invited to the Commonwealth Festival in London. There, I met a Norwegian woman who expressed her interest in helping disabled people in various parts of the world, including Ghana. Her group was working to break social barriers in local communities where people with disabilities were often marginalized. Leprosy, a chronic infectious disease caused by *Mycobacterium leprae*, primarily affects the skin but can also impact peripheral nerves, the mucosa of the upper respiratory tract, and even the eyes.

In some communities around the world, lepers were considered societal outcasts. Some areas in Ghana were no different, and it broke my heart to see how a person's life could be deemed almost worthless because of a disease over which they had no control. When people avoided any association with you due to an unfortunate illness and the accompanying social stigma, it was easy to feel like an outcast. Lepers in many towns around Foase felt the same way. This left a deep sympathetic feeling in me, and I wanted to help. If there was anything I could do to ease someone's pain, even for a moment, I was glad to do so.

When I returned to Ghana, I fell ill in Kumasi and spent the next few months struggling with pain in my left calf muscle. During a visit to the hospital, I met Mrs. Peggy Appiah, who first introduced me to a disability center. The conversation I had had with the Norwegian woman in London came back to mind, and although nearly two years had passed since that encounter, my desire to share a warm smile and love with those in need only grew stronger.

In Jachie, the disability center offered several vocational programs for disabled people, including one that taught guitar making. Mrs. Appiah was unsure if I would have time to help, but she hoped that, if anyone could share something about the guitar, it would be me. They asked if I could teach guitar to the disabled men and women, and very soon, I found myself doing just that every Saturday morning.

I decided to return to Jachie, a small town in the Ashanti Region of Ghana, which is home to an institution designed for people with physical handicaps. As part of their programs, the disabled worked to produce acoustic guitars as an attempt at self-sufficiency. Although I could not fully put myself in their shoes, my upbringing had given me an empathy that went beyond merely acknowledging their emotional hardships from a distance.

Whatever small impact I could make to offer comfort, I knew it had the power to put a smile on someone's heart. In a world where many actions are driven by the expectation of something in return, I discovered that one of the most fulfilling acts of life was sharing your gifts and talents with those who cannot reciprocate. All I had were my guitar, my words, and my time, and in that moment, I realized that was all they truly needed. There was a quiet satisfaction in giving without expectation, in offering something that came from the heart.

At the time, researchers had started experimenting with natural remedies to help minimize the spread of leprosy. The more we learned about these diseases, the more we all wanted to help. When I was in secondary school at Adisadel College, I had been part of a group of boys assigned to plant trees from which these natural remedies were derived. We ended up in the Ankaful area. The more I learned about the plight of people whom society had pushed aside due to their disabilities, the more I wanted to help them. What might seem insignificant to me could make all the difference in someone else's life.

This was a time when people would overtly shun lepers in society. The idea of Koo Nimo volunteering his time to teach them music was unheard of. I was at the peak of my career, but I didn't want to rush forward so fast that I missed the priceless lessons along the way, especially those intertwined with the lives of society's less fortunate members.

I often find myself reflecting on one of the most defining moments of my life, when we visited the lepers, and I took the lead in shaking their hands and touching them, just as we would with anyone else we welcomed into our presence. In that moment, it wasn't just about offering a physical gesture; it was about breaking the invisible barrier that often separated us from those whom society had cast aside. The act was simple, yet profound, a reminder of our shared humanity, and of how a small, seemingly insignificant gesture could carry so much meaning.

As a young boy in Asawase and Zongo, I knew two lepers. Without their thumbs, they couldn't perform some of the simplest, most routine tasks. They couldn't even strike a match. I would always have to fill their lanterns with kerosene and help keep the lanterns lit at night. Whenever I was tempted to take anything in life for granted, I would remember the misfortune others had to live with, and it inspired me to appreciate whatever I had.

Our society often clung to myths and social perceptions unlike any I had ever seen. In some communities, leprosy was believed to be contagious. Even though looking at a person or touching their shoulder or hand didn't transmit the disease, many people either didn't know this or chose to avoid contact altogether. Touching a leper's shoulder or arm might seem like a simple gesture, but we certainly didn't want them to feel more ostracized than they already did.

At Jachie School for the Disabled, we started making guitars for sale. I remember one disabled craftsman who made a beautiful guitar and gave me the privilege of playing a song on it. The guitar eventually found its way into the hands of musician Ivor Mairants in London. He had written the book *Encyclopedia of Chords* and took the time to examine the quality of work produced in Jachie. After his objective review, Ivor wrote a report about the guitar's acoustic capabilities and sound. Anyone who played one of our guitars shared a similar viewpoint.

From where I stood, the smiles on the faces of the men and women at the facility were irreplaceable. More importantly, for every guitar chord I shared with the lepers, they gave me an even richer outlook on life in ways I could never have imagined. I also spent time visiting the Ankaful Leprosarium in Cape Coast and, later, the Agogo Hospital in the Ashanti Region. We entertained children at the facility, some of whom had been infected with Buruli ulcers. My humble beginnings had nurtured an unpretentious empathy for people whose plight in society was often less fortunate than mine. It was an encouraging sight to see large auditoriums packed with people with some form of handicap - people who would otherwise be social afterthoughts - enjoying an evening of music, dancing, and celebration.

As I shared stories about people who had inspired my song *"Yaree Ye Ya"* and sang it for those whose sickness or handicap had become their normal life, the song gave them something to smile about. Some wondered why I took so much pleasure in entertaining at Jachie when I could have been performing at more sophisticated venues in Kumasi and Accra.

For my part, I believed that if the people at the Disability Center couldn't come to hear us play, it was our responsibility to bring the music to them. I had never lived in their world, but I knew that all I needed to be someone who could truly understand their pain, something fundamentally human. Even many years later, that experience remains one of the most rewarding moments of my life, a feeling I will always cherish. I can only hope that, in some small way, I gave them something to sing about, a reminder that they, too, deserved to feel the joy and connection that music can bring.

An enduring thought, especially earlier in my career, was the realization that once a song was heard, it would take on a life of its own.

There was very little I could do but strive for excellence. The pursuit of creative perfection meant doing my very best because I might not get another chance to make a good impression. My unique experiences would create meaning for the audience. If I had done my work well, the words would mean something deeply personal to them, and their appreciation would be born from their own experiences. Unlike being on stage, in recording music for radio, I had no other way to affect emotion, which gave me an even more compelling reason to let the messages in my songs leave a lasting impression.

I remember a few years ago when I had a conversation with my old friend Professor Mawere Opoku. He had spent his life around music and had seen some of the greatest composers and performers of his generation. He asked me what I found to be the most basic motivation and source of joy for musicians. Maybe it was the love for the words or the sound. Maybe it was the love for the rhythm or the melody. In my eyes, my life had been immersed in music from an early age, so my affinity for song had its roots in my childhood.

I had fallen in love with my mother's voice as she sang Methodist hymns, and with my father's fingers strumming the guitar strings. That set in motion my unadorned inspiration for music. Then I discovered that I also loved music's power to express what lived in my heart—sometimes even to my own surprise. Other people might have stumbled into their passion, but they never turned back. Whatever the reason, the lyrics and rhythms satisfied a deep urge in my heart. It gave an almost indescribable feeling and satisfaction that an artist can never fully express in words alone. And so, we sang.

From what I had seen growing up, the idea of songs and dances as expressions of hope and love was the perfect medium to connect with humanity's inherent craving. Music is a natural part of life. In the villages, we sang to worship our God and show reverence to our chiefs and kings. When we sang, we were able to communicate emotions and thoughts that language could not accurately convey.

The notes and harmonies filled in the gaps where we couldn't in any other way. They lifted our spirits when life's gloom weighed heavily on our feeble shoulders. So, even though there were many reasons why we sang, there was none more poignant than the thought that perhaps we sang to remind ourselves that we were alive.

In his 1992 book *Music and the Mind*, author and psychiatrist Anthony Storr made observations about the human mind, not much different from what I had known as a little boy. "The perception of music as a central part of life is not confined to professionals or gifted amateurs," he wrote. His words coincided with something I observed after years of dedication to creating music and performing around the world. Music is very much a part of the fabric that clothes us.

At times, the creative structure of tunes and harmony stood out to me more clearly than it did for most people. I set out to play guitar and create music, but a deeper understanding of music theory magnified my joy in the sound. From my days as a little boy, I saw how many people, from different ages and local cultures, would sit around palm wine tappers listening to songs from people whose inspiration came far from the bright lights of any stage. Some used traditional diction or a vocabulary rich in poetic imagery as the only way their lyrics could reach the listener's ear. I grew to become a man who also saw tremendous worth in using the same traditional language.

The melody and harmony were certainly enough to bring dreams and hopes together. I discovered early in life that despite social differences, the language of music could be understood by people from all corners of the world and all walks of life, with little effort. My love for singing came from an unpretentious desire to encourage ailing minds and soothe grieving hearts. Sometimes, that pain was my own. That is why I sang.

Beyond its entertainment value, and before I ever considered pursuing it as a career, music had become central to my life at a very young age. As I reflect on my own fascination with it, I realize that it gave me a sense of connection to something that had always been a part of my identity. Harmony sends a heart, even if only fleetingly, into a world of its own. I latched on to the creative elements of sound itself, and in every moment of my life, I found a song to tell my story. Music was profoundly natural. The late Ghanaian composer Philip Gheho affirmed, "Music is the only language spoken in Heaven, and which angels use to communicate with God."

We sing because music has an overwhelming power to connect emotional chords in a way nothing else can. Someone like Philip Gbeho would know. As a legendary creative artist, he spent a great deal of his life absorbed in the art and science of song. Every time he and I spoke during the later years of his illustrious career, he added depth and clarity to how remarkable music had been to him. Long before the world knew him as the composer of Ghana's national anthem, he wanted nothing more than to preserve the value of our indigenous music.

Every second for a composer like Gbeho was a chance to transform a note in his imagination into a classical tune. Just as the world heard George Frideric Handel's famous *Messiah* and was forever enthralled by the masterful interplay of creative excellence, Philip Gbeho had an audience in Ghana whose ears also yearned for timeless compositions and found them in the African streets where the meaning was not too far from their grasp.

He sang for a vision much bigger than his own and a future beyond where his imagination could travel. I saw how his work lived through time because he loved what he did. I discovered that his passion reflected an inner glow, a deep sentiment for the world he knew and the life around him. His songs were meant to remind generations to come of who we had been as a people and what our destiny ought to be. That is why he sang.

After an Afrofest concert in Toronto, Canada, I was sitting behind the stage watching other bands hurriedly set up when a thought came to mind: there would always be differences in how our highlife music traveled through different communities in the world. The differences, perhaps, might lie in the translation and context. The local Ghanaians and Ashantis understood almost every word I uttered.

Other people listened patiently to the rhythm and musical arrangements, waiting quietly as I explained the meaning of the words in English. No matter how carefully I tried, I knew that some of the meaning would inevitably be lost in translation. Yet, it was always my hope that whatever was lost in my delivery, or in the audience's interpretation, would be restored by the sound of my guitar. The music, I believed, had a way of bridging gaps words alone could not, conveying emotion and intent in a language beyond translation, where the heart could understand what the mind might not.

Often, this realization made it seem as though we and the audiences were in different worlds, two ships sailing past each other in the middle of the ocean, briefly encountering each other only to exchange a word, before continuing on their way. From the very start of my career, I truly enjoyed the challenge of reconciling the two worlds. It was not hard to do.

Perhaps it's because I've always believed that we're all born with an innate ability to express emotion, and music is simply an extension of that ability. In the same way, we all have a remarkable sense of others' emotions, especially when we take the time to listen—not just to their words, but to the subtle nonverbal cues that reveal what they may not say.

My storytelling style sought to bridge the language gap, filling it with the emotional depth of the songs, allowing a wide and diverse range of cultural audiences to connect with the music in a shared understanding. It was never just about the notes or lyrics, it was about the feeling that transcended words and reached the hearts of anyone who listened.

When I played music in Alice Tully Hall at Lincoln Center in New York, the audience would tap their feet to the tunes and sway their heads from side to side. They gave standing ovations after the performance, but the words left a bit of a mystery. The guitar's strings filled the air with both strange and familiar notes. It was fascinating that the reception we got was no different from when we played for audiences at the Smithsonian in Washington D.C., or at summer festivals in Milwaukee, Wisconsin, and in Nashville, Tennessee. That was also no different from the performances under the big tree shades with the palm wine tappers and the audiences in the quiet woods of the village. It was always a joy to see audiences packed in concert halls, arenas, and open spaces, just as it was to see them at firesides in a distant town.

Audiences appreciated the sound of music from Koo Nimo's guitar from their unique vantage points. In Jack London Square in Oakland, California, I met crowds of music fans who, although they did not understand the lyrics, became some of the most captivated audiences I have seen in my life. Often, the brief interpretation of the songs I gave between the performances seemed to give them an even richer trajectory to travel along. The joy in the journey never waned, and my fingers never got tired of picking the strings. So I sang.

It was after a performance at the prestigious John F. Kennedy Civic Center in Lowell, Massachusetts, that I observed another intriguing sentiment. The lyrics hadn't changed, and the *kente* cloth was still draped around my shoulders, yet a subtle difference remained. The acoustic experiences in the huge auditoriums were strikingly different from those in the quiet woods of my hometown. Some of the large auditoriums held several thousand people, and the sounds were transmitted through the spaces and columns, amplified by the enormous speakers surrounding us. They cheered when the song ended. It was magnificent in its own way.

In performances back home in Ghanaian towns, or even in other less formal arenas, audiences sang and danced along. Unlike in parts of the world where the audience usually cheered only when the music ended, the feedback was almost immediate. Sometimes, I was too lost in the chords to notice the difference. Perhaps what is most beautiful about music is how the melodic swings evoke authentic feelings in audiences, allowing them to appreciate a song in a manner most familiar to their own culture and style. That is why we sing.

The heart of my music career lies in the realization that I learned to sing about what I truly knew. I discovered that using Asante figures of speech allowed me to express meaning in ways I might not have been able to otherwise. It wasn't just about the words or the music, it was about capturing the essence of my experiences, my culture, and the world around me. In my quest to understand the world that had shaped me, I unearthed a joy so pure, one that only a creative artist can find in the faces of a crowd. Each smile, every silent moment of connection, was a reminder that my music was no longer just mine; it belonged to all of us.

The experience was truly remarkable. Even with the cultural expressions I had yet to fully understand, I was fortunate to have spent a great deal of time with Asante elders who had a deep knowledge of them. Their wisdom and insight added a vibrant layer to the words I sang, imbuing my lyrics with meaning that went beyond language. It was as if the images in my songs were painted not just by me, but by the rich stories and traditions they shared, transforming each note into a vivid reflection of our culture and history.

Our songs were not just about what we knew but also about what we hoped for. It's often the uncertainty of life that prompts us to reflect most deeply on our existence. This uncertainty drives an artist to discover notes and harmonies that once lived only in the realm of imagination. It is in these moments, born of doubt and longing, that we find our richest experiences, those that shape and define us. But they also bring with them the most painful moments, reminding us that creation is often born from both joy and sorrow, and that the full depth of life is felt most profoundly in the spaces between.

For me, that introspection and appreciation began a process of unraveling what lies beneath life's layers. It was like finding the hidden sounds between the guitar's strings and the unexpected musical notes across the frets. We sang in those moments too, and our songs were our stories.

In writing music in the Twi language, we would often prefix our thoughts with another word: *sɛbi*. It has its origins in the Akan orator's attempt to avoid using improper words or inaccurate references to people and things. We said *sɛbi sɛbi* to convey a specific meaning in public without offending the listener. This was particularly the case with the Asante language, where we used imagery and figures of speech in our dialogue. The connotation was seldom literal, but even then, the inference could distort the intent of a creative presentation.

Sɛbi sɛbi was our way of asking permission from the elders and audiences to make references that might be deemed inappropriate or inaccurate. The orator might have no other way of presenting the idea, but the words still had to be heard. This knowledge lived at the core of my creative work because, even in our songs, we were sharing a culture and a great deal about how we perceived the world.

We said *sɛbi sɛbi mprɛ aduasa*, loosely translated to asking a listener to accept apologies thirty times over. The literal interpretation was part of an effort to appeal to the audience's inclination to use metaphors to convey meaning. Just as in the presence of elders and chiefs, an artist would work his hardest to be cognizant of the language used. When I learned to sing, even as a young boy, I learned how our songs often made references to animals and inanimate objects to pass on the song's intent. There were messages woven into the creative work from which all of us could learn something. For instance, it was impolite to compare a person to any animal, so we hoped the metaphors, with the help of *sɛbi*, would keep the message without tripping over our own culture's feet.

Music connected the faces in the places in a way that reminded me of one of the most popular sayings about music from the poet Henry Longfellow. The classic quote, "Music is the universal language of mankind," has found variations of meaning in different societies around the world. The truth is, there is a universal appeal to music, regardless of the differences in cultures and beliefs, so we can all somehow find an intrinsic connection within it. The all-encompassing nature of music comes from its ability to allow all of us to add our own interpretations to a sound without losing the relevance and value it holds for others.

As a young boy in Foase, I discovered something amazing about music's unusual ability to impress a thought in a person's heart. We sang because a deep harmony slowly found its way into our most desperate situations. Nothing else could do the same. We sang about the things we wanted to remember and the people who touched our lives. Often, even without a great deal of thought to the words we sang, the messages still stuck with us.

I had traveled across the world and seen a curious tendency in many people to miss the poignant messages in music. I did not want the heart of the music to be muffled in the pulsating rhythms because, even if no one heard the song, I would have heard my own voice and heeded my own advice. In what had been a fulfilling journey for a musician, it was my hope that the songs would birth a lasting reminder about those things in life that mattered most. For many, the songs certainly did, and that is a satisfaction beyond what words could fittingly describe.

Later in my career, I wrote another song with the wise King Solomon's words from Proverbs on my mind: "Go to the ant, thou sluggard, consider her ways and be wise." The song *Akoko mon Brekuo mon* was about how wise people carefully thought of their future and lived for a moment beyond today. They lived in the present, yet were completely aware of what their life's journey would require in order to achieve their goals. In the proverb, the ant storing its food in the sunlight provided an easy story for most people to visualize. It fit well with my hope to always have my lyrics convey messages that uplifted as much as they instructed; hence, I fell in love with nuggets of wisdom such as these.

And I sang.

I once performed at an event in Houston, Texas, to a crowd that included as many Ghanaians as Americans from various cultural backgrounds. With applause, I walked onto the main stage with my son, John. After every song, while some of the audience clapped, I tried to explain the Twi words to those whose curiosity had been piqued by the smiles on the faces of those who understood the lyrics. I told stories, as I always had. The audience listened intently. It was as though every song connected the lives of people in the room, like many strands plaited together. Then, I played the tune to a popular song, "Aburokyire Abrabo."

The room lit up as the audience cheered. "Aburokyire Abrabo" means "Life Overseas." I had written this song while living briefly in London during a cold winter. It was frigid, a place so cold that I often joked that even the elephants in the London Zoo had to drink champagne to cope with the weather. The snow and rain were unusual for visitors like me, but equally unbearable for people who had spent their entire lives in such conditions. A desperate man who had left his home in search of a better life had few options.

In my short stay in London, I could only imagine what kept my brothers and sisters in a place where the weather was too cold to be bearable. Surviving the morning winds, with ears cracking and knees buckling, and frozen tears running down the corners of one's eyes, life overseas was undeniably a tough ordeal. The audience, many of whom I imagined had never been to London, had lived their own frigid moments. They knew what it must have felt like. In fact, it wasn't the lyrics themselves that suddenly changed meaning; rather, it was the shared experiences. There were a myriad of life's challenges that all of us had learned to cope with, occasionally even with our knees buckling, and we continued to do so every day. The song reminded all of us of the paths we had walked. It also reminded us of how we survived and triumphed. That is why we sing.

From what had been a career filled with its own sun and storm, I came to realize that what often gives a song its worth is its ability to connect us with our imaginations and allow an audience to travel along with the artist. I saw how people living in a foreign country dealt with a range of unfamiliar emotions. But beyond country and home, the song could just as easily have become a metaphor for life in an unknown world. In a strangely familiar way, songs like this held a different, yet equally gripping meaning for the person who had never left home.

"Aburokyire Abrabo" struck a chord with everyone who had left a familiar atmosphere at one point in their life. Back home, much of life had been familiar, and even the unknown would not have seemed strange. Many Africans, like the people in the Houston auditorium that evening, had ended up in a new world as students and walked through the magnificent hallways of large universities. Some had left home with expectations of glamorous professions, but all turned in different directions. While they did their best to hold on to their dreams, they saw much of life through the paces on the sidewalks and in the never-ending cycle of a hurried life.

In their world, they discovered how life's subtle nuances make the most significant difference in every endeavor, beyond the knowledge we acquire. "Aburokyire Abrabo" was their story in music, a metaphor for a journey that was different for each of us, but not without its troubles. Long ago, as a young boy, I heard stories of families who sent their loved ones overseas for medical treatment. The situation was often dire, and the hope was that the medical facilities abroad would perform the miracles that local ones had been unable to. As some returned with their health, and others came back into a casket to be buried, perhaps destiny had much to say about how our lives turned out. The journey to *"Aburokyire"* was often filled with joy, but in other cases, filled with tears. It was a reminder of how our lives were even more fragile than we had made ourselves believe.

For many who left their homes in search of a better life abroad but never had the opportunity to give their life a moment's fighting chance, there was always some consolation in the Asante adage, "Se ebewie, nana Nyame na onim," meaning only God knows what tomorrow holds. So, whenever I sang "Aburokyire Abrabo," I thought about the people I had known, or even those I had heard of, who left their families and memories and never came back. They may have ended up on a deportation flight back to Kotoka Airport, or given up on life altogether. So, when I sang "Aburokyire Abrabo," all these sentiments were woven into a song that became incredibly touching but also gratifying for me as an artist.

When I picked up my guitar and looked into the crowd in the Houston auditorium, the first words that left my lips were a reminder to live out our days and live our version of life well. I had always learned that everyone had a different story. Some came home with genuine smiles and elation, while others were saddled with pain and regret. Wherever they had been, "Aburokyire" had been anywhere but home. This was the reason for the smiles and cheers from the audience: they found their own stories in mine, and the music helped us all share that moment. That is why we sing.

Many have made astute observations about the cognitive interplay of music. Some have sought to identify the connections between music composition, how we listen to it, why we enjoy it, and the human brain. Scientists describe how the increasing rate of development of the brain and its emotional states have their roots in music.

When many musicians pick up an instrument, they know very little about the therapeutic influence of music. Not many children playing musical instruments around the world know that music activates certain regions in the brain and can strengthen neural connections in ways that are sometimes difficult to explain. They play because they enjoy the art. It is refreshing to discover the unintended effects and learn how music resonates within us and uplifts the human soul.

Music's uplifting nature lives in its ability to alter depressive moods and affect our emotional states. When medical professionals encourage a sick person to listen to music as part of the therapeutic process, we find a beautiful art that has remarkable effects on the human body and mind. Most of us often remember patterns in music much better than patterns in words alone. Maybe the underlying chords connect more than musical notes; maybe they connect hearts too. When people with Alzheimer's disease or other dementias are able to respond to language and memory through music, we find a creative work that is indeed powerful at its core.

In a perfect world, the universe would exist in flawless harmony, with no dissonance to disturb its flow. In such a world, the chords and progressions from a guitar would always be in tune, playing the perfect song every time. There would be no torn strings, and each stage would be as flawless as the one before it.

But the reality is, our world is far from perfect. It is in the chaos, however, that we find something beautiful, rhythms and melodies slipping into our emotions, quietly soothing hearts that race with worry. I often reflect that, even when pain doesn't fade, the weight of the moment on the soul does lift, if only for a while. For some creative artists, this alone is enough to inspire a song to sing and a story to share, proof that even in imperfection, there is beauty and meaning to be found.

Long before I fully understood what music could do to our shared human experience, the lyrics had already become guideposts through dark nights and shade on the brightest days. Music, in its essence, was a refuge, something that spoke to parts of me I couldn't always articulate. I had fallen in love with an art form that, though experienced by each listener through their own unique perspective, created a universal connection. No matter where I went, the audience I encountered found something of their own in the music, and that shared experience became a powerful reminder of how deeply art can resonate across time, space, and circumstance.

That is why we sing.

Photo taken by Boadi at U.S.I.S Centre, Accra

Koo Nimo and a musician from the USA, being taught how to play the petia drum at a workshop at U.S.I.S, Accra

Koo Nimo at the Photographic Studio in Imperial College London, UK, 1963 Photo taken by Koo Nimo

From left to right: Stella Amponsah, Kwaku Gyasi, Kwabena Ampomah, John Amponsah, Koo Nimo, Ebenezer Koo Nimo Amponsah, and Little Kojo Noah. Photo taken in 1972

Koo Nimo Awarded Doctor of Letters, D. Litt (Honoris causa), Kwame Nkrumah University of Science & Technology, Kumasi, 1992

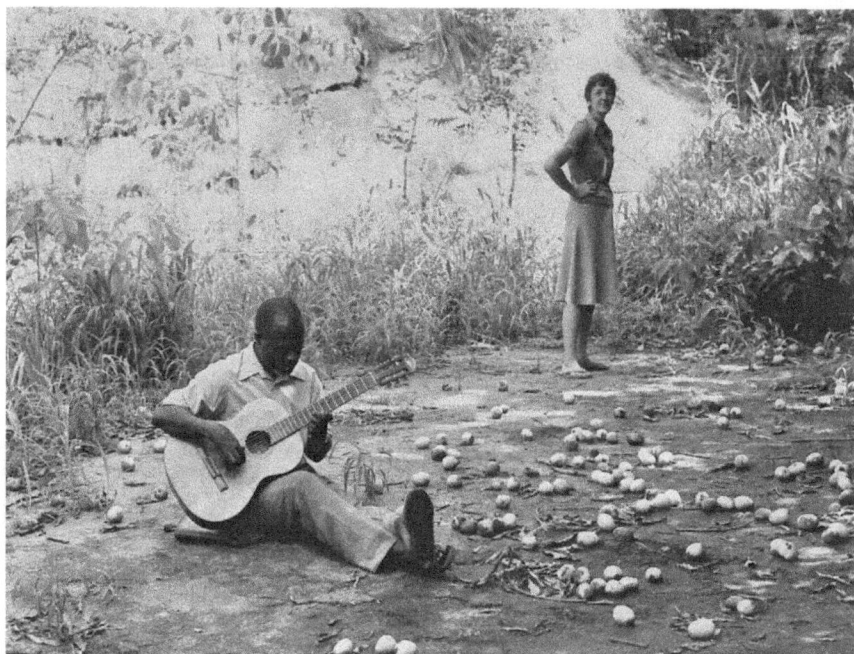

Koo Nimo and Mrs. Valerie Sackey in Nkoranza, Brong Ahafo, 1980
Photo by Hannah Schreckenbach

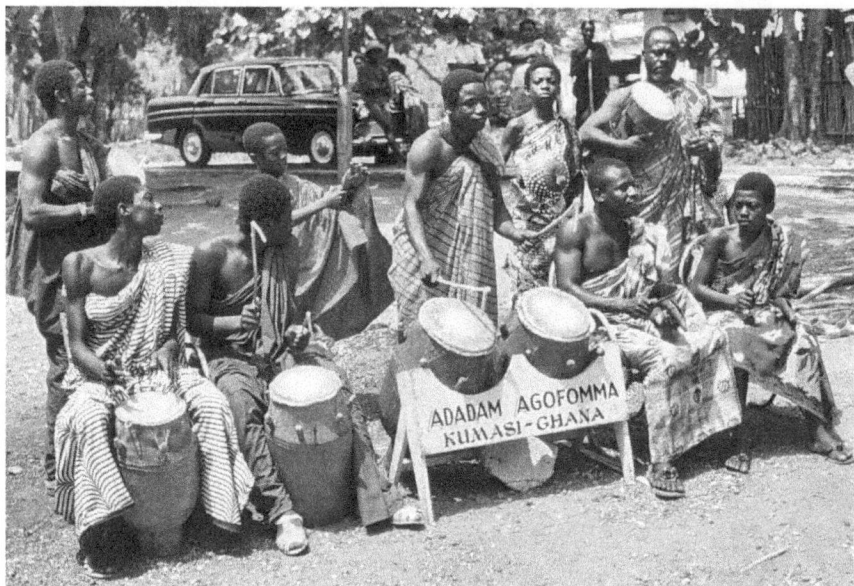

Adadam Agofomma performs in Kumasi, 1979

*Koo Nimo in his office, Chemistry Department, Kwame Nkrumah
University of Science & Technology, 1960*

*Koo Nimo, Acquaic, Stanley Jordan, Professor Leo Brower and Eli Kassner
at the International Guitar Conference, Martinique, 1990*

I.E. Mason, Appiah-Agyekum and Koo Nimo in Accra, 1985

Koo Nimo's Adadam Agofomma, Akosua Frimpomaa, Felicia Abena
Manu and Tawiah, at the Massa Festival in Abidjan, Côte d'Ivoire, 2007

Left to Right: Mr. Dick Moore, Nat. Amarteifio, Koo Nimo and Art Bennin at U.S.I.S Centre (workshop) Accra

Adadam Agofomma at Holland Park, London at the Commonwealth Festival, 1984

*Leo Sarkisian and Rita Rochelle from Voice of America,
with Koo Nimo at the Centre for National Culture, 1980*

*Vishal, Yaw Amponsah and Koo Nimo perform at
Cornish College of the Arts in Seattle, Washington, 2000*

Performance at Massa Festival in Abidjan, Côte d'Ivoire, 2007

Koo Nimo with children at the Cultural Research Centre, 2009

10

THE SUN SETS AWAY FROM HOME

Beyond Ashanti Ballads to the Edge of the Winds

A young couple met at a funeral and fell in love at first sight. The trouble was that Abena was already married to another man. Whatever affection instantly gripped her, or whatever spell Ampon cast over her, they could not resist the urge to be together. Driven by their own desires and selfishness, they hatched a plan to kill Abena's husband so that the two of them could spend the rest of their lives together.

On the day of the fateful and wretched plot, Abena was to sit by the fireside with her husband. The cue for her betrayal would be to fan the fire, allowing Ampon to aim perfectly and kill the innocent man when the fire was lit. Abena was to lean forward and gently blow air over the fire. Ampon hid behind a tree, never thinking about the consequences of his actions. Love had blinded his heart, and he could not think beyond the lustful moment when he was overtaken by Abena's evil grin. Even in the face of a gruesome murder, Ampon did not imagine what a tragedy it would have been if he had been the one sitting beside the fire, unaware that a wife could do such an unthinkable thing to her husband.

The plan worked. Ampon shot and killed Abena's husband. The two dragged the lifeless body into an old mine pit and left him there. Abena soon reported that her husband was missing. A funeral was held after the search party could not find the man's body. Without anyone knowing the truth, it seemed that Abena and Ampon had gotten away with their evil plot. They married soon after, but it was to be a cursed marriage.

No sooner had the initial thrill of their infatuation faded than Ampon found himself sitting by the fire one quiet evening, seeking its warmth. His past lingered, a constant companion that haunted him with every passing day. A single moment in one evening gave him every reason to pause. He had just returned from the farm, weary from a long day's labor. Abena, his wife, quietly joined him. Without a word, she leaned forward, gently fanning the fire.

Ampon jumped in fear. His mind suddenly traveled back to the day he hid behind the tree to kill an innocent man because he had been smitten by love and could not help himself. His heart raced with suspicion, and gripped by sudden fear, he exclaimed, "Abena, is there a man hiding behind the tree to kill me?"

Shocked, Abena wondered why her husband would accuse her of such a terrible act. She had tried her hardest to bury the weight of the callous act she had committed, pushing it deep within herself, hoping it would remain hidden. Now, perhaps bewildered and hurt, she couldn't understand how her husband could suspect that she might repeat the same mistake only a few years later. Ampon suspected that the way Abena was fanning the fire could be another sign of betrayal. In Akan, the song title became *"Me suro wo gyamu fite."*

The lyrics to the song had their roots in a popular Akan saying, *"Me suro wo gyamu fite,"* which conveys the feeling of having a reason to suspect a person's actions. I crafted the story of Abena and Ampon to illustrate how the consequences of our actions always seem to find a way of returning to us. The good deeds we sow, even unknowingly, may have an effect on our own lives someday. This simple truth is the meaning behind the lyrics, with Abena and Ampon's story setting the stage for what we must all protect our hearts against. Opening one's heart to live honestly and free of self-serving compromises brings a fulfilling reward without the discomfort of a dark past.

There have been men and women whose selfless investment in my life reminded me that, no matter how we act in life, we will face the consequences or rewards of our actions someday, when we least expect it. There is so much in our lives that we cannot control, and I have learned that the best thing I can do is to live simply and truthfully with the people whose paths I cross. If my heart is pure, I will allow myself the freedom to be amazed by the wonder of the unexpected.

When I set out to record *Ashanti Ballads,* I could not have fathomed what an important body of work that would become for my career. There were songs I had written and originally performed in the Twi language that had carved out their own identity, and some that told of life's truths as I had learned them. The virtues and values that had become the underpinnings of my life were no different from those others might have learned, so it was not hard to find an audience.

In 1966, Joe Latham, who was working in Ghana at the time, arranged to help translate *Ashanti Ballads* into English. My group later recorded 21 songs at the Ghana Film Industries Studios in Accra. I reflected on what a fascinating opportunity that was and how I was convinced that every song on the record would have its unique stanza to share. I was in Kumasi at the time, as were the band members. We could not use E. K. Badu's studio as we had done in the past, but we thought a change of venue would be refreshing.

We hopped on the state transport bus early in the morning, the STC, as we called it, for a long ride to Accra. We arrived in Accra later in the afternoon, and our band stayed at the Nkwadum Hotel in Kaneshie. I had been to Accra on numerous occasions, and it was always a special experience. This time, we planned to be in Accra for about three days and did our best to finish the recording on time and head back to Kumasi. One benefit our group always enjoyed was that we had rehearsed many of the songs over and over through the years. It turned out that whenever we were to record a song, it did not take us long to get the result we hoped for. I often joked about how most of my first takes in every recording ended up being the best.

Our work in Accra proved to be hugely successful, and if that success was any indication of what the future held, it promised to be filled with both surprises and euphoric moments. Yet, none of this might have come to pass if it weren't for people like Joe Latham and the studios, who poured their best efforts into ensuring that the melody of my dream found its perfect beginning.

Even before the recordings for *Ashanti Ballads,* one interesting coincidence in the songs I wrote was their length. They fit well with radio play. Radio stations in Ghana preferred shorter songs because of their programming constraints, and while I had not set out to write songs with that in mind, it became an unintended promoter for my music in those early years. It was as if the friendly stars had quickly gathered to align on my behalf when I wasn't looking.

We went back to Accra ten years later to record four more songs. They were all published in English, French, and Esperanto a few years later. I had also met a young journalist, Kwabena Ofosu Mensah, whose knowledge of media law and international business became incredibly instrumental in getting the recordings to a larger audience. In those pivotal years in my career, there was always a comfort in knowing that all I had to focus on was creating music and trusting that serendipity would open doors for me. Maybe every helping hand I had given to someone else had slowly found its way back into my life.

The record *Ashanti Ballads,* became the first professional compact disc produced in Ghana. That in itself was a remarkable achievement at the time. The compact discs and cassettes were sold in Britain, the United States, and as far away as Japan. *Ashanti Ballads* opened the door to many international performances.

Every stage had a different sense of satisfaction for me, and it may have been because audiences brought their enthusiasm, the likes of which I could not have anticipated. The influence I would have on people was soon to be more than I could ever have dreamed of, perhaps because I was still waking up to the cresting waves of curiosity rushing my way about my culture, my people, and my songs.

I enjoyed performing in front of live audiences. I always thought that an audience's participation had an unorthodox way of encouraging a performer to reach down into the richest part of their art and display it. The smiles spoke even louder, and even more so as people's lips moved to the lyrics they had heard before. Performances felt like an intimate conversation with audiences who spoke back in the moment. Even on the days when I was so tired and felt my knees dragging, I was never too worn out to pick up my guitar for one more song.

A performance in front of several hundred people still required dependable band members, like an orchestra working in unison. After the release of *Ashanti Ballads,* I traveled often for shows. I still did not enjoy performing in television studios and for radio as much as I liked being underneath the calm shade of a tree on a sunny afternoon. When there was no pressure to fit into an allotted space and time, there was an artistic freedom to follow where the strings led. It felt different. Yet with studio work, there was a curious satisfaction that, as soon as I walked away, many people would hear the music and, hopefully, enjoy it long enough to understand the deeper meanings behind the words.

Regardless of which city and stage my music took me to, I was particularly cognizant of my intent not only to entertain but also to educate anyone who took the time to listen to me. This influenced my creative process entirely. I needed the band to lend their talents to every song, and I have been truly blessed to have had such a brilliant group of individuals in my world. The stage lights never got so bright that I forgot what a unique opportunity life had afforded me, to live my passion and see the world in all its color. The sound never got so familiar that what had once been amazing in my heart became ordinary.

My memory often takes me back to when I was younger, before time had made my feet heavy with age. Back then, I played every song with a boundless energy, even when the melodies were calm and soothing. The chords and rhythm flowed effortlessly, yet deep inside me, there was a young man bursting with words, eager to express everything I felt. I never could have imagined a future where the grey in my beard would symbolize the depth of a journey so rich and fascinating.

Looking back, those years hold a special place in my heart, filled with excitement and purpose. It was a time when I embarked on this journey alongside some of my closest friends, sharing in every triumph and learning from each step we took together.

There was an unusual joy in every song, and they never missed a chance to ask me why I had chosen a particular tune or tone. It almost didn't feel the same in the later years of my career. The passion never faded, but often, the memories of my contemporaries, many of whom I wished were still sitting on stage with me, weighed heavily on me. If I had known where my creator would take me with my palm wine guitar music and on which stage he would grant me the chance to share Asante culture and Ghana's story, I would have begged them to stay a little longer. What they gave of themselves to me, I could only wish I had half the opportunity to give back to others.

That nostalgia brings a quiet pain that only an artist whose path has been enriched by such an outpouring of kindness and friendship can feel. Many years ago, there were Kwabena Onyina, Gyasi, and Kwaku Kwarteng, all of whom influenced my guitar style and lyrics in their unique ways. Akrasi, a trumpeter and good friend, also added his unforgettable style to performances. Now the sun has set on their lives, and only the memories remain. I had the honor to stand by their side when they last saw the world, and I will always carry with me an image of the world with their voices still loud with song.

On some of the records for *Ashanti Ballads*, I introduced notes and progressions that were a bit different from what I had often played. I ventured to play with a variety of complementary keys and fell in love with using chords to amplify the lyrics as a messenger whose lips are covered with lovely fragrance. Like an artist descending on a canvas with color to paint a beautiful image, I wanted my fingers to find their way to whatever could keep the tune authentic.

All the subtle variations, at least in my mind, added a particularly magnificent depth to the otherwise regular tune. I often found that many in the audience wouldn't care much about the technical nuances, but it made a big difference to me in how I heard the sound, even when I had played it over and over again. The men and women with whom I stood on stage dug deeper into their talents too, so that every performance would be a journey of its own, not only for the audience but for each of us as well.

The more I gave of myself, the more friends and mentors poured every little bit of knowledge and experience into mine. They fanned my fire so that my passions would not turn into vapor and vanish.

I had set out to create a unique style, and it brought me much joy, especially at a time when a new wave of audiences would be hearing my music for the first time.

Early in my career, guitarist Kofi Twumasi played alongside me at many events. His style was an excellent complement to mine. I would often be engulfed in the singing while also playing some of the most intricate guitar chords. I didn't want my divided attention to affect the music and the message, so Kofi's skill was a tremendous help. Like him, in many ways, the band members had all become an important part of my still-unfolding story.

I learned one of the greatest lessons about having a trustworthy person standing by my side during a performance in front of perhaps one of the largest crowds of my career. It was in Oakland, California. The day was cold, and the pain I had sustained in my knee as a young boy came back to haunt me. I could barely move my foot earlier that day, but I hoped the discomfort would soon wear off. The sharp ache lingered throughout the performance, so I tapped my feet often when I could. I must have been the only person in Oakland that day who did not enjoy the music. I was in so much pain.

After the performance, the audience stood to cheer, their applause filling the air. As was customary for performers - and something I had done for many years - I stood up and graciously bowed in appreciation. But in that instant, the pain in my knee became unbearable. I couldn't stand. I had to sit back down. What had always been a simple, graceful gesture turned into an awkward moment: Koo Nimo, sitting on stage, as the curtain slowly closed on him. It was a stark reminder of how swiftly things can change, even in the most familiar of rituals.

I had managed to get through the performance and did all I could to stretch my leg in such a way that it wouldn't hurt too much. But when I needed to stand, even for a moment, I could not. My group stood, but I gripped the guitar's strings as I sat in the chair. I was doing my best to stand up, but it was as if my knees were bent on not letting me go. The tall curtain gradually came down, and the band members quickly helped me to my feet before it went back up. It was a scene everyone may have forgotten in an instant, but one that would live with me for as long as I held onto my guitar's strings.

To this day, I remember how humbling it was, a stroke of kind fortune, that a falling curtain made it look as though my sitting down was part of the act. It taught me an incredible lesson about accepting a helping hand, and I saw fate as a friend, because you never know when your own strength and wisdom will not be enough to carry you along. That evening also taught me that I had entered a world where I had to turn a disadvantage or even a letdown into a teaching moment.

Whenever I replayed that scene in my mind, I couldn't help but hope that the band members who stood beside me that evening in California also carried away a thought that would shape their own attitudes. I wondered if, in that moment of vulnerability, they saw something beyond the performance - humility and the unpredictable nature of life. It was a moment that, for me, transcended the stage, and I hoped it left a lasting impact on them as well.

The years in the international limelight nudged me even more to embrace a relentless pursuit of unprecedented diligence and to make a conscious effort to strain every muscle in doing so. The story of a creative artist is occasionally filled with chance happenings that may have seemed like a stroke of genius when, in fact, they seldom feel that way. Over and over, I had seen how musicians would adjust on stage when their plans for a show fell apart, and without uttering a word, the collective judgment of the band would be to improvise quickly.

As a bandleader, I had found how important improvisation was, like when some band members did not show up, and I would quickly have to harmonize to fill that void. I had come to terms with the fact that any success at a given stage in a person's life would come along with its unexpected low points, and I had to be ready to live through those as well.

Even before Joe Latham talked about what he hoped my recording *Ashanti Ballads* in multiple languages would become, my experience had been marked by a string of surprises. My only comfort had been that I had truly guarded myself against a culture where image over-shadowed a heart's truth and where instant gratification could tempt an artist away from living honestly and selflessly.

If my closest confidantes could stand and speak in my place, they would remind me of how I never imagined the excursion I have been so fortunate to embark on with my music. My feelings mirrored those of my mentors and of the remarkable individuals whom Nyankopon had brought along my path. Maybe they had been my reward for something I had done for someone else but which I took to be a kindness I probably could not have earned.

I knew I had been given the gift of music, but I would never have reached the shores of my own ambition if I had only been eager to swim past all the people swimming alongside me. I recall memorable encounters with many people from different walks of life. Sometimes I traveled to Fiema and surrounding towns with Ms. Hannah Shrekenbach, who was working at the time as a professor of Architecture at the University of Science and Technology, and Mrs. Valerie Sackey, a teacher at Saint Louis Secondary School.

Our work involved a collaborative initiative with the local animal welfare organization. The region, with its breathtaking landscapes, was also renowned for its sanctuary monkeys, the Mona monkeys and the black-and-white colobus. These monkeys had become captivating hosts, their interactions with humans leaving visitors in constant awe. The way they engaged with us was nothing short of mesmerizing, drawing curious onlookers who were always amazed by the bond that seemed to exist between the animals and the people who cared for them.

Once, I was invited to perform at the shrine of Abudwo in the twin towns of Buabeng and Fiema in the Brong Ahafo region. Nana Kwaku Firi, an extraordinary drummer at the shrine and seperewa player, lived there. Not many people had heard of the talent he possessed, and he had never found an audience bigger than just a few people who passed through the village.

We arrived at a residence near the sanctuary for monkeys, where we would learn more about the town and visit with some of the elders. In the courtyard, I was playing a few songs on my guitar when Nana Kwaku Firi came out with a seperewa in his hand. The strings were all torn. He had found out that I was interested in the harp lute and that I always found a way to add traditional sounds to my music. He loved music and played the traditional drums with such magnificent skill, just as he played the seperewa, completely lost in its sounds and rhythms. For Nana Firi, he was looking forward to a day when all the music in his heart would come alive. I was impressed by his skill, and my mind began to race in search of a way I could help the man live his dream.

I came back to Kumasi and arranged a visit with Dr. Craig Woodson, a research candidate at the University of Science and Technology. Knowing his shortcomings, Nana Firi advised that we go to a nearby village called Busunya, several kilometers from Fiema. We met Agya Atta, Kwaku Firi's former teacher, and soon learned that although he had been a phenomenal singer for much of his life, he was weak with old age and could no longer play any instrument.

He told us a story of when, as a young boy, he had once walked with his father to buy a sack of salt in Kumasi, only to find, as they neared the city, that there were still clashes in what became the famous Siege of Kumasi. Agya Atta recalled the events of his history just as he had lived them, and was glad to share them with a young man who hoped that someday he would get the chance to tell the rest of the world. I saw a heartwarming example of a man who wanted to share every little ray of sun with anyone he knew could enjoy its warmth. We decided to mesh their talents and record their songs.

I invited Nana Firi to come to Kumasi for a concert we had organized for him at the city's Cultural Center. What had started as a chance meeting back in his village, Fiema, ended up opening a new chapter in the lives of these men who had gone as far as they could on their own. All they were looking for was someone who would lean forward, take them by the hand, and urge them to dream again beyond where they stood. I had the great privilege of helping in the small way that I could.

I have found that in life, there will be moments that will profoundly amaze us if our eyes and hearts remain open, and we walk humbly. If we have not killed another's dream but instead have fanned their fire, we will not be saddled with guilt or wonder if the shadow behind us is our own. Meeting Nana Kwaku Firi was unforgettable. Perhaps keeping an untainted heart as best as I could had led me to this.

Once, on our way back from the region, we made a turn from the Techiman main road just before Forikrom village. There stood an outcrop of rocks piled high along the roadside. The Brong-Ahafo area was full of stunning natural sites, and it was as if every hill and dip on the side of the road had its own story waiting to be told. Mrs. Sackey had read about the vibrating stones rumored to be in the area, and thought we should seek out this once-in-a-lifetime experience. These were unique rock structures and other unusual land formations. My curiosity had been awakened, and the place was already living up to the expectations I had come in with.

We made our way up until we came to one tree sitting atop the hill. It was covered with mangoes.

"*Koo, play something,*" the two ladies said.

I tuned my guitar, adjusting the strings and tightening the knobs, then began to strum a few chords. As the sound filled the cave, a powerful reverberation swept through the space around us. I was astonished. Chord after chord, the melody seemed to loop and echo through the cave's corners, as if it were announcing our arrival, one that, I imagined, was unusual, given that not many would come to this place with a guitar in hand. As an artist, this was the kind of experience I had always hoped for, one that would take my breath away. And it was nothing short of extraordinary.

"I will play you a nice Presbyterian hymn," I said.

I played the chords to *Glorious Things of Thee Are Spoken*, the 18th-century hymn made famous by the English clergyman John Newton. I had heard this song over and again at Adisadel College, together with a handful of hymns, and also in church as a boy. I wanted to play a tune familiar to the women who had come with me. Ms. Shrekenbach, who was German, looked up in surprise because she was very familiar with the tune, her face glowing with a smile as she burst into song. The mangoes began to fall from the tree one after another.

The incredible reverberations continued. The prolonged echo blended with the chords from my guitar, creating a magnificent sound that I could never have imagined. It was splendid. We were far away from the city noise, tucked away in a serene and refreshing little world. The whistling sounds through the cracks in the rocks also added their voices. We were filling the village skies with more beautiful melody.

No matter what I had accomplished in life, I could not believe I deserved such a moment. I've often thought that someday I would go back to the quiet Brong Ahafo town, to that same area, to see if anything had changed. I would be curious to see if the sons and daughters in places like Forikrom, Nkoranza, and Tanoboasi managed to keep the treasured beauty of their world, or if the passing years had stripped away the miracle. To this day, I remember that afternoon as if it was only yesterday, and it still takes my breath away.

Whenever I took my turn on stage, I was keenly aware of how my own path had been littered with opportunities to let people hear our brand of music and be inspired by its meaning. My paths crossed with extraordinary men and women who had, in their hearts, a voice for the whole world to hear, and it was such a joy to stand with them and see their dreams live too. There was nothing I had found more fulfilling than helping others find their tune, style, and song.

During my early years as a boy at the Presbyterian school, we went to catechism class and studied the Bible's teachings, some of which inspired my singing. The stories stayed with me. It was not only a fascinating excursion into how life must have been in that time in history, but also into how the characters still live on in how we carry out our work every day. The teachings of the Christian faith kept my dreams alive and often became a reminder of what had unearthed a passion in a young boy. It was these that gave me a song from the heart.

I often quoted the Apostle Paul's 1 Corinthians 13: "If I speak in the tongues of men or of angels, but do not have love, I am only a resounding gong or a clanging cymbal." For me, these words emphasise that love is the overriding emotion we should carry in every facet of life. They would leap off the page each time the guitar's chords accompanied them.

When I first performed the song *"Naa Densuaa,"* I paraphrased these words from the famous Apostle Paul and spent a few moments sharing what they meant to me, a humble reflection. Fortunately, some of these Christian verses had already become popular sayings many people knew, but they hadn't taken the time to understand how these meanings applied to them personally. When the words merged with rhythm, they stirred the heart, giving meaning to even the simplest thoughts, and made people feel alive again. That is why we sang.

The song *"Naa Densuaa"* evokes an image of a mother's endurance and her love for an ailing child. When she must find deeper strength to console a child in pain, a love that knows no bounds keeps a smile in her heart. With love, a mother gently cares for her frail child, finding the grace to endure long, sleepless nights. For those we care deeply about, we learn to overcome unimaginable odds to see them live their dreams. The song "Naa Densuaa" builds on this reflection to tell a story about one of life's most important virtues, - love.

The meaning of "Naa Densuaa" was always piercing. Unlike Abena's role in "Me Suro Wo Gyamu Fite," "Naa Densuaa" speaks of heartfelt faithfulness - the kind that sacrifices for the happiness of a union. When I first sang "Naa Densuaa" in a recording session, I was so overwhelmed with emotion that I couldn't finish. It was difficult to sing a song that meant so much to me, and the memory evoked sentiments that gave the lyrics a life of their own. It felt surreal.

In one of the recording sessions, the sound engineer stopped the recording so I could compose myself. He realized that the lyrics had perhaps guided my own life. He suggested we could resume at another time. In hindsight, those are the moments I wish I had had the strength to sing through the heartache.

For his part, the sound engineer always recalled that moment as one he wished he could relive because it was a genuine event in a performer's life that connected with emotions he could not articulate, even on his best day. Whenever I reflect on it, I realize how much of a difference it made that someone cared enough and, with a simple gesture, took a moment to see another man breathe.

Much of the work done on *Ashanti Ballads* became the foundation for most of my later work, even during times when ideas were elusive and the words didn't come as quickly as my fingers traveled on the guitar strings. I had chosen to write a song that bore a deep feeling for me, but one that I hoped would also resonate with every face in the audience. *"Naa Densua"* was such a song.

Naa Densua, my dear, listen to me
Though I speak with the tongues of men

And of angels and I have not charity,
I am becoming as sounding brass or tinkling cymbal.

Do not sell our marital issues outside
Because to do so means others would buy
And resell it for extra profit.
Observe the pillow; it hears every laugh and what goes on in our minds
But it neither breathes nor coughs to create awareness

Love is like measles
It takes patience to cure
Without it you lose your child
Naa Densua, listen to me and be patient and stay with me
For marriage is no child's play
Someone is envious of the fact that I am self-employed
My enemies want my downfall

Someone is envious of the fact that I am well and not sick in bed,
But illness was not made to be experienced by an individual,
Nobody knows how the termite gets water to build its hill.
Life is like sugarcane,
Not all the joints of the stem are sweet,
Be patient and stay with me
Afua Yentumi says "Behind every successful man, there is a woman!"
Women are like common salt
You recognize their usefulness
When the salt is not in the preparation

Kwaku Addo, my good friend,
Never despair for there is always hope
Amma Asibuo, I am grateful to you

Please listen to this advice and listen to me
Naa Densua, listen to me. .

In music, I have been fortunate to find something I truly enjoy. My hands never grew so weak that I couldn't play, even more than 70 years after my first performance. I could not imagine a life without the six strings. It has helped that my preference for nylon strings has been gentle on my fingertips. Occasionally, studios and music auditoriums were equipped with sound amplifiers, so I didn't have to force the strings to scream their notes.

I had learned to play guitar with my fingernails. I never used a guitar pick, and perhaps I had convinced myself that I didn't want to be on a stage with my destiny in the hands of something so small. I hadn't given it much thought when I first began, but I had never learned to play any other way. My fingernail had become an extension of my thumb, and it was always a good companion. As best as I could, I didn't want my sound to be harsh, and I did everything I could to let the strings speak gently for themselves. The more I practiced through the years, the more I found that every time I picked up my guitar, I could achieve the perfect note and tune I was hoping for.

My career in music thrust me into the limelight, but it did not take away the joys I found in ordinary days. I played my guitar freely. There were years when I would jump from fret to fret, as if trying to peel away any mystery that was tucked into the guitar's neck. In my older years, I discovered new ways to reach the same tones, and these thrilling exercises brought a refreshing love for the art form. I knew I had to keep learning, find creative paths along the frets, and search for my notes as painstakingly as I always had. But every moment was still a delight, perhaps even more so because I was not living with secrets that tugged at my heels with every step.

As I walked onto different concert stages, my mind raced through time and every experience, eager to share my heart with the audience.

This feeling never went away, no matter how many times I sang the same words. It was the gentle strokes that spoke the loudest. There were days when I couldn't play a song because of a torn string or the strangest of unexpected events. Once, I watched the great American guitarist Stanley Jordan dive into his creative versatility in Martinique, with a torn guitar string in hand just as he began his first song. But he handled it just fine, and I learned to do the same.

Like any guitarist, I spent days weary of a sound falling apart when the dryness in a room wreaked havoc on a guitar. There's only so much a person can do because, by its very nature, solid wood shrinks when it dries. That, in turn, affects the frets, and soon, the sound slowly changes from what the artist expected to hear. I did my best, so that even in moments I could not have prepared for, I might still get through the song. But all the preparation in the world would have been for nothing if my life away from the lights and the crowd had been filled with its own emotional chaos.

I never thought being born left-handed would influence how my life turned out. Whatever complex interaction between genes and environment endowed me with this trait, I didn't have much of a chance to explore it. My mother, Akua Fukuo, who had been a strict disciplinarian as far back as I could remember, did not like to see me play an instrument with my left hand. I had no choice but to relearn whatever little skill I had developed early on. Whatever her reasons were, I would never know. But she was adamant that I use my right hand to play the guitar, and I will never know where life would have taken me if I had played the same guitar with my left hand all those years. This may have been a fascinating turning point in my life, but it was perhaps *Nana Nyankopon's* way of pushing me to build resolve and strength in pursuing excellence.

Who knows if my story would have been different from guitarists who flipped their guitars and played them upside-down, with the bass E-string sitting at the top? Maybe it wouldn't have become as fun through the years, and I may have returned to explore another hobby. But maybe I would have encountered people like Jimi Hendrix, who were known for using right-handed guitars after having them re-strung to make them comfortable for left-handed musicians. Whatever I could have become or whatever shortcomings I would have had to live with, I will never know. I practiced over and over with my right hand, and soon, that became all I knew.

There were days when the winds would carry my songs away before the audience could hear them. There were also days when nostalgia and memory brought me to the stage with a heavy heart, but through it all, I had to find the strength to reach for the furthest star. Even on those days, I could only hope that the genuineness of my heart would restore anything that had unraveled with time and that the voice from my mended scars would still be loud.

The years after the release of *Ashanti Ballads* set the stage for a career that had been incredibly eventful, even if occasionally turbulent. I was blessed to share the spotlight and gaze into the future with a remarkable group of people. An artist often has a pivotal moment he looks back on, realizing how it probably influenced or even altered his creative path. Like a note underpinning whatever tune we play, what we give will eventually come back to us.

I have poured all my life into the guitar's strings, but have I ever woken up surprised by where I am? On the contrary, I go through each day knowing that the sun will set when its work is done, ready to give way to the moon in the evening. I, as a man and a guitarist, have no influence over where and when it does. At the end of the day, even if I chose to chase the sun to the ends of the earth, it would still set away from where I stand, and give me a chance to be amazed. I truly hope that in finding my voice on an international stage, I have given many artists in the crowd a reason to keep their fingers between the guitar's strings.

There is no telling where inspiration will come from. No one knows which day will bring the extraordinary or what new experience will take our breath away. Over time, I've learned never to let what I cannot fully understand stand in the way of what I know to be true. A truthful heart has guided me through my career, helping me navigate even the most uncertain of times. I've also come to realize that no path is carved without its share of remorse and regret. But each day, as the sun rises, I give my life's honest effort, allowing the day to unfold as it will, trusting that the darkness of night will come and go, without worrying about what it may bring.

11

ON THE SHOULDERS OF LEGENDS

Nketia, Mawere Opoku, Ellingson and
Many Who Paved My Way

There is a quote made famous by renowned scientist Sir Isaac Newton, though it may date back to the 12th-century theologian and author John of Salisbury. He said, "If I have seen further than others, it is by standing upon the shoulders of giants." This serves as a reminder that who we have become in life has only been possible because, at one point or another, we stood on the shoulders of giants.

We have benefitted from the improbable voyages of men and women whose experiences have served as invaluable lessons, guiding us toward the fulfillment of our dreams. While this truth is undeniable, the human mind often discounts or fails to fully appreciate the profound impact of these giants. Too often, we find ourselves acting from a place of self-belief, as though we have navigated life entirely on our own, forgetting the invisible threads of influence that have shaped our journey. It iis a humbling reminder that our progress is not solely our own, but built on the wisdom and struggles of those who came before us.

I have had ample experience to know that we all need a helping hand to carve a path through the dense forests of life and to achieve our dreams. Had I not had the good fortune of learning from some of the most remarkable men and women in Foase and around the world, my passion may have never seen the morning light. In my mind, the truth of John of Salisbury's words lies in the fact that we are all beneficiaries of our ancestors. Even our modest successes owe much to the great thinkers and world-changers who came before us. In Asante, we call them *Adikanfo*.

Many of the *Adikanfo* left their own trails for us to follow. Everything we have become, and everything we have discovered in life, has come from a view of the horizon that we did not discover on our own. Many climbed as high as they could so that we would know how far we stood from the summit. Some of the men and women who came before us lifted us when we fainted, with songs deeply tucked away in our hearts. Others gave us every reason to press forward in whatever skill we chose to pursue.

The love for the guitar never faded from my heart because there were giants in every corner of my world who would not let it weaken. From this most significant realization, whatever I have become, I am indeed grateful to have had legends who made progress in various aspects of life and stood tall long enough for me to stand alongside them. I am forever thankful for the chance to say that it was upon the shoulders of our own *Adikanfo* that a man like Koo Nimo turned philosophies into poetry and passion into rhythm.

From the quiet woods in Foase and surrounding villages like Nkawie Kuma, Nkoran, Trebuom, and Nweneso No. 1, there were brilliant minds always willing to share their knowledge, if only one would ask. From the dusty roads in Afrantuo and Kokoben to the busy streets of Kumasi's Kejetia and New York's Times Square, every smile and sacrifice from mentors guided my footsteps. I remember the people who took the time to invest in my life and inspire me when my own wisdom was not enough to tell a story. When my skill was not enough to reach a world with music, it was such men as these whose courage and support pushed me further.

Emeritus Professor Albert Mawere Opoku served as a professor of Dance and Choreography at the University of Ghana in Legon, Accra. He is one person I always hoped never got tired of hearing about my gratitude because he made such a selfless and tremendous investment in my career. It means the world to me to have had his words to hold on to, and his encouragement to stand on. I think back to when he first saw my childlike enthusiasm for playing guitar. There was such willingness in my heart to commit myself to acquiring the skill, and Professor Mawere Opoku urged me on with more than just his words.

Often, I reflect on having chance and serendipity as two of my closest friends. Some doors opened for my vocation when I least expected it, but this was made possible through the lives of people whose footpaths I had stumbled across. Professor Mawere Opoku was one of the true heroes of African culture, and my memory will never lose sight of the man he was and how influential he was on my own accomplishments.

I think back to the very start of my career when I was still searching for my own sound and a unique style that would hopefully set me apart from my contemporaries. The conversations in those years would set the stage for the rest of my journey. Professor Opoku advised me that, in his opinion, the best way to learn guitar was to practice often. The easiest way to continue practicing without your fingertips giving you reasons to quit was to use nylon instead of steel strings. A simple idea, but one that added richness to my technique throughout my music career.

When it came to guitar strings, most people - and even guitar experts - still argue which is better for a novice. When I began my career, I was not particularly concerned with the technical subtleties of guitar strings or whether steel or nylon produced a cleaner sound. I had fallen in love with the instrument and did not care much about anything else. I smile at the thought today, nearly seventy years later, that I didn't know enough to argue against Professor Mawere Opoku's opinion, but I'm glad I didn't disagree.

Adikanfo reassured young minds like mine of a nirvana that came along with devotion to one's craft. What in one instant may seem gloomy may very well be the rain that clears the sky for the newness of another day. Someday the pain would be gone from one's mind, and all the endurance would pay off.

Usually, when a person first plays the guitar, the calluses that form at the fingertips from plucking the strings force many people to give up on the instrument. In my case, I was fortunate to have heeded the advice of someone with the experience and genuine heart to share what he had seen over and over. I loved the guitar too much to give up on it. I found great joy in the sound, and I also found that every fret held an inimitable story waiting to be told. The guitar gave the words life, just as the great mentors had assured. I found out many years later that nylon-strung guitars, or classical guitars, were often ideal for people with a preference for classical music. People like me.

What particularly strikes me is that maybe Professor Mawere Opoku saw a specific music genre in me long before I did. This would turn out to be one of the most overwhelming observations I would make in my life as a creative artist. The mellow tone and gentle responsiveness of the nylon strings gave me immediate satisfaction with whichever chord or progression I learned. So, I played even longer. His 60-pound sterling investment in my life turned my passion into a lifelong journey of entertaining people around the world. It was on shoulders like these that my passion grew wings.

People who had dedicated their lives to the paths we hoped to travel became a rich source of wisdom. As Sir Isaac Newton wisely said, if we stand on the shoulders of giants, we can see much farther into the distance. By leaning on the self-sacrificing musicians who came before me, and with a deep commitment to honing my craft, the joy of following a humble dream allowed my words and my sound to reach far beyond what I could have imagined at the beginning of my career. It was through their guidance and my own dedication that I found myself on a journey that took me to places I never dreamed possible.

Anytime I have been given any credit about my knowledge of Asante traditions and culture, I have been quick to talk about how it was rather great men like Professor Mawere Opoku who truly deserve all the accolades. I had become a beneficiary of cultural knowledge only because my life had been intertwined with men who had spent a great deal of their lives peeling back the layers of our history. I call them libraries on fire and walking museums. This is what Professor Mawere Opoku became for me. I have been fortunate to have legends like him invest in my life. I owe them a great deal.

I worked my hardest at a career that consumed every waking moment and challenged me to sacrifice the leisure of an evening for long stretches of practicing chords, octaves, and matching melodies. I thank Almighty God for legends who showed me the value of hard work through their own example. I saw elders wake up at dawn, as if to prepare the day for a still-sleeping village. Their dedication was greatly admired by all, and even they never stopped learning.

Throughout my career, every time the cheers grew louder, I was reminded of the men and women who never had anyone to cheer their efforts. It was their quiet tenacity, their perseverance in the face of obscurity, that sparked a fire within me. Their struggles became the foundation of my own passion, inspiring me to pursue my dreams so that someone like Kwabena Boa Amponsem, just a young boy at the time, could one day find a voice through songs and strings. I often reflect on how their journeys, unseen and uncelebrated, made it possible for me to express myself in ways I never thought possible.

Koo Nimo's music would not have been anything worth listening to if my mother Akua Fokuo's favorite Methodist hymns had not echoed in my head. It may have taken many years for me to appreciate the blessings in every day if my father Opanin Kwame Amponsah had not taken the time to teach me some of life's core values. My parents shared what they had learned in music and in life, and gave me a leg to stand on. Most important of all, their integrity reigned in a home where honor guided our actions, so my career found dedication from a probing mind nurtured over the years.

The faith my parents left me with as a little boy became my guiding light, the gentle wave that carried me to stages across the world. From my parents, I learned to reach for every opportunity. I often talked about how we did not have much, but we did not need any more than what we had. With a family who taught a child to give thanks to our creator for the good days and to be even more thankful for the not-so-good days, I walked away with instrumental lessons later in life that saved me from inevitable disappointment. I have them to thank every day.

I nurtured my talent in the shadows of brilliant thinkers whose humility soon became a guiding light and taught me the practical value of not only building lasting relationships but also embracing shared learning experiences. It was such open hearts of legendary musicians that added clarity to the pursuit of my dreams, allowed me to tap into their creative reservoirs, and set me on a path to artistic discovery.

When I first met Professor Emeritus J.H. Kwabena Nketia, he was the Director of the Institute of African Studies at the University of Ghana. He soon became a friend and mentor whom I have always looked up to. I had chosen a career fraught with uncertainties, but his words were always the tools that helped me sculpt my craft. Professor Nketia, through the decades, had become a star across Ghana, Africa, and beyond, a star that stays through the night and glows to show dreamers the way back home.

A mentor like Professor Nketia celebrated even my modest successes and saw the truth in my every pain, even when the rest of the world only saw Koo Nimo, the musician. Audiences only heard the soothing music and beautiful harmonies, but it was the integrity of such friendship that became the central nerve for the creative artist in me.

One of the biggest highlights in my evolution as a musician came from Professor Nketia's invitations to perform at cultural events on the University of Ghana campus. It was an opportunity to share my ideas and my message through traditional palm wine guitar music. Before long, those performances earned me popularity beyond recognition. Beyond entertainment, the university audiences particularly appreciated the didactic element of every song, piecing together many of the anecdotes and folklore they had heard from their own towns and villages.

If, indeed, as in the words of famous British politician Sir Winston Churchill, "We make a living by what we get, we make a life by what we give," I have been given a great deal and have a lot to give to any listening ear. The traits I saw in mentors significantly affected my career and my life. Whether I was playing guitar to audiences at a United Nations concert, a little girl on the side of a Kumasi street, or in front of large crowds in San Francisco and Melbourne, the legends who walked in the shoes where I now stood never strayed too far from my mind.

Much earlier in my career, I embraced the fact that every performance on stage would be a chance to perfect my skill. Koo Nimo's voice might join with that of an entire generation whose story was yet to be told in the history books. I have had people remind me that if history was unkind, our lives and works might not find their way onto any paper to be remembered. So much of the songs and work may even be lost through the years, but the hope is that our traditional sounds would become a part of musical compositions and a permanent slice of culture.

Again, it was Professor Nketia who urged me to preserve the African harp lute, *seperewa*, one of the most ancient musical instruments of the Akan people. Men like him had worked tirelessly to stir the appreciation of this music genre, and it was our generation's responsibility to continue - through every song, every performance, and every opening - to add our voices to the legacy.

Music was much more than the words the audiences heard and the rhythm to which they tapped their feet. Every element in a sound spoke in a different way, yet all were tied together in the musician's heart. The audience would watch me sing, and even my appearance would have its own words to say. I had to be conscientious of the image I projected in every moment. Professor Nketia often said that even my fingernails, my beard, my traditional cloth, and my footwear all spoke to the audience in ways my lyrics could not. That counsel made a difference, and whenever I was tempted to treat an event as ordinary, his words would ring in my mind, helping me push forward.

"Legend" is a term often used casually in contemporary society to describe people whose work, impact, and worth we admire. I believe it also aptly defines those whose legacy inspires us to leave our own. When we have had the chance to sit and learn from excellent teachers of remarkable character, we continue to draw from their wisdom long after they are gone. They become the legends whose storylines shape our own.

When you've traveled far from home and become a stranger in someone else's land, there are inevitably days when the dark alleys will make you wonder how the future will unfold. In the faces of such men and women, life taught me about persistence. In distant lands, away from the comfort of familiar places, the shoulders of legends emerged for us to stand on.

Had I not taken the chances I did, perhaps fate would have been kind enough to find me once more. Yet, it was the helping hands along the way that nudged me forward through winding roads, just in case I lost the tailwind in my sails. Maybe, in another place and another time, my destiny would not have wandered too far, and our paths would have crossed again. Still, I never regretted choosing to live my life in pursuit of a passion born from a guitar string, rather than watching life pass me by as I lingered in the shadow of an unfulfilled dream. But I knew, deep down, I could not have done it all on my own.

Without even knowing their impact on my life, many extraordinary individuals helped me build the faith that I, too, could write my story with courage and resilience. It may be long, and perhaps even difficult, but when the sun sets, I would look back at every memory of a flower's bloom and be happy I held on to hope when I wasn't sure where it would lead.

Professor Duncanson was an Australian physicist working at the Kwame Nkrumah University in the late 1950s. I met him early in my life, and he became instrumental in my decision to pursue a musical career. His words, "This is your life," created a turning point, like a bright morning sun in open fields waking a farmer to a new day.

I think back to that evening and wonder what it was that made this man notice such talent in me. Maybe this ought to be my life, I thought to myself. Just as negative words have the power to affect a person's life and actions, I've always believed that positive affirmation can be the fuel that energizes a person to unlock their true potential.

From the day he heard me playing guitar, the challenge for me was to apply myself diligently to learning all I could about it and become the best professional I could be.

If people like Professor Duncanson were betting on me, I had no choice but to bet on myself. I've long held the opinion that the desire to excel at any craft is like a seed, and it takes encouraging thoughts and positive affirmations to nurture it until it blooms. While some argue that persistence can substitute for talent, I learned later in life that, on the continuum of growth, persistence is an excellent companion for talent.

A few years after we met, I got a new job at the same university, but Professor Duncanson had retired. Still, he had left in me that same tendency to motivate young people in whom I saw opportunity and talent. I heard his words over and over again: "This is your life." Anytime I walked past the small hallways at the university, I was humbled by the inspiration and privileged to have found my future on these same grounds.

The word *"legend"* reminds me of musicians like Akwasi Manu, who paved the way for many of my contemporaries. Long after he played his last tune, I wished the rest of the world had the chance to hear him perform songs like *"Nkwankwaasem," "Agyanka Bra," "Kanoa Wakum Mpempem,"* and *"Yaa Serwaa."* All of these songs had distinctive musical arrangements that showcased talent both rare and mesmerizing. Other well-known guitarists at the time were household names like Kojo Mireku, Kankam, Appianin, Appiah Agyekum, Kakaiku, Kwasi Peprah, Kwabena Mensah, Yaw Kune, Jacob Sam, Kwaa Mensa, and Peasah.

They all mastered their crafts and became standards of musical excellence in Ghana and across Africa. This was a time when an artist could only earn the respect of a generation of brilliant musicians by devoting great effort to learning. The creative artists who inspired me to pursue my passion did not walk past an opportunity to ignite boldness with their ingenuity and indefatigable craving for classic highlife. They had been Akwasi Manu's contemporaries, but they all put a unique spin on guitar techniques and breathtaking progressions. In all of their styles, I found great motivation to expand my own rendition of chord progressions with the infusion of rhythmic chords that would enrich the harmony.

Around the world, prominent guitarists like Italian composer Mauro Giuliani had become famous for their broken chords and arpeggio style. It was as unique as it was beautiful, and not everyone could play his style. Another, Andrés Segovia, captivated the world with his conviction that a guitarist playing scales for about two hours every day could fix any tendency for incorrect hand positioning. Their work was celebrated globally and became popular in classical guitar. They set new standards for creative artists in different parts of the world. But in the remote towns and villages of Ghana, we had our own legendary trendsetters of the guitar style.

Musicians across Africa discovered their own styles and honed their talents to suit their unique cultures. While I listened to and appreciated internationally renowned artists, the biggest influences came from my own backyard. Musicians like Kwaku Kwarteng, who sang many of Akwasi Manu's songs and often imitated his style, had developed their own technique and a repertoire that distinguished their sound from other guitarists. Kwaku Kwarteng's voice won audiences across Africa, and he remains one of the greatest musicians I have known. These artists not only gave me concrete examples to aspire to, but I was most affected by the way they never overlooked who they were and where they had come from. That is why they became legends in our eyes.

I was particularly moved by how these musicians took pride in the creative process and immersed themselves in the sounds from their guitar strings. When we learned to play music, it was those techniques that we used as our launching pad until we developed the skill to carve our own. Just like the legends whose work had been an inspiration, I became almost obsessed with patiently creating an inimitable sound.

At the start of my career, what mattered most to me was not to mimic someone else's song or style but to discover my own unique flair, one that would make even the most familiar songs feel fresh and new. Reflecting on this journey, I realize I've been fortunate to have had incredible people to look up to along the way. The greatest blessing of all, however, has been their encouragement to let go of limiting beliefs, urging me to push past self-doubt and embrace the full potential of what I could become. Their faith in me helped shape not only my sound but the way I see myself and my place in the world.

One of the beautiful tapestries of life is living through the years and having a rich memory of life as it used to be. Long before there were music unions and organizations to provide career roadmaps, we could only learn by example. For many of my peers, well-known musicians like Akwasi Manu and his contemporaries were crucial in our development, setting benchmarks for African music to the world. It is on the shoulders of these legends that I stand today.

For a man who spent some of my most defining years around traditional Asante culture and in the royal courts, it would not come as a surprise that some of my greatest influences came from those hallways and verandas. When every strand of my personality is knit together with the culture that made me the man I am, my music could not stray from that center. My humble beginning always held a certain nostalgia that swept over me every time I needed a reminder of how far I had traveled. I continued to play my music as though I still sat in the presence of those brilliant personalities I had once known.

I am immensely grateful to people like Opanin Kyirifufuo, who once served as the Asantehene's *Atumpankahene*, a master drummer.

His wise counsel carried me as a musician, even through a career and future in flux. There was a time when Nana Prempeh I, the Asantehene at the time, embarked on an effort to revive several cultural areas in the Ashanti region. From what I learned from Opanin Kyirifufuo's account, when the Asantehene returned from the Seychelles Islands, he arranged for him to go to Kokofu to study *Twene Ka* - the drum language - under Agya Agyei Owusu. The experience changed him, stripping away the distractions that did not add value to the rich cultural stewardship and all that he had been entrusted with.

Late into the night, he memorized proverbs and adages. If there was any one thing I wished for above all, it would be to know everything Opanin Kyirifufuo knew. Even as a young boy, watching the dedication of men in the courtyards became one of my fondest memories, especially with the warmth of language from the treasury of kind hearts. I knew I could ask anything and learn anything about Asante philosophy.

I learned to examine my life constantly, a practice instilled in me by the elders in the royal courts, who took turns admonishing and encouraging a young boy with a growing awareness of the world around him. They pushed me to think beyond my current station in life, reminding me that one day, I would be the old man with nothing left but words to offer. They made me realize that those words would only hold weight if I had lived in a way that made them meaningful, if I had done my best to ensure they mattered. Their wisdom became a quiet guide, urging me to live with intention and to shape a life that, in the end, would be worth reflecting upon.

Throughout my career, I have never missed the chance to tell the world about the remarkable lives of people like Nana Opoku Ware II, Nana Kwame Bonsu, Nana Osei Kofi, and Nana Osei Kwabena. Like a rudder steering a ship in the direction it should sail, Nana Akua Mansa and Asantehemaa Queen Mother Nana Ama Serwaa Nyarko were exemplary figures in crucial stages of my life. Listening to their words and reflections gave me a window into their minds. Many prominent people in the royal palace - dating back to the 1940s - poured their wisdom into me, igniting a tiny spark that would grow into a great wildfire of ingenuity. Their hopes have become my voice.

Regardless of how far around the world my music has carried me, the one constant in my life has always been the foundation laid by these influential people. The longer I live, the more I am convinced that my life would not have amounted to much without the priceless gestures from the village elders. Their humility shaped my character and exposed me to great wisdom. The elders in the royal courts may not have had all the answers to life's enduring questions, but they generously shared insights on Asante traditions and values from other world cultures that would have taken almost a lifetime to discover on my own. They were legends in my eyes.

I cultivated a reading habit, which began by seeing the members of the royal family read in their leisure moments. I had a child's natural instinct to emulate them. They encouraged me to read anything I could find. As my life progressed through the heights of happiness and the depths of tragedy, their words brought comfort and lifted my spirits to carry on. With a commitment to the pages in a book, I nurtured valuable traits that would deeply affect the next stage of my life. These habits have become a central part of who I am more than 80 years later. I am lucky to have been in the presence of people who knew how to lead, but even more, how to nurture young minds.

When I moved to live with my sister at the royal palace in 1942, Nana Opoku Ware II advised that while I attended Adisadel College, I should also learn Greek and Latin. I had always been intrigued by world cultures, though perhaps not enough to learn their languages. Nana Opoku Ware II emphasized that it was not enough to simply learn English words. It would be far more enriching to understand the origins of the vocabulary we used. I quickly became fascinated by the derivatives of words, much like I was captivated by fables. In particular, Aesop's fables introduced me to a form of satirical story-telling that also provoked reflection in the reader.

My imagination, my development of musical style, and my knowledge of Asante poetic imagery were greatly enhanced by these encounters. As my career evolved, I began telling stories through songs, always hoping to share some of the prolific and fascinating anecdotes from my part of the world, even though they had been worn thin by time. I owe a deep debt of gratitude to Nana Opoku Ware II and his brother Nana Kwame Bonsu for what became one of the most significant elements of my music.

Nothing breathed more life into my dreams than the opportunity to listen to and learn from people whose imaginations never skipped a beat. One such person was Sir Mark Oliphant, one of Australia's most renowned nuclear physicists. He was a man of extraordinary intellect, remembered not only for his groundbreaking contributions to science but for infusing his work with a creative vision that changed the world. His ability to blend imagination with scientific discovery left an indelible mark on me, reminding me of the power of creativity in shaping the future.

In 1969, Sir Mark was invited by Professor A. A. Kwarpong to Ghana for the Aggrey-Fraser-Guggisberg Memorial Lectures, where I first met him. The annual event celebrated the legacy of James Kwegyir Aggrey, a Ghanaian scholar, educationalist Alexander G. Fraser, and Gordon Guggisberg, Governor of the former Gold Coast. It was his comment about mankind, that "Knowledge is not wisdom," that drove home one of life's most powerful yet simplest truths for me. He continued, "Wisdom can come only from the interplay of science with society; from the evolution of ethics, morality, and law to govern the actions of all men."

I had the opportunity to visit Sir Mark when I traveled to Australia to perform as part of a fundraising effort to purchase medical diagnostic equipment for Ghana. I used my time there to talk about scientific innovations and shared my thoughts on living life with a determination to excel. Oftentimes, individuals who treasure knowledge find ways to immerse themselves in activities that compel them to think beyond the status quo. In their company, those passions are awakened within oneself and carve an even brighter path for creativity.

It was always refreshing to witness the minds of true thinkers. They always encouraged me to stretch my imagination and create value through ideas that others might find ordinary. Knowing facts and being well-educated are two different points along the intellectual path, but creativity transcends the modest steps along that path. It was from these encounters and conversations that I came to appreciate the unimaginable value of human imagination, something for which I will always be grateful.

Another influential contributor to my career was Dr. E.K. Osei Kofi. He was incredibly invaluable to the creative artist I became. Dr. Osei Kofi had been an industrial sociologist and later a lecturer at the University of Science and Technology. His knowledge of culture and the genuineness of his heart were among the most admirable traits I encountered. Much of the wisdom by which I have lived my life, and which I encourage others to heed, came from his reassuring words over the years.

During his years as Director and Chairman of the Center for Cultural Studies in Kumasi, Dr. Osei Kofi remained focused on promoting traditional music and instruments in parts of the world where our genre and culture were still unknown. Some of the most significant exposure in my music career came under his leadership at the Cultural Center and because of his recommendations. I am forever grateful that he believed in the power of music to connect hearts and bring Ghana's story to an international audience.

My encounter with Dr. Osei Kofi was remarkably similar in many ways to one I had with Dr. Alex Atta Yaw Kyerematen years before. Dr.

Kyerematen had also attended Adisadel College in the 1930s. In my first year at the school, I saw his name on the Prize Winning Board, which showcased brilliant students through the years. The young Alex Kyerematen had been one of Adisadel's exceptional English students and later turned out to be one of the brightest minds I would have the good fortune to call a close friend throughout my career.

A few years later, he served as Director of the Ghana Cultural Center, which became known as the Center for National Culture. My band had performed at some of the events at the Kumasi Cultural Center, which he oversaw, and so our paths crossed. He was always reassuring, as if he knew that Koo Nimo, the musician, carried the weight of a culture on his shoulders and might need a helping hand along the way. I remember how the heavily attended Anokyekrom event gave me another platform to hone my creative skills, and Dr. Kyerematen never missed a date with Adadam Agofomma.

During my performances, I would occasionally tell a joke, which Sir Mark Oliphant found particularly entertaining. A part of me was driven by the desire to use every communication channel to convey a deeper message. While humor is often employed to capture an audience's attention, I think I leaned on it because there were proverbs and pieces of wisdom embedded in stories that couldn't be expressed any other way. It was as though laughter opened the door to something greater, allowing the truth to seep through in a way that felt both natural.

Dr. Kyerematen had earned a remarkable reputation through his scholarly writings and his impact on relevant social and cultural issues throughout Ghana. I remember reading one of his articles about the royal durbar in 1961. Durbars were state receptions given to British sovereigns when they visited countries that had once been colonies of the British Empire. The article recalled the year Queen Elizabeth II visited Ghana and painted a vivid picture of those moments through Dr. Kyerematen's eyes. I admired his writing even more because of his ability to convey messages in such great detail.

Over the years, I never grew tired of saying that Ghana should be proud to have a native son who displayed such excellence in his life and work, and I am certainly thrilled to have had such a man influence my career. His memory lives on, not only through the Dr. Alex Atta Yaw Kyerematen Memorial Lectures held annually but also through the many people whose lives he positively impacted. Dr. Kyerematen was an ardent visionary and supporter of culture, an immeasurable value to society. His impact on my life lives on in every note from Koo Nimo's guitar strings.

In 1976, I was invited to the celebration of America's 200th anniversary at the American Folklife Center, organized by the Smithsonian Institution. It was first unveiled as the United States National Museum, nicknamed "the nation's attic" for its eclectic holdings of millions of objects. The Smithsonian Institution in Washington, D.C., was established "for the increase and diffusion of knowledge" through its museums and research facilities. I traveled to the United States along with 27 other African musicians to perform at various venues across the country. We toured from Washington, D.C., to Milwaukee, Wisconsin, and to Oakland and San Francisco, California.

It was through people like Joe Latham, Professor Ter Ellingson, and his wife Linda that I had the opportunity to share palm wine guitar music with some of the most vibrant crowds in the heartland of America. For a musician engrossed in the thought of sharing my traditional guitar style with the world, I was always deeply appreciative of the work these individuals did behind the scenes to make these performances possible. We entertained crowds in parts of the United States where the guitar's influence on blues and folk music was popular, and we received some of the most amazing audiences any musician could ask for.

We later traveled through East St. Louis, Illinois, Memphis, Tennessee, and small towns like Evansville, Indiana. American audiences had heard various styles of African music before our arrival, but we walked away from each venue with audiences cheering for more and eager to learn about the places we sang about. I was fortunate to witness a panoramic view of music across world cultures, which refreshed my perspective and shaped my character.

In September 1998, Andrew Kaye recommended me to become an artist-in-residence at the University of Washington, Seattle. This was my first time in Seattle and my first such position in academia, and it turned out to be an incredibly pivotal moment in my life as a creative artist. I worked under the leadership of Professor Ellingson, a professor of Ethnomusicology, Anthropology, and Comparative Religion. I have often spoken of how Professor Ellingson became a great help to me and turned Seattle into a home away from home.

Occasionally, Professor Ellingson would assist me in promoting concerts and other musical events around Seattle. I was in a place where, no matter how captivating my music could be, there was still much work to be done to stir excitement for something that the people knew almost nothing about. What made the biggest impression on me was his gesture when I told him that I would be performing songs in the traditional Ghanaian palm wine guitar genre. He arranged to have several palm trees brought onto the stage, as if to recreate the perfect scene for the audience, who had never been to a village where guitarists entertained crowds under such trees.

Professor Ellingson invited me to give my first lecture at the University of Washington-Seattle, on Performance, Power, and Dignity. The turning point in my life as a musician had begun, far beyond what I had envisioned many years before. It was profoundly humbling and brought me much joy. Later, after I moved back home to Kumasi, the university arranged for students from various American universities to enroll in courses I taught in Ghana, including "Music Appreciation, Traditional Music, Ethics, and Etiquette."

When I reflect on the people who helped thrust me into some of the most fulfilling aspects of my career, my appreciation for Professor Ellingson's impact on my life's work continues to this day. I was a beneficiary of a genuinely good man who did not expect anything in return. He saw in me an artist who had sacrificed all he had and all he could to tell a story, and he didn't want my toil to become a futile undertaking. He did everything he could to make that stage of my musical career and life in the United States memorable.

Over the years, I would sometimes visit him in his Seattle home, and I would see a book in his library, which he would quickly ask me to take. I am convinced that one of the hardest things to do in life is to keep a vivid mental picture of every smile, handshake, and pat on the back to remind a person that there were always people in the crowd rooting for them to win. It was the selflessness of such people along my path that propelled me to new heights—beyond genre and country. Some of the stories I read from Professor Ellingson's library inspired a creative impetus and new things to imagine. I smiled every time I thought about this: maybe another song was tucked within the pages.

My life as a musician was gradually becoming an incredible adventure - often more than I had wished for. I remember the waves of thoughtfulness, and my gratitude would never be enough to embrace them. Like Professor Ellingson, Cynthia Schmidt, a Professor of Ethnomusicology at the University of Washington in Seattle, had attended Otumfuo Opoku Ware's Silver Jubilee in Kumasi and used that opportunity to visit me as well. Cynthia was immensely helpful in my experience as an instructor in the United States.

I recall one evening when she drove from Nebraska to Minnesota, a journey of over 500 miles, just to watch me perform for a single hour. Though she may not have understood all the lyrics, that certainly didn't stop her from fully embracing the music. Her presence, her willingness to make such a long trip, spoke volumes about the support and love for the art. But it was a reminder that sometimes, the heart understands the music in ways words cannot.

If there is one thing I always say about Cynthia Schmidt, it is that I learned far more from her life and the value of her words than she probably did from mine. The legendary musician John Lennon wrote, "Count your age by friends, not years. Count your life by smiles, not tears." The smiles from people like Cynthia gave me an uplifting and almost indescribable sense of calm, knowing that I had her friendship and support at every turn. I am forever grateful for friends like Cynthia, whose smile from the crowd gave inspiration to the man on the stage.

In music, just as in life, we stand on the shoulders of mentors and friends to climb along the gentle slopes and steep hills of life. Our human nature often assumes that people hear enough appreciation from others, so ours might not mean much. Many of us miss the chance to express our gratitude to those who sacrificed to give us our voice. Oftentimes, we assume that somehow, by coincidence, those who poured so much into our lives will know how grateful we are. For every act of kindness, a seed is sown, and the fruits of that will come alive many decades later. Gratitude never overflows in a heart; rather, while we express what lives in our hearts, we open ourselves to more people responding by pouring wisdom and knowledge into our lives.

I always made it a point to tell the men and women whose shoulders I had stood on how much I appreciated their contributions. It was the miracle of ordinary and unassuming moments that built character and honed talent, away from all the adulation. They made time to listen to me when I needed direction and affirmation. They valued my talent and person. Long after their voices had fallen silent, they still stood as mute reminders of why I pursued the dream the way I did. I hope that anytime I play a tune on any stage in the world, the audiences will join me in giving tribute to the people who helped shape my dreams and define my music career.

Because I spent most of the early years of my career on university campuses, my interactions with academic scholars compelled me to continue learning. Professor W. N. Laing at Okomfo Anokye Hospital had a calm way of conveying ideas, and he seemed to truly enjoy seeing perceptions and meanings uncovered. Long before I recorded a song, those relationships sparked my pursuit of what I imagined with chords and harmony, letting the guitar's strings take me on a journey. Even seemingly mundane conversations occasionally veered onto a deeper intellectual path. I found it truly refreshing to lean on their knowledge where mine fell short.

A man like Emeritus Professor F. Addo Kufuor, who had been a professor of Chemistry, recruited me to the University of Science and Technology from Okomfo Anokye Hospital. The date was November 1, 1960. I remember that Tuesday morning, after having worked through the long night before, how eager I was for the new opportunity to work under Professor Addo Kufuor's guidance.

Whether it was Oliphant, Ellingson, Schmidt, or another influential figure, the years of rich interactions with those I had admired throughout my career illuminated far more than just scientific experiments. Their guidance extended beyond their fields, offering invaluable lessons on life, perseverance, and purpose. One of the most important pieces of advice I received was about the unwavering commitment to a passion that drives us forward. It resonated deeply with me, shaping my own journey. I always made sure to thank them for the opportunities they gave to a young man eager to make something of his life, opportunities that helped me grow, not just in my craft, but as a person.

If I stand today, it is because of men like Vice Chancellor R.P. Baffoe. Ever since the afternoon in 1962, when he walked into a laboratory and spotted a curious young boy arranging equipment with such unusual patience, he saw in me a young man eager to discover anything that keen observation would lend itself to. I had found that my imagination in those arenas opened doors in my mind and allowed me to soar as high as my creativity would take me.

I think back to when I shared with Dr. Baffoe how much more I would love to learn, and my interest in any training courses that would help me develop my understanding of science and some of the absorbing experiments I was helping with in the laboratory. Three weeks later, he had partnered with department head Professor Whittaker to select me for the Inter-University Council Scholarship, which took me to England for three years. Much of my career as a creative artist soared after my exposure to new techniques while there.

I put a great deal of effort into what had once been a hobby, perhaps because I knew how much my heart felt awakened whenever I held my guitar. The opportunity paved the way for palm wine guitar music to find audiences far from my home. I had stood on the shoulders of others to reach the heights of my life's ambition, and I cannot forget how every bright day and shining moment had been made possible because they gave me a chance to discover my unique station in a vast universe.

Some of the most defining moments in my life and career came about as an outgrowth of some of the habits I cultivated; others happened through chance meetings. When I met Mr. Owusu Prempeh of the Ghana Broadcasting Corporation, he was working with Osei Mensah Bonsu and Nana Osei Owusu. They were, at the time, the producers of the program *Ene Ye Anigye Da*, a weekly radio show produced in Kumasi. They allowed me to use their stage as a stepping stone and gave me an opportunity to entertain the world with my music. The program was Kumasi's premier variety show, where many talented musicians had performed, so any effort to distinguish myself was undoubtedly going to yield great dividends later in my career.

Some of my chance encounters left indelible marks on my heart, with prominent people whose hearts were even bigger than their fans may ever know. Jazz trumpeter Clark Terry had encouraged many household names and performed with celebrated entertainers like Count Basie and Duke Ellington. At the time we met, he was famous for playing both the trumpet and the flugelhorn, and he had done so for decades. Clark Terry had come to Ghana when I was serving as president of the Musicians' Union (MUSIGA) in the late 1970s.

As part of the U.S. State Department's tour schedule, the Ghanaian musicians participated in an educational workshop organized by the United States Information Service (U.S.I.S.). Not long after Clark had returned to the United States, Cape Coast University invited me to teach traditional guitar. I fused traditional rhythms with jazz and other musical influences, with some of my conversations with Clark Terry lingering in my mind. This became my effort to give the students a broader, richer appreciation for how all these sounds and styles continually drew upon each other.

In one session, I introduced some of Terry's works to the students. Some of them found his technique exceptionally intriguing. I shared stories of how he had also been an encouragement to me, and of how, although we played music of seemingly different genres, our paths merged into a friendship and a rare chance to learn from a legendary musician. I sent word to Clark about the young people who had developed a genuine admiration for his work. I remember the day he sent a trumpet to one of the students to motivate the young musician to pursue his passion and not let the sound of music fade through the years when it would seem as though no one was listening.

Clark's passion for education etched his legacy not only as a trumpeter but also as a jazz educator. At many points in his life, the world-class trumpeter found joy in teaching, conducting clinics, and jazz camps in a classroom setting. It was no different from what he had done in Cape Coast. Contemporary musicians still spend a great deal of time learning Clark's skills and some of his remarkable finger movements. Clark is still revered as one of the legendary musical minds in American music history. What made the difference for me was the friendship we formed over many years and the inspiration I drew from his life's work.

Like a star that waits patiently through the day for its turn to shine bright at night, there were also people who picked up the torch of creativity and passed it through uncharted waters to show others how devotion could produce such brilliance. Until his passing in 1981, William Anderson, the famous American jazz trumpeter known around the world by his nickname "Cat," had been one of the foremost figures in jazz music.

No one surpassed Cat Anderson when it came to playing the higher registers on the trumpet. Any trumpeter will attest to the immense difficulty and skill required to navigate those extreme pitches with the ease and precision he mastered. For over four decades, from 1935 to 1981, Cat consistently played in the extreme upper register, pushing the boundaries of his instrument every day throughout his career. This included the legendary 26 years he spent performing with the Duke Ellington Orchestra, where his extraordinary talent became a defining feature of the band's sound. His ability to effort-lessly conquer such challenging territory on the trumpet remains an inspiration to musicians everywhere.

From the little I knew of him, I saw a disciplined determination, such a moving encounter that prompts my memory every time. A brilliant musician and inspiration, Cat Anderson was one musical genius whom I never missed a chance to visit when he was in town. Whenever his band would perform at venues in London and Manchester, England, during the time I was studying in the country, I would find a way to connect with him.

Cat Anderson was a man I have been unreservedly fortunate to have as a friend, and what was even more interesting about him was that there was never an inopportune time to talk with him about musical technique. It could be a brief moment backstage or sometimes in the musicians-only dressing rooms, but Cat understood that my curiosity came with a host of never ending questions. The conversations were always fascinating, and they meant a great deal to me. Meeting such remarkable talents of their generation and genre fanned the flames in my heart, and the same pursuit that fueled their commitment fueled mine too.

An honest appraisal of how far we have come in life often brings us back to our modest beginnings, especially with the emotional memory of the people who held the door open ahead of us and invited us in. Hindsight evokes an even deeper gratitude, as in the moment when Mr. Faisal Helwani sent my friend Ani Johnson to ask me to join the newly revived Musicians Union of Ghana in 1978.

Lebanese-born Faisal Helwani had made a name for himself as a music producer extraordinaire in Ghana and around the world. I saw in him a man whose vision was to see other people reach their highest potential. When the group needed to buy chairs for the Arts Council meeting room, Mr. Helwani took it upon himself to help. Similarly, for the MUSIGA elections, he volunteered to pay the transportation costs of all the musicians who had been invited.

His unwavering desire to help anyone he could in the industry, and even beyond, made him a remarkable person for people who worked with him. In his own way, his success did not allow him to ignore the challenges faced by artists. He believed that every creative artist reaches a corner of the world with his or her unique talents, and if he could help many people achieve their dreams, he would have also done his best in life. Mr. Helwani founded the Adikanfo Band and worked tirelessly to encourage Ghanaian musicians to work together under a unified umbrella. It is for this legacy that he is fondly remembered by many Ghanaian musicians, and I remain thankful for having met him.

As a man who carried his longing to share traditional guitar style with the world for several decades, it is almost impossible to recall every step I have taken through the pouring rain and the scorching sun, and every heart that has helped me get there. The relationships I forged defined the path I was able to follow.

The men and women on whose shoulders I have stood played music in the proverbial sands of time and dedicated themselves to their chosen profession to be known for having lived to the best of their abilities. I have had the benefit of intellectually challenging personalities whose wise counsel helped me climb the heights I would be fortunate to reach as a creative artist. I am certain that when future generations read the works of some of these men and hear their songs, it will reiterate the honor that I am privileged to bestow upon them. They were the shoulders I had to stand upon and the helping hands that became a constant companion in my pursuit of a future.

Throughout life, many will accomplish great things, but often for their own careers and personal ambitions. There are others, however, who bring forth success in the lives of those around them, seizing every opportunity to offer encouragement and support. Koo Nimo is the man the world knows today because, through the grace of the Almighty God, these men and women allowed their influence to connect one man's passion for the guitar to a destiny in music.

12

AKORA DUA KUBE

A Father's Hope for a Culture's Tomorrow

A young man came to me, eager to learn how to play the guitar. He admitted that he had witnessed extraordinary performers who played with what seemed like effortless grace. Their music was beautiful, and it sparked within him a desire to play just as effortlessly. As their fingers moved across the frets, his eyes lit up with the dream of what he, too, could become. His enthusiasm was palpable, and he could hardly wait to begin his first lesson. Like many eager learners, he imagined that in no time, he would be plucking the guitar strings and effortlessly playing popular highlife tunes, as if it were second nature.

The young man was at the point where many creative artists stand at one time or another. The only difference was that he was more enamored by the outward presentation of the end result than by the quiet rigor of the learning process. The magic, for him, had to happen instantly. That was an observation I did not find surprising, because I had seen it over and over again. There was no patience left to unpack the elements of the sound and understand the guitar in its most basic form.

I asked the young man to go to the local market and buy another local instrument, the *dawuro*. His face fell with complete disappointment. The *dawuro* is a banana-shaped metal bell with a small opening at one end. By all standards of music theory, it was a rather simple instrument that did not require much skill to learn. In fact, not many musicians set out to learn how to play the dawuro. The young man had set his heart on an avid desire to play the guitar. He had formed a glamorous image of his creative self and was desperate to see that come to life overnight.

In his disappointment, he went back home to his father to tell him how mistaken he had been. The man his father had recommended to be his guitar teacher was asking him to buy a simple metal bell that even a child with little training could play. What skill did one need to hit a metal bell and make a sound? How could the *dawuro* bring his ambition to life? The young man had developed the eagerness, but he was missing the patience to unearth the creative process, which would take time. Excellence often requires the commitment and patience of a snail, without trampling over the seemingly simplest stepping stones.

The father, without knowing anything about why I had asked his son to buy the *dawuro*, advised him to follow my instructions, even if it seemed odd. "Maybe Koo Nimo has something unusual in mind," the father suggested. Indeed, I had a good reason for the seemingly odd idea. I was using a process that would get my idea across clearly.

Music theory is intricately woven together through a series of artistic interactions that elevate what could have been an ordinary sound into something rich with rhythm and meaning. The young man would later come to realize that the lessons in percussion were the foundation not only of jazz and highlife but of countless other musical genres as well. In the same way, the basic steps, much like those taken by most creative artists, became the linchpin to my guitar style, offering invaluable insight into how beautiful sounds emerge from what initially seems like nothing. It was through this simplicity that I learned to build complexity, finding depth in the most basic of movements.

The sound of a guitar weaves its way into intricate melodies and harmonies, each note telling its own story. The true challenge for a player lies in learning to tune one's ear to the subtle nuances of every string, and understanding how chords bring depth and character to each note. In my own journey, studying with some of the world's renowned guitar teachers, one lesson that deeply resonated with me was the profound impact of every fret on the guitar's neck. Each shift, each touch of the fretboard, has the power to transform sound into a rich, complex musical journey, unfolding with every note played.

The logic holds, at least in my mind, that if a person cannot master the simplest instrument, it will be difficult to grasp the core arrangements on the guitar. I have seen people who attempted to play the *dawuro*, our supposedly effortless instrument, with their preconceived expectations, only to find out that their concentration waned quickly, even with what appeared to be simple repetitions. The guitar demands the use of several mental faculties at the same time, so the ability to create a sound and listen to it simultaneously goes a long way in determining one's ability to learn.

My encounter with the young man was unnervingly similar to a prevalent viewpoint I often come across, especially in young aspiring artists. Somehow, there seems to be a new wave of thought that creative excellence will emerge even when a person has thrown every caution to the wind, without patience to learn or dedication to an art. It was my hope that the young man, and many like him, would force themselves to work through the agonizing days and nights, even when the path wasn't glamorous, and there was no crowd standing at their doorstep with fame and accolades.

I wrote "Akora Dua Kube," a song made popular by the story beneath the title, "The Old Man Plants a Coconut Tree." A grandson asks his 90-year-old grandfather why he is busy planting a coconut tree when he may not even live to see it grow and reap the fruits of his own labor. Quite an intriguing observation, the old man must have thought to himself - and candid too. The old man replies, with a big smile, "Grandson, I know I may not live long enough to see the fruits of my labor. But it is because of you, and the children yet to be born, that I plant the coconut tree."

One important element in the lyrics was the use of the colloquial term *"akora"* in place of the Akan word *"akokora."* The song is about the *akokora*, which means the old man, but the more informal vernacular fit the song more easily. The meaning did not change, however, that if all that matters in life is what we have and do right now, much of our life's work will be futile even before it begins.

Throughout the years, I have held a deep conviction that the future of any society depends on its youth, who must build upon the foundations laid by those who came before. The work of our forefathers, along with the contributions of the great men and women who shaped our lives in unique ways, has provided valuable insight and set the stage for a future that is still unfolding. Their legacies are not just part of the past, they are the blueprints for what is yet to come.

Our greatest challenge would be in our ability to stay silent long enough to learn from them. It is because of what our grandfathers had seen, had known, and had learned that they planted the figurative coconut trees for a future they could only imagine. A country's potential and a culture's value are brightened by the preparation given to sons and daughters by fathers and mothers who understand the weight of their footsteps.

By nature, a coconut tree may take nearly a decade, and sometimes much longer, to reach its full maturity. When the conditions are right, the once small tree can rise high into the air, its leaves stretching several feet, displaying the strength that comes with time. Yet, it all begins with a humble seed, planted many decades before, with patience and care. I have come to appreciate how easy it is for any of us to overlook this simple truth: even the tallest coconut trees that soar into the sky didn't grow overnight. Their growth is a slow, deliberate process, rooted in the quiet patience of time.

This was the message in *"Akora Dua Kube."*

We gaze at the tree's towering stature and realize its years of standing through the sun and rain. When we stand at its side, quietly, we marvel at the days and nights that seem to have flickered in time, but which the tree needed to slowly find its place in the earth. Someone made the time to dig, to till, to toil, and to plant. Such is the story with investing in generations to come after our work is done. Who they will become and the value they will add to a nation will have their roots in the words and actions we sow into them today. The coconut trees we plant today will define their first steps and go a long way in affecting how high they will soar.

Life gives us a myriad of opportunities, and we owe it to ourselves not to let them outlive us. The events that unfold in the world around us can quickly feel like a desperate dream that will soon overturn life as we know it. Our mindset should be tilted towards and consumed with seizing the present, not out of fear, but to take advantage of what will soon become our past. The caution is that at every conceivable turn in our lives, we should be humbly reminded that we would never want to look back and find that we drowned our own voices in our hurry to live for today.

In my humble plea for living, I had convinced myself that my talents had a lot to offer. I made reference to a Bible verse I had known from my days as a young boy in the Methodist church, Psalm 90. It mentions the lifespan of a person being 70, or at most 80 years. Perhaps this is all the time a person needs to leave a mark on whatever vocation consumes his days. I always found 70 years to be a fascinating number, which I assumed would give me ample time to accomplish whatever I set out to accomplish. Even if the number in the verse was only a generalization - like a figure of speech - to express the thought that life is short, the significance shouldn't be lost on us.

If 70 years could pass in the blink of an eye, perhaps it would make the most difference if we left the world a little brighter than the one we stumbled into. I was convinced in my early days that I wanted to do more with my life and let the later years be the best years.

The first day I held a guitar in my hand feels now like an eternity ago. Strangely, it also feels like it was only yesterday. I think it is only when you get a chance to stand at the 80-year mark that you can look back at how quickly the years have flown by. It's a summit only a few get the chance to reach, but however long we live, we can never get back the golden moments we watched slip through our fingers. Such opportune moments will someday become a distant memory, the years will turn into a blur, and in no time, a foggy shield will surround the legacy we wish to leave behind.

Over the years, I have had priceless opportunities to share with my sons and daughters how every moment ought to be cherished, especially those that compel us to see beyond our own immediate satisfaction. The next day, or even the next second, is not promised to any of us. Koo Nimo, the musician, is from a place where our children will carry on our name, our dream, and our culture so that whatever the proverbial old man plants in the earth will live to see the light of day long after he is gone.

Sowing seeds with a future generation in mind demands an undeniable optimism about the fruits of our labor, the gratitude and growth of those who will come after us. It is this deep sense of responsibility that drives us to dedicate ourselves to causes greater than our own lives. This is why the old man plants a coconut tree, knowing that while he may never see it reach its full height, his actions will create something lasting, something that will nourish and support those who follow in his footsteps.

More than the crowd's applause, I came to realize the need to absorb the same desire that pushed our forefathers to be diligent in their craft, so that we could look to their counsel and pursue our own. When Professor Andrew Kaye, as a Fulbright Scholar, wrote *Koo Nimo and His Circle: A Ghanaian Musician in Ethnomusicological Perspective,* it spoke of the same deep passions that I hoped I would find just the right words to express. In his time at Columbia University, he had been instrumental in my invitation by Jed Wheeler and Associates to attend the Serious Fun Festival, where I played side by side with Puerto Rican cuatro player Yomo Toro.

The journey to that stage had been a long and particularly grueling one for me. Patience did not always speak the loudest when I was uncertain about where the woody paths were leading. I often reminded myself of the reasons beyond my own, and that alone was sufficient to reignite a dream. Andrew Kaye introduced me to the ethnomusicological departments at some American institutions, and I was invited to teach Ghanaian highlife, including Asante Court music and dance, fontonfrom, Adowa, kete, seperewa, and Apirede music. These were all opportunities to help inspire young hearts to love the art of music, as others had kept the door open for me.

In 1992, Andrew spent a great deal of time profiling me as part of his dissertation at Columbia University. Interestingly, whenever I had the chance to share stories of my past, I relived some of the most remarkable moments in my journey. The most fulfilling of these moments came whenever I found fertile ground to sow seeds of a desire to learn, explore, and create. My hope was that someday my life's work would be of value to generations yet to come.

Thirty years earlier, I had developed a sound known by many as the *Up-Up-Up*. The influences on this rhythm were a blend of traditional sounds and unique guitar patterns. Music observers at the time attempted to describe the uniqueness behind my sound and style, which helped it gain recognition and admiration. It had come with the passage of time. I reasoned that as long as we do not thwart our own attempts to become passionately engaged in our art, our voices will stand distinct in the crowd, and the trees we plant today will have the chance to soar to greater heights.

In the words of Andrew, the *Up-Up-Up* was about music with a youthful and buoyant rhythmic appeal, with lyrics of noble beauty, infused with elegant and powerful Asante poetic imagery. The pace was often a bit faster than most of the songs I wrote at the time, although the satisfaction for me was no less. He described the rhythm in a newspaper article as "a pulsating mix of melodious and intoxicating guitar patterns, harmonious vocals, and mesmerizing percussion."

One of the most fulfilling rewards of my life's work has been watching my music take on a life of its own, enduring through the years with the same authenticity as the moment I first played the note. I often thought to myself, if I was fortunate enough to live long enough, I might witness the seeds of perseverance I planted begin to blossom. I envisioned their branches reaching high into the sky, their roots digging deep and enduring even the harshest of life's storms. And in those moments, I realized I would never want to look back and wish I had planted more. Every note, every effort, would be a reminder of the legacy I hoped to leave.

Names like Akwasi Manu, Kwame Gyasi, and Kwabena Onyina sink further into the depths of a culture's history. The longer I lived, the more questions swirled in my mind over and over. Whose voice would preserve the works of our forefathers if we did not embolden talented young minds to keep them alive? Could we touch more lives if we took the time to pour our energy into developing the gifts of a future generation? Could we find strength in ourselves to watch a few more magnificent branches sprout across the skies someday?

As the years passed, I found myself, Koo Nimo the musician had become Koo Nimo the teacher. I was particularly determined to teach music not only as an art but also as the art of life itself. I often could not get past the reality that I may have done some of my most challenging and finest work in my later years. There is more to learn, and even more for people who live in the aftermath of what they could have done with their lives when they had the chance. If I had my way, I would like to live as long as I can and maybe bring a ray of hope into the hearts of young creative artists in their search for their own sound and voice.

For my part, I would give life my best effort to celebrate the gloomy days just as I do the sunny days. I would remind my sons and daughters to celebrate the simple joys and opportunities, because one of life's misfortunes would be to look back after many decades and wonder how we walked past the glow in every day with our eyes tightly shut. I am forever mindful of the responsibility to prepare those who come after me and leave a legacy of learning. As we ascend to the apex of our ambitions, there will be more work to be done, and I thank Nana Nyankopon every day that I get a chance to be part of this magnificent journey called life.

A thought-provoking yet fundamental truth I embraced early in my career was the realization that my ideas held an inherent potential to travel far beyond my own reach. The young people I inspired would go on to explore places and opportunities that I, myself, would never have the chance to experience. What was important was the impact of my work to ripple outwards, touching lives in ways I could never have imagined, extending my story and song.

Like the branches of a tree in search of a home in the gusting winds, when I am able to add a thought to students' minds, they in turn will go to their cities and towns to build on the tiny seed I planted. They will interpret the little bit of Koo Nimo they met from their unique vantage points. I know this because many years ago, I latched onto an enthusiasm for a traditional style of music and hoped that every encouragement along the way would lead to a gratifying end. I wanted to understand all I could about drums, and I turned to Okyerema Opon, a remarkable historian and drummer.

Okyerema Opon was arguably one of the most prolific Asante drummers the Asante kingdom will ever know. He did his best to teach me everything he knew about Asante drums, and a great deal about the talking drums. For all he invested in me, he did not get the chance to see my performances in Melbourne, Seattle, and London. If I had been able to share our culture through the beating of the drum, Okyerema Opon's life, wrapped up in my voice, would have lived again through me.

I had been taught a great deal by many brilliant people with whom I crossed paths. For many years, I traveled to villages in Ghana and spent time listening to the older people and learning different guitar techniques. I found these to be some of the most refreshing and enlightening experiences of my life. A peculiar thing about such trips was hearing incredible wisdom that seemed to have been kept safe by the old people, waiting for me to find. They had seen history unfold and had become repositories of cultural knowledge. I thought to myself, "They must be recorded before they are lost forever." I called them libraries on fire.

The Asante people taught through stories and tales. As far back as I could remember, we grew up listening to *Anansesem*. The Asante people called our folktales *Anansesem*, which meant "tales of a spider." The word *Ananse* means spider in Akan, but the character often represented a person in whose actions many moral values were displayed, or lacking. Kwaku Ananse, the central figure in the stories, was seen as a trickster. For his ultimate ambition, Kwaku Ananse wanted to be the most important person in the world, and he would stop at nothing to see his dream come to life. Even Ananse learned the lesson that no person would ever have a monopoly on wisdom.

We heard one folk story of Ananse pleading with God, Nana Nyankopon, to gather all the wisdom of the world into one pot that only Ananse would keep. God granted his wish. Ananse decided to climb a tall tree in what he thought to be a crafty maneuver to hide the pot. He was so sure that he was the wisest man in the entire world. He placed the pot on his chest, making it difficult to climb the tree. His son Ntikuma watched as his father struggled and called his attention, "Papa, I think if you placed the pot on your back, climbing would be easier."

Ananse was furious. He realized immediately that in his attempt to put all the wisdom in the world in one pot, he had inadvertently left some wisdom for his own son. Ananse was not the only wise man in the world, after all. In anger and frustration, he dropped the pot. It hit the ground and broke into pieces. Wisdom spread all over the world, so that neither Ananse nor anyone else on earth could claim monopoly over it.

The late Dr. Efua Sutherland, in the foreword to her play *The Marriage of Anansewa*, tells us, "Ananse appears to represent a kind of Everyman, artistically exaggerated and distorted to serve society as a medium for self-examination." From their start by the fireside in villages in Ghana, stories about Kwaku Ananse were passed down through generations and spread throughout many other parts of West Africa. Men and women gathered under the stars with the children and grandchildren to tell them stories. They shared truths about their people, their way of life, and their God. They were sowing seeds through the tales, in the hope that lessons would live on through the imagery.

For much of my life as a creative artist, my lyrics evolved from entertainment to a different dimension of appeal to the listener's intellect. I reasoned that it is through wisdom that we can inspire a generation to seek the best in every action. It is through this wisdom that the next generation of creative artists will embrace the responsibility to affect the future.

If we can unchain ourselves from the belief that all that matters in life is the present moment, we will all find a yearning to pass on rich values to people who will come after us. We will educate a village and in turn, make a difference in a generation. These are the coconut trees we can plant with our lives - roots that will grow, deepen, and provide shade long after we are gone.

Not long ago, I stumbled upon how the fortitude to endure a learning process can help a person truly embrace some of music's fundamental traits in order to harness their own talent in a much deeper way. Like the young man interested in playing the acoustic guitar, it's best to discover that the best way to excel at musicianship is to understand the logic behind the sound. I emphasized through the years that the trick is not to memorize the notes and the chords. Just as in life, the miracle in perseverance is in learning over and again from our own footsteps.

The patience to observe and understand gives us a much better appreciation and develops a much richer skill. I have always thought that one of the biggest problems with music education is how students often have no basic understanding of the logic behind the notes. It follows that without an unpretentious appreciation of the creative guideposts of music theory, they would give up at the first sign of sweat.

John Miller Chernoff invited me to a viewing of *Repercussions*, a film by Dennis Marks. John wrote a chapter, *Africa Come Back*. He is the author of *African Rhythm and Sensibility*. We both contributed to a workshop in Denton, Texas, in 2012 at the invitation of Professor

Steven Friedson, who at the time served as the Distinguished Professor of Music and Ethnomusicology. While the film investigated the West African music influences in America, there was also a part of me that hoped another generation would be able to carry on from where our strength and age took us. Some of what I reflected upon in *Repercussions* often came back to mind in the quiet moments before a performance.

While I sat in the corner of the stage strumming along the chords behind one of Ghana's most popular tunes, "Yaa Amponsa," I was reminded again how much of our life's work had a tremendous impact on the young men and women who quietly watched every fret and every strum. I like to think that human beings are remarkably similar in our quest to find logic. We look for meaning and patterns. As in music theory, once the logic appears, communication follows and meaning is generated even without much effort. This is probably why we instinctively dance to rhythms that click in our minds, long before we know the lyrics to the song. This is the same kind of connection that I hoped our traditional instruments and highlife music made with the generation who took to playing guitar.

I have been a little saddened through the years by the many people I came across who have not been exposed to the simplest yet most critical components of music. As is the case with music or even life, the variations become incredibly simple if we understand their logic and recurring footsteps. Many contemporary guitar bands were struck by this handicap, and their style ended up being very monotonous. A song completely done in the E-Flat or F scale doesn't give the work any color. I told the story of an Indian at a Ghanaian highlife music concert who curiously quipped, *"Kofi, do you have only one style in your music?"*

The song, as entertaining as it must have been, had used the same harmonies throughout, and it didn't take much for an objective observer to want more. Often, the lack of multifaceted arrangements prevents any variety or range of expression. Unless a generation of creative artists embraces fundamental music theory, our culture will soon be stained with the scars of stale, outdated music of yesteryear. Hardly a day passes by that I do not hope, more than anything, that my music and the experiences I share with other musicians will outlive me.

I recall one morning in Kumasi when I interviewed more than 40 people to join a band. The work required an understanding of scales, musical notations, key signatures, inversions, and a range of progressions. I came to find that none of the people could read music and that even the concepts were completely foreign to them. Even if they had natural talent, they needed this kind of creative depth and discipline to bring it out.

It is true that even prominent musicians like Django Reinhardt and Wes Montgomery were famous even though they were unable to read music. But unlike the people who had been eager to jump at the opportunity for fame, what they lacked in knowledge of theory, they made up for with an unimaginable patience for understanding every nuance of the guitar and an indefatigable drive.

The old man plants coconut trees because he knows how much of the future depends on both the water and food from their fruit. In the world of a musician, one after another, the crowds will dissipate and soon the tunes and lyrics will find a place to rest in the minds of all who had once been the audience. If the old man's sons and daughters are patient, the shadows cast by the sprawling branches will give them comfort.

Dr. Thomas Kruppa, a German biologist, was the director of the Kumasi Center for Collaborative Research (KCCR). Years ago, we discussed an African Music Village, a music training facility I had started in Kumasi. Thomas and Henrick Betterman offered much-needed support by establishing a center to train children in the community.

A few years later, I received financial support from the Ghana Cultural Fund and the Danish Government. It was through Dr. Kruppa's influence that the center developed into a training ground for young guitarists and musicians from all corners of the world. Some came to watch me play guitar, but others came to learn instruments such as the atumpan, seperewa, and drums.

We had the privilege of teaching children the basics of music, encouraging them to share stories, learn proverbs, and embrace the values of ethics and etiquette. They also engaged in drawing, painting, drumming, and dancing, allowing their creativity to flow freely. One of the most humbling realizations in my early career was coming to terms with the fact that I was not yet ready to carry the weight of a culture's song and the traditional African guitar genres to audiences worldwide. I had to learn patience. Like these children, I had to explore my own creative journey, using whatever instrument I had at my disposal, trusting that, in time, I would be ready.

When the opportunity arose, Dr. Kruppa's guidance and effort became instrumental in the creation of the Koo Nimo Cultural Resource Center. The center was intended to be a venue for creativity and to provide an environment where the next generation could learn what I knew. With this venue, we could share the wisdom we had been fortunate enough to stumble upon through the unfolding paths. If the resources were available, I was willing to take a leap of faith that the children would learn.

Mountaineers climb mountains because the rocks and cliffs are there, offering both challenge and opportunity. Without these natural avenues for adventure, there would be nothing to push them to explore. In much the same way, there is no greater purpose for any generation than to build the mountains for our children to climb. In the lives of the accomplished guitarists I've met around the world, I've seen how we can create a platform of learning and growth for the next generation of musicians, poets, and creative minds. There will be a stage for them to stand on, not by chance, but because we've worked to build it, providing the foundation for their voices to rise and their talents to thrive.

The Koo Nimo Cultural Resource Center was born from an unassuming conversation with Professor Nketia. I made it my humble contribution to the community and country. I had been blessed with mentors and compassionate visionaries who helped me live my dream. My hope was also to help the Akan philosophy live one more day through the gifted young minds who found their own inspiration in musical instruments, just as I did.

One of my greatest joys was spending time with young people who were often eager to tell me how much I had taught them. Young men like Little Noah, who became part of my family at an early age, learned to play the atumpan and quickly became a master drummer. I found it very reassuring to know how much these young people learned on their own, often with very little instruction. This brings joy to any teacher's heart. My investment paid off, as once the environment was created, in different parts of the country, it nurtured extraordinary musical talent. This is the only hope of saving the creative works of our predecessors.

It was refreshing to continue the journey side by side with some of the incredible young talents of future years. Every lesson I had mastered, from Manchester to San Francisco and everywhere in between, would be theirs to grasp. Nearly 80 years after my first lesson in music, it is the awareness that I could miss a miracle moment if I sail too quickly past the oncoming tide that keeps me learning and gives me a reason to pass on a skill. I want to be one of the old men who plant a coconut tree and are fortunate enough to live to see its branches dance in the winds and in the skies.

As I became more aware of my own musical influences, I also grew increasingly mindful of the responsibility to influence others. One of the most fulfilling and creative moments for me has always been during rehearsals and performances, when we have the opportunity to truly pass on our skills. I made a conscious effort to teach everything I had learned, knowing that it was important to offer anyone with a genuine curiosity the chance to embrace the silence and solitude required for deep learning. It was always essential to me that those who sought to understand had every opportunity to see their own ambitions take shape and come to life.

Who a person sets out to be and what they become are often not the same, and so their legacy can be contrary to what they intended. In Walter Lippmann's words, "The final test of a leader is that he leaves behind him, among men and women, the conviction and the will to carry on." For the men and women who carry on a legacy, their audiences may be much different, and perhaps even their genres will differ from mine. But the next generation would have the chance to excel, even in areas that were blind spots for some of us.

I've learned the importance of nurturing creativity and encouraging young musicians to embrace their own originality. As a teacher, there's always the delicate balance between sharing from my own experience and urging students not to simply replicate a style. At its core, talent is something innate, it's a gift that can't be fully taught. While it's easy to convey an idea or concept, true growth comes when a person digs deep within themselves to interpret that idea in their own unique way. It is this personal journey of discovery that truly defines their artistic voice.

Long before we left Foase, my father often said that human beings seldom use their minds to their fullest potential. I often thought he was referring to something I had not done well, until I learned later in life that his remark was true for all people. He wanted me to stretch my imagination and expect to uncover new heights in any effort. That expectation erased mental barriers. I grew up to believe there is limitless potential in young minds as they embark on a journey to find their own voices and unique creative paths. One of the most intriguing mysteries of life will forever be exploring and discovering the supposedly infinite creative power of the human mind, and it is my sincere passion to help the people I encounter to do so.

As my career took shape, I found that retaining information and transforming it into knowledge worked very differently in each individual. While I studied music, teaching also became a pure source of joy. Individual aptitude and a person's desire to learn often determined the outcome after days and nights with a guitar in hand. Oddly enough, the more I knew about others, the better I understood my own self. For this reason alone, whenever I taught music, my instinct was to carefully study a person to identify how best to plug into their artistic outlet.

It was true everywhere I had been. The village is filled with individuals on their unique pathways, and I am confident in a future where they become the storytellers and artists we desperately need. I saw the differences in artists like George Darko and his peers in the early 1980s, and in George Spratz and his contemporaries decades later. I taught excellent guitar students such as Mike Ofori, Paa Joe, William Afreh, Emmanuel Agyare, Akah Blay, Eugene Oppong Kyekyeku, and Professor F.O. Akuffo.

What I fully appreciate is that different people grasp the comprehension of music theory in different ways. There are people who hear information in one moment and understand it perfectly, only to forget it in the next. Others struggle to retain information initially, but something inexplicable happens once the information clicks in their brains. Like the old man who set out to plant the coconut tree, our role is to ensure that its fruits are plentiful enough for all individuals, no matter what their differences are.

I have often reflected with humility on how music is taught in Ghana and across Africa as a whole. The memories of my time at Adisadel College remain vivid, and in many ways, they echo the realities of today. Unfortunately, one thing that stands out is how we did not teach Ghanaian music with the same passion and urgency as we did other forms of music. The rich history of our native musical legends became increasingly overshadowed by the pull of popular culture and the passage of time, leaving their stories at risk of being forgotten.

The songs that had so much significance for a country and its people became relics of the past, and not many people cared about them. There was usually very little time allocated to historical music education from elementary school to university levels. The void was not because there weren't enough teachers to impart the knowledge, as there were certainly dedicated teachers all around us. Perhaps, as an illustration of how familiarity breeds indifference in human nature, the curriculum treated music as an afterthought, eventually placing it at the bottom of any priority list. In recent years, guitar music has earned more creative appeal at the hands of prominent musicians showcasing their skill on stage with flair and incredible style. I remember when I had just arrived in Ghana from teaching guitar at several universities in the United States.

I was back in Kumasi, teaching a Music Appreciation course at the University of Science and Technology. The students in the class had the enthusiasm to learn the music, but unlike what I saw in other parts of the world, not many were conscientiously seeking to inspire a new generation. The students had been exposed to music in elementary school, but any knowledge they had acquired had faded quickly, just as the sunset fades into the evening's dusk. The old man who plants the coconut tree hopes its seed will outlast the dawn and dusk, day after day, until it blossoms into something magnificent.

Western education has had a profound impact on our African society, and music is no exception. I have always encouraged musicianship in Ghana, urging young people to recognize and appreciate the rich creations we have cultivated. We don't need to abandon the authentic creativity that runs in our blood, nor should we seek validation from those who may never fully grasp the depth of our story. The possibilities within us are endless, woven into the very lives of our fathers and mothers, our brothers and sisters. It is in these roots that we find the true essence of our expression, and it is from here that our music can flourish and resonate.

By exposing young people to the rich heritage and skillfulness that gave birth to our traditional music, we ensure that their cultural ingenuity will not be muted. If the next generation does not know about past legends or understand what they did, it will be almost impossible to hope that they will continue from where their prede-cessors left off. This is why an old man plants a tree whose fruit he knows he may not live long enough to see, so his sons and daughters will live in the echoes of the brilliant artists whose work preceded their own.

There is certainly nothing wrong with the African child learning about legendary and prolific composers like Ludwig van Beethoven, Wolfgang Mozart, or Johann Sebastian Bach. Every music student I came across in Ghana knew all there was to know about German-born British Baroque composer George Frideric Handel, famous for his operas, oratorios, and organ concertos. The only nagging reality is how quickly we embrace and adore strangers, yet so easily ignore and fail to acknowledge our own legends.

On a tour in England years ago, a good friend shared his opinion that perhaps Handel and Mozart had no idea where Ghana was. Beethoven and Bach probably knew nothing of our culture, and understandably, none of them would have cared in the least about our music. As important as it is to learn from a broad range of influential musicians and composers to appreciate the transcendent nature of music, what value will our lives have if we know nothing of ourselves and from where we have come?

Our music is more than the guitar and piano. Our instruments have deep cultural significance that lives at the core of the sound itself. In Ghana, and for the Asante, adowa, kete, and fontonfrom are all integral elements of our musical culture. The complexity of the fontonfrom could potentially become a great area of learning. I have always been intrigued by how foreigners came to our countries, from far and wide, with great curiosity to learn all they could about African music. What about our unique sounds carried them across the shores into our towns and villages? What hides in plain sight from us?

The story of the young man who was eager to learn the guitar but wouldn't be patient enough to embrace the underlying structure of rhythm and sound is a reminder that we must gradually and deliberately rethink the Ghanaian and African musical mindset. The challenge is for the natives to cultivate a deeper appreciation of what our forefathers did and to be able to continue the journey. It may be difficult to bear the thought of a culture's entangled future, but without the seeds in the hearts of our young people, all that was once treasured will dissipate before our very eyes. It would be disappoint-ing to come to the end of the trail with no stories to tell or songs to sing.

Looking back on my life, I find myself deeply grateful for the painstaking efforts of my mentors, who so thoughtfully passed down the wisdom of generations before us. Their guidance has laid the foundation for a brighter future. It fills my heart with warmth to encounter young people who, despite the noise and distractions that surround us, continue to dedicate themselves to honing their skills with unwavering perseverance. Their commitment serves as a reminder of the power of persistence and the enduring value of the knowledge we pass on. *"Akora dua kube"* because of what they see in a future that beckons in the distance.

When I first set out with a guitar in hand, filled with creative dreams, I was not starting from scratch. There had been others before me, dreamers, visionaries, and ancestors, who had laid the foundation, whose efforts had planted trees long before I came into being. They were the old men, the "*Akokora*", for me. Their roots run deep in the earth, in ways I could never fully comprehend or see. Yet, even though their work went largely unseen, it was for me, and for those who would follow, that they planted those trees. They did so knowing, one day, someone like me would come along and need the shade of those branches to rest.

I was, in every sense, a beneficiary of those who had dared to dream before me and part of a larger tapestry woven over time. I carried with me the legacy of their hopes and their triumphs. They had carried the torch for me, lighting the way and making it possible for me to find my own path in this world. Their courage created a space where I could explore my passions and express myself freely. And, at that moment, I embraced the profound responsibility that came with this gift.

As I continued to walk my own path, I found myself deeply grateful for the torch that had been passed to me. But I also realized that my duty wasn't simply to carry it. It was to keep the flame alive, to elevate it, and to ensure that it burned brightly enough for my sons and daughters to see. I hoped that I had carried the torch high enough and bright enough so that it illuminates the path for the dreamers yet to come.

I always hoped that my work, my music, and my story would be the kind of beacon that could guide others, just as I had been guided. It had become my privilege to inspire a new generation to find their own creative paths, to dare to dream, and to excel in ways they may never have thought possible.

Creativity is much easier to stifle than to nurture, but if we can invest in our next generation, future artists will look back at these years and remember them as the times when we defined our future and our destiny. African countries, Ghana, and certainly the Asante are engaged in a quest to ensure our culture does not fizzle away.

Social groups and musicians are beginning to truly appreciate the value of the creative works from our past. We are going to great lengths to capture classic tunes and preserve all we can, so we can hand them down to the next generation of guitarists, pianists, songwriters, drummers, and other creative minds. All will not be lost.

The true measure of a tree's height and strength is often best understood when it lies on its side, resting on the ground. It is only in its fall, as the life it once held fades away, that the full magnitude of its presence becomes even more profound, striking a deeper chord in the hearts of those who witness it. I have been fortunate to live long enough to see the fruits of our labor rise, reaching towards the skies. It is my hope that all the efforts to preserve our history and music will one day bear fruit in the hearts of young African musicians, inspiring them to carry forward what we have worked so hard to nurture.

It is my prayer that for the next generation of creative artists, the legacy of their forefathers will not fade with time. Instead, may it live in their consciousness, guiding them to understand that all the work they create will be rooted in the songs, the words, and the culture that have come before them. Their artistry will be a continuation, a testament to the strength and depth of the foundations laid by those - the *akokora* - who came before.

13

A CHARGE TO KEEP

WE LOSE THE SONG WE DON'T TREASURE

Researchers and sociologists who sought to understand life in the world I come from walked away with unique insights into Asante society. Some arrived in Ghana for anthropological studies, aiming to explore the interconnections between social elements, cultural attitudes, folklore, and art. They were intrigued by how the songs we sang conveyed meanings far different from what they had anticipated. In the lives of the men and women they encountered, they discovered the embodiment of courage, honesty, and an unwavering passion to pass on a rich culture to the generation that would follow. What they found went beyond their academic expectations, it was a living testament to resilience and purpose.

To truly understand the Asante from an Asante perspective meant immersing oneself in the culture, living alongside the people, and experiencing life as they did. These encounters offered our guests a unique and captivating window into our way of life, revealing the subtleties and idiosyncrasies we often overlooked in our daily existence. In doing so, they came to see the richness of our traditions from a deeper, more intimate vantage point, one that brought both discovery and appreciation.

Over the decades, as I used my music as a means to connect with more and more people, I found myself making observations that deepened my understanding and sparked a curiosity to explore our culture in ways that no outsider ever could. To become the man I was destined to be, with nothing more than six strings and my voice, I had to dig deep within myself, tapping into the roots of all that had been planted in my heart. It was there, in that quiet place, that I found the courage to let it all bloom.

Back in Kumasi, I first heard a story about the respect we ought to give to our elders. It often replayed in my mind whenever I was away from home. It reinforced much of what we otherwise took for granted and illustrated the importance of greetings, a seemingly insignificant gesture, in Akan tradition. In one story, a man went to visit a friend who had only described the general location of the house he was looking for. He arrived in the neighborhood, but while walking along the narrow, dusty road, it dawned on him that the directions he had been given were of little use. He did not know which way to turn.

The man found himself facing two identical houses, unsure of which one was the right one. He retraced his steps and asked an elderly woman who was quietly washing clothes in the courtyard nearby. The old lady had been sitting in the same place while strangers walked by. Some stopped to greet her, but others did not take the time to do so. "What difference did that make?" they must have thought as they walked on. The man had also walked past the elderly woman, but in his preoccupation, he had not taken a moment to greet her.

As chance would have it, the man needed help. He retraced his steps to where the old woman sat and asked politely, "Nana, where is the house I am looking for?"

The woman lifted her head slowly, and with a surprised look in her eyes, wondered to herself what hope there would be for a society if we are so consumed by what we want that everyone and everything else along the way becomes insignificant. The man missed a simple gesture, but that may have been because, like him, we have given ourselves permission to see much of life as inconsequential, allowing its worth to slip through our fingers. *"Wo firi he?"* the elderly lady asked, which translates in Twi to mean, *"Where do you come from?"*

In a society where a person's family name often identified him, it didn't take much for the elderly woman to learn who the man was and what family he belonged to. He was supposed to know how to conduct himself in society because his father or mother had taken the time to teach him. He was supposed to know that in our culture, we show respect to elders irrespective of their station in life. You treat everyone with the utmost respect because you never know when they might be the only person whose counsel you need to help you find your way.

When I first heard of this short exchange, the metaphor was striking. In much the same way, we hurriedly walk past many pathways. We may acknowledge their worth, but we race past the simplest things we should hold dear in our hearts. Because of our haste and disregard for her values, fate forces us to retrace our footsteps and cross paths with her again, so we may hang our heads in shame for ignoring life's guideposts that had been there all along. You and I may be the next people of whom our culture asks, *"Wo firi he?"*

For every one of these stories, I learned that the knowledge of our history guides our actions in the present. Oftentimes, the only way to understand how we became who we are today is to have a better sense of where we have come from. We should not be in such a hurry to miss the guideposts that lead us in the passion we choose. The charge for all of us is a debt we owe our culture, a duty to the villages where our roots live. We must remember how much of our culture's posterity rests on our shoulders.

The more I thought of what it would require to pass on culture's song, the more I realized that none of us can go through life as a blur and expect to gain any value from it. Perhaps the truth hinges on the fact that there are many nuggets of wisdom sprinkled throughout every experience.

One day, we will stand before the Almighty God and be held accountable for the lives we have lived. Perhaps, if we have lived with integrity and purpose, the legacy we leave behind will shine brightly for others to follow. Our country, our community, and our families will depend on us, and we will know in our hearts when we have given our very best, - because it is conscience, that unwavering judge, that we cannot silence. In that quiet moment, we will understand whether we truly lived with honor and intent.

Throughout my career, I encountered individuals from all corners of the world, many of whom knew the Ashanti only through what they had read. For some, I became the embodiment of the ideas they had about us. In those moments, I often felt the weight of that responsibility, not just as a reflection of my own identity, but as something much larger. It was a heavy burden, but one I came to realize was essential to the role I played.

Our culture remained remarkably constant through the years, and so did the profound impact it had on me, day after day. I understood that we were called to be heroes within our own towns and villages, and moral guides for our sons and daughters. While my music and words might bring a smile to someone's face, I always hoped their true power would lie in inspiring the next generation to not only appreciate but also deeply cherish who we are as a people. In that, I found a sense of purpose, knowing that through my work, the essence of our heritage could continue to shape lives for years to come.

In all the work undertaken by these researchers, I wonder if encounters with men like Okyeame Nuamah, Bantamahene, and Nana Totoe altered their worldview. Foreigners seldom paused to consider the enormous value that Africa's past has for its future. We sang our father's songs and lived our mother's hopes. Our lives will not just be our own, but those of our children too.

What would we pass on to a world that will only hear about who we had once been? I have been driven by the conviction that if we give every effort our very best, our character will lift a cultural veil, not only so the world can understand us, but also so our sons and daughters can appreciate that our traditions and culture must be handed down to them. In a world where community and dignity give a man his pride, the counsel of ancestors will always hold weight in every heart.

This is what we clung to, the essence that gave meaning to everything we poured our hearts and souls into. At international music festivals in Australia and Canada, I encountered men and women who shared that their understanding and perception of Ghana had been secondhand, shaped by others' stories, until we arrived and told our own through the language of music. They would have never known any other way, had their feet not unconsciously moved to the rhythm of the same music that once filled the Asante skies, and if the overwhelming warmth and human kindness they felt hadn't gently shifted their worldview. This is why it is so crucial that we guide our children to nurture their character and let their unique voices shine, so that they may authentically reveal who they are at their core.

Like the elders in Foase would say, who we were as a people came with a great responsibility to affect our generation in whatever we did. Our resilience in our time would be for the sake of our children's future. Throughout history, when a man is pressed on all sides by life's unrelenting challenges, it is easy for his heart to crumble and his dreams to fade away. But a tiny seed of fortitude can build his hope and keep him fighting, not only for himself, but so that the sounds echoing in Asante and African hearts will not fade into silence. Whatever adversity my forefathers lived through, they cautioned against indifference that could transform the most promising pillars of a nation into a passive generation.

Even through the uncertain terrain of a music career, I did not want an observer to tell me who I was. This deep desire, not an obligation, led me to learn more and to use my music as a platform to share our stories. Making an original contribution to one's culture requires a quest to find the fundamental awareness that drives its people, what makes us dream and makes us sing. It is only then, perhaps, that one can truly understand and appreciate the culture for what it is and the value it serves in our lives. This is what my father told me, and what I get to tell my children and their children too.

I had perhaps one of the most interesting conversations of my life with my father before I left home. I was wearing a wristwatch, and he asked me to hold it close to my ear. "Listen to it carefully," he said. "And remember how quickly the sound is replaced by another." Just as soon as you think you have heard a sound, there will be another, and then another.

Tick tock, tick tock. He talked about how life moved on just as quickly as the sound of the tick and the tock. Even when the sound seems the same, every tick owns its time and carries its own life and opportunity. We have no knowledge of what tomorrow will bring and no assurances of what we will get to do, but there is a life we need to realize. Even in our unguarded moments, we must conduct our lives with a sense of purpose.

If I had only one thought to leave behind, it would be my father's caution: Every minute and every day we are alive is truly a special occasion, for our lives are but vapor, a wisp of fog. It is easy to slowly drift into a view that time is eternally cyclical, and that a lost moment will somehow find its way back to us. I once heard the adage, "You cannot bathe in running water twice." The moments that pass us by are gone forever. This is the truth our next generation will have to realize.

Even in what often seems like a limitless landscape of time, the moments will soon fizzle away, and the only lasting work will be that which we have carefully set in motion to live on. It will be as if the future has already happened, and we are watching the story replay around us. Odomankoma Nana Nyankopon, the God who gives grace, gave us the days we have on earth but left it to each of us to make each new moment count.

For musicians, when we have walked away from life's stage, audiences will only hear our music and not have our presence to nudge their thoughts. So, with every recording and every performance, we must showcase our best so that the men and women who come after we have sung our last will have something worth holding on to.

A journalist, Kwabena Fosu Mensa, once asked what I thought of being known as "the repository of Asante music or culture." A humbling compliment, but I always thought of Asante music and culture as an eagle with sprawling wings that could not be kept in one man's heart. Despite my ceaseless effort to acquire a great deal of cultural understanding over the years, my life's work does not qualify me as a repository. My life will only be part of a collective duty that rests on society's broad shoulders. I can only think that it will take many more people, all with an authentic awareness of the value of our history and its posterity, to give life to our culture and turn each of us into one vital contributor to that repository.

As I pause to reflect on the long path that has led me to some of the world's most prestigious international stages, I find no greater fulfillment than in the understanding of how each chapter of my life has shaped the person I am today. Looking back on the many accomplishments my band and I have been blessed to achieve over the years, I find myself hoping that, above all else, a new generation will rise to carry the torch even further, pushing beyond the limits of our strength, talent, and passion. There is still much work to be done to propel the sound forward. The Asante village where I spent my early years gifted me with invaluable treasures of life, treasures that I, in turn, hope to leave behind today, hoping that these gifts will endure and resonate long after I am gone.

In the late 1950s, there was a cultural shift among social thinkers engaged at the frontlines, focused on advancing Ghanaian culture. For musicians, preserving our genre and our story demanded an even more conscientious desire to sing aloud. When I began my career, it was important to the leaders of that generation that the young people who would inherit the mantle had a firm grip on the reality unfolding around them. They were to inherit their land and cherish every bit of it. They never stopped reminding people like me of the unique opportunity we held in our instruments to connect our world.

One thing I found particularly striking was their unbending conviction and hope for an Africa where our identity would truly be a reflection of who we are and from where we had come. This was what I had seen modeled for me many years ago in Foase, and I knew someday it would be my turn to do the same.

Our history and heritage have always been a rich wave of authentic rhythm and sound. At their very core is the unique inspiration that gives us our songs. The world will look on as we all make the work of our predecessors our stepping stone, one beat and one rhythm after another. The drumming and the poetic appellations echo the courage to live out our dreams and the opportunity to make Ghana the land our sons and daughters will be as proud as we are to also call their home.

I was following the example of people who personified such a profound sense of duty, and I had an indelible impression of what my people expected of me. Our history is ours to cherish; else we walk through life as though we had never seen the sun rise.

Standing here at what feels like the pinnacle of my career, I can't help but reflect on how some of my greatest strides emerged from the smallest steps, those moments I never imagined would make such a profound difference. Wherever I performed, I adhered to a disciplined routine, understanding that every second mattered. This commitment to punctuality extended beyond my music; it became a principle I applied to every part of my life, because the tasks at hand were too important to waste a moment. Over time, I learned to cherish even the simplest moments, finding meaning in the flow of life's currents, where the essence of each experience never lost its richness. These are the virtues I hope to leave behind, through my character and my work, I hope to inspire someone else, just as I have been inspired along the way.

The ticking of time must give us a sense of urgency to live with purpose. When we are fortunate enough to see another day, we should not lose sight of the fact that the day behind us is gone forever, along with anything we could have done with it. All we have left is the moment we have now. My hope is that Ghanaians will learn to be disciplined in their actions and value time. I re-echo the advice that a mentor gave me: *Ɛberɛ wɔ na hyeɛ, yɛnnɔ ɛntera.* Time has its boundaries; one cannot plough beyond.

Tick-tock, tick-tock, the moments will vanish like a whisper. If each of us had to leave behind a stone upon which to build our culture's future, would our life's work be enough to leave a lasting foundation? We wouldn't have to wait for the sun to set before sharing all our deep-seated gifts in whatever vocation we chose. We could not take for granted any opportunity in hand. Everything we are and all we have has been bought at a hefty price, and that realization alone should weigh heavily on all our shoulders. That is the challenge, but also the charge, ours to keep.

In retrospect, the worldview of our Adikanfo called on mothers and fathers, and their sons and daughters, to fully express their African identity and pride. Koo Nimo held a guitar and its six strings in hand, doing his best in the way he knew how. I do not recall having much talent for doing anything for which I did not have an honest craving. It made it easier for me to choose friends, to have a clear intention to write music, and to develop a strong appetite for creativity. I cherish the long nights cradling guitar strings to find the perfect tune because every minute of it helped leave a legacy for our children to build upon.

Time and again, I have seen the indescribable worth of every platform I've had as a musician and the opportunity for our music to tell our story to the world. With all the superfluities pruned away over time, I became keenly aware of the tremendous gift handed down to us, having come from a village in obscurity to stand in front of large audiences across Africa, Europe, and America. All these people would look deeply into the songs to paint their images of Africa. If I did well, it spoke loudly of where I had come from and everything my people held dear in our hearts.

During a 1976 tour in the United States, I witnessed a man experience a life-changing encounter with a part of African culture, unlike anything I had seen before. At the invitation of the Smithsonian Institute, my band Adadam Agofomma had the chance to perform on one of the world's most celebrated stages. We took along some clay soil, a mortar, and a pestle to use as a backdrop during the performance. There was nothing special about any of these objects, certainly not in our eyes. We planned to use the clay to decorate the walls of a traditional priest's house in the museum.

After two weeks in Washington D.C. and a hectic travel schedule, we could not carry all the leftover clay with us as part of our luggage.

We had finished our work, we would soon be returning to Ghana, and there was no need to take it home. Without giving it much thought, we discarded the clay soil in a nearby open space at Georgetown University, where we were staying. After all, it was just soil, just dirt. Some of the people who had seen us perform earlier in the evening also saw us pouring the clay.

The next morning, I saw our tour guide gathering the clay from the ground. He rubbed it on his body. It was the strangest thing, and other onlookers stood completely astounded.

"What are you doing?" I asked.

"You do not understand," he tried to explain, breathing heavily with a smile beaming on his face.

"Don't understand what?"

"This is the soil from Africa." He struggled to find the words to explain.

His thoughts seemed to race without pattern or pause. The soil we had discarded the day before was an important symbol of a place his heart called home. The act, as strange as it may have seemed to us, symbolized a deep affection for a motherland he had never seen. This was a man in search of a culture he could call his own.

His grandfathers had told him how a part of them was left in Africa or even stripped away during the horrid years of slavery. The soil that held no particular significance for me was of grave importance to someone who thought this might be the closest he would get to the soil in his motherland. Maybe, in his lifetime, he would get the chance to visit the land of his ancestors. But until that day, in this moment, he cherished the music, the language, and the earth we had brought to him.

I became convinced that many people in different parts of the world cherished the traditions I embraced and celebrated, the very same ones that colored my life with music. The same intrigue that once motivated anthropologists and sociologists to uncover life in distant places lived in the faces I saw. I was often amazed and inspired by the interest in African art, objects, and ideas.

As I emerged onto the scene in the 1950s, I saw such a remarkable display of culture throughout Ghana and Africa. I never wanted its familiarity to dull its worth in my eyes, or in the eyes of my sons and daughters. It would be sad if we stopped appreciating the ancestry to which we owe so much of our passions and dreams.

Our treasure lives with us. The task is left squarely on our shoulders to relive all that our ancestors hoped for and to ensure their message lives on long after our work is done and we are gone. In Ghana, our challenge in the coming years will be to preserve our core values and make them the centerpiece of a collaborative effort to build upon what our fathers had begun in pride. The charge is for us to find a way to expand the narrowness of our own compass in whatever profession or vocation we undertake, for what matters most is that our rich history always sees the light of day.

As I traveled the world throughout my music career, I was consistently humbled by the people I met, - those who admired some aspect of my life and expressed a desire to follow in my footsteps. Whether it was through the songs I sang about culture, the way I wore my traditions like a cloak, or the vivid images of beautiful villages I painted on stage, they saw something in me that resonated with them.

But the guitar's strings had much more to say than Koo Nimo could ever imagine along the frets and in the scales. Long after Koo Nimo is gone, the flame ought to burn brighter still for the creative artists who find their own voice and follow their unique passions. This is why the next generation of guitarists and musicians should only aim to be the best they can be on their inimitable path in life. They should not wish to become the "next Koo Nimo."

Just as sure as the sun's reappearance in the morning gives life to a day, so too does a person live the most fulfilling life when they do not sway from their true self. Young people today will have their own fears and carry their own hopes. I had mine. I never had any doubt that they too would have their own words, their own music, and their own audiences. They will have their own arenas of influence which will require the discipline of time and the clearing away of the debris of the superfluous. Their contributions will be tangible, and their voices will earn their own centrality and relevance.

Everything that Ghana has been for them will serve as a guiding light, shaping their own stories to share with the world. It will be their responsibility to transform any platform, no matter how humble, into an opportunity for growth and expression. One day, the curtains will fall on their father's work, but it will then be the turn of a new generation to carry forward the dreams and hopes that their fathers once envisioned.

I have spent the later years of my life reminding my children that they cannot afford to let the memories of our heritage fade into the murky depths of forgetfulness. I especially encourage the young men and women who will be fortunate enough to win the attention of audiences wherever their music takes them. In the pursuit of keeping pace with changing musical tastes, the tunes and rhythms may also change. There may never be Adadam music that travels back into the years quite the way ours did.

My deepest prayer is that the messages I've shared do not fade into meaningless artifacts, lost in the tides of change. It fills my heart with warmth to see young people who genuinely appreciate the traditional music styles, for in them, I hear echoes of my own experiences, as well as those of our ancestors. These connections will inspire their music and empower their voices, making them even stronger as they carry the tradition forward.

Many of the trends in what has become the digital age become archaic just as quickly as they are new, but an understanding of the underlying music arrangement will stand the test of time. The opportunity to explore has never been easier, and creative artists will have a new world open to them to hone their skills. As I traveled throughout the country, I encouraged people, both young and old, with my humble observations in life that everything worth achieving boils down to a person's attitude. A dedication to hard work will still be the proven path that transforms God-given talent into a fulfilling story.

I smile at the thought that, in the years to come, artists will look back, rediscovering songs from times gone by, reimagining them for a new generation. Musicianship will stand at the delicate crossroads of honoring the masterpieces of our past while striving to create something fresh and original. Yet, it is my hope that, in the midst of this journey, musicians will seek to carve out their own identities through their creative work. Their talents will guide them on a path that is both magical and deeply fulfilling. This will be their choice, though they will no doubt encounter challenges, and even the brightest days may be clouded by moments that test their spirit. The next generation has the potential to offer profound contributions, not just to music, but to society and the world at large.

Ghana has to lead its own charge, and it will be rooted in what our sons will cherish. Our people will have to remember our own heroes and courageous leaders. Our people will have to remember their fathers' dreams, what the battles stood for, and what the triumphs meant for the moment in which they live today. Musicians like Sam (Kwame Esiar), Kwasi Manu, Kakaiku, Kwaa Mensah, E.K. Nyame, and Kwabena Onyina hoped for a day when Ghanaian musicians would celebrate the incredible work done through the years and seek to add their voices. There is no better moment than now, and I am privileged to have climbed a step higher in time to see all of the marks their footsteps left in the sand.

I look back at my own career and I realize that everything I have become and everything I've discovered has been born from sacrifice.

I remember the times when we practiced the guitars, feeling the pain and frustration, yet we kept pushing forward, never stopping. Now, when I meet fellow musicians along my path, I find myself sharing the same advice: keep practicing, even when it's tough. Go beyond what feels comfortable, push past your limits, and embrace every opportunity life brings, just like the waves that shape the shore, each experience has something to teach you.

I am blessed to stand at the edge of my own career and tell another generation that while others sleep, you stay up and stretch your imagination. What other musicians may do for an hour, take on the challenge and go the extra mile; do it for an hour more. Take pride in developing your skill. Stretch yourself even in the camaraderie and competition with your peers to bring out the best in you. The competition awakens and ignites the hidden creative avenues you couldn't have pulled apart on your own. Just as in *nnoboa*, a man can weed alone, but he cannot weed an entire forest. But many men together, working side-by-side, will accomplish much.

As far back as I can remember, in Foase, the village where I spent the early years of my life, we relied upon one another. This interdependence filled the void any one person might feel, because a community's members lifted each other up in times of need, celebrated each other's joys and happy days, and shared in each other's pain. If there ever was a place where people depended on community and each other, and trusted the people around them to carry them along the way, it would be the village. Our lives are best lived in the company of men and women who also embrace the charge to pass on culture's song.

I remember a woman who told me that my music was old-fashioned, just as I remember the words of the man who said that when he first heard my music, he thought I was an old illiterate man in a corner store somewhere in a remote village. My lyrics and style had not been as colorful as these people may have wanted, but perhaps they did not ignore the message. Those are only reminders that our journey will be laden with views and noise from people whose lenses color the world differently than ours.

I was fortunate to have mentors who assured me that I would encounter people who would understand my journey. They also reminded me that if I poured my heart into every song I wrote and gave my all in every performance, the words of our culture's song would resonate with an audience far beyond the familiar grounds of my village, Foase. Their belief in me planted a seed of trust that, with dedication, my music would find its way to the hearts of others.

As a country, the task will remain ours to uplift our next generation. I saw in my own life the frailty of our human capacity to forge ahead through a world we cannot yet fully comprehend. Often we look back and wish we had stared into the face of the thoughts that once jostled us, and like a farmer, plowed ahead to fulfill our heart's ambitions. It may be that what we give to the next generation may not be as important as how we encourage them to also contribute to a generation following theirs. The beauty of our heritage is that if the current generation can hold on to their spirit, future generations will benefit immensely. I have always thought of preserving one's culture as a rare chance to keep a country or its people glued to its guiding principles and an identity that defines who they are as a people.

Our beginning in life is shaped by forces beyond our control, but we always have the power to decide what we leave behind. We can all find meaning in living in a way that reflects the lessons we hope our sons and daughters will one day learn from us. For Ghana, the legacy of our music and cultural heritage would be a tragedy if it were reduced to mere relics of a bygone era, nothing more than lifeless specimens in an art museum.

The sons and daughters I will leave behind will touch lives that I may never have the chance to reach. I have been fortunate to have walked nearly the full spectrum of the human experience - the joy and sorrow, the laughter and the pain. With a guitar in my hand and a passion entrusted to me as a young boy in a remote village in Ghana, I've been given the most magnificent opportunity. Along the way, I've come to understand the fleeting nature of life and felt the deep urgency to truly live it, fully and with purpose.

In the end, my hope is that I have not overlooked any opportunity to bring a little more laughter, joy, and meaning into my life, nor failed to leave behind something more for the world to carry forward. I hope that, in every step I took, I added something of value, whether through a moment of light, a spark of inspiration, or a contribution that will endure long after I am gone.

14

HOW FAR THE SOUND TRAVELS

A PORTRAIT OF KOO NIMO: FRIENDS, MENTORS AND MORE

The memories of my life, if I have done all I could to live it well, will undoubtedly weave into the lives of the people with whom my path has crossed - those I met, those I lived next to, and those with whom I shared a song. I am grateful that Nana Nyankopon did not let me forget music's ability to leave a profoundly moving trail, perhaps even into the hearts of many around the world.

These are their words.

Professor Kwesi Yankah, Accra, Ghana

"Few know his real name, Daniel Amponsah. I came across the name when I began engaging with him in closer encounters. But I felt blessed to meet the gentleman who is a hero in Ghanaian folk music. My first serious encounter with his musical recordings was during my days as a Legon University student, and then in my years as a doctoral student in the 1980s, when I was exploring the content and lyrics of Ghanaian highlife music.

Agya Koo stood like a colossus in the world of musicians. What made Koo unique was the folk foundations of his lyrics, which floated over an ensemble of indigenous Ghanaian instruments, further enhanced by a rich embroidery of acoustic guitar. The outcome was enough to sweep you into a universe of palm wine music. His nimble fingers produced a wailing sound that would momentarily yield to a baritone voice singing lyrics on wide-ranging themes.

But Agya Koo's intimacy with his guitar cannot be mistaken as a metaphor. He confesses that he visualizes the acoustic guitar as an ideal female body that deserves gentle handling and cuddling. Never a coarse stroke or rough handling from Koo Nimo's fingers. Nothing that could hurt his intimate love. She could write in pain, wince, and recoil in tender protest, and that could ruin an Agya Koo concert.

But Agya Koo's concerts are well measured. He would take his audience along in guitar song and dance, ably aided by his Adadam Group of artists (including his dancing wife), and treat all to a feast of Akan folk songs and philosophy. His dancers would gracefully toss, turn, and gyrate to indigenous rhythms while Koo sang tale after tale, waxing philosophical in song and narration.

Yet Koo is often sensitive to the aesthetic distance within his universe and would curtail a performance even while the audience was just about warming up. His dramatic ending to a song performance, just as it peaks on stage, partly defines the artistic persona of Koo Nimo. It also partly explains the constant yearning for an encore whenever he is on stage. Never a dull moment, never a dull concert with Koo Nimo.

His folk songs are largely creative renditions of folktales, as well as *mmoguo*, song intervals artistically seized by participating listeners during storytelling. This is an intrinsic feature of Ghanaian folktale performances, where a flagging performance suddenly receives a boost from a listener, who volunteers a song interlude, comment, or dance sketch to enhance the narration. But Koo Nimo uses his *mmoguo*, not as a catalyst or stopgap, but as a full-blown menu with a life of its own.

Koo Nimo goes beyond Akan folktale routines; over the years, he has re-created tradition within the context of modern life and sung lyrics that encapsulate the woes of the African migrant in the West, as well as the plight of the modern-day student burning the midnight oil in search of knowledge. It's often a delight watching Agya Koo engage with students or tourists through music.

The personality of Koo Nimo is that of a rare artist, philosopher, and teacher. Eloquent in both Asante and English, Agya Koo has sung his way across the world and lectured in several universities, where he brings Ghanaian wit and wisdom to life, through words and his fingers."

Professor John Collins, Accra, Ghana

"I first met Koo Nimo in 1973 at his home on the campus of the Kwame Nkrumah University of Science and Technology in Kumasi, where he worked as a biochemist technician. I had wanted to meet him for several years, ever since being bowled over by his music in 1970, which I first heard on a tape recording made by a British music photographer friend of mine, Jak Kilby. Koo Nimo's style of highlife, which is rooted in the old palm wine music that developed in the Akan areas during the 1920s and 1930s, led me to expect an older guitarist. However, the first thing that struck me about him was his youthful appearance.

We played some music together, and then I interviewed him and arranged to meet the following week at the Phillips Recording Studio in Kaneshie, Accra, where he and his group were going to record six singles. The seven-man group consisted of Koo Nimo on classical acoustic guitar, Little Noah, his twelve-year-old adopted son, on talking drums (atumpan), and George Kusi and Yaw Nimo on the premprensiwa, a large variety of hand piano on which the musician sits and supplies the bass line. There was also Nyamekye, who played the long, thin gyama drum, and Bawuah, who provided the gong patterns. On four of the recorded tracks (including "Densu"), I played a small gourd rhythm instrument called the "asratoa" (in Akan) or "televi" (in Ewe).

In the late 1980s, I had the pleasure of traveling to Kumasi with the late Beattie Casely-Hayford to record some of Koo Nimo's instrumental pieces as background music for a United Nations developmental film called "The Secret of Wealth." Some of these recordings, made with my Bokoor Recording Studios mobile unit, were later released in 2003 as part of the "Vintage Palm Wine" CD by the Dutch Otrabanda label.

In June 2000, I accompanied Koo Nimo as his second guitarist on a United States performance and lecture tour of New England's universities, including Yale, Harvard, Wesleyan, Boston, and Trinity. A party was organized for us at Harvard by historian Professor Emmanuel Akyeampong, who had extended invitations to many prominent Ghanaians, including economist Dr. Kwasi Botchway and philosopher Dr. Anthony Appiah.

In my 1973 interview, I asked him about his future plans in music, to which Koo Nimo replied, "From my corner, I would like to develop percussion, then insert heavy chords into highlife, rhythmic chords that will enrich the harmony. I'm going to marry the traditional highlife guitar with Spanish and Latin American music, an Afro-Spanish style using traditional rhythm and arpeggios, for I always use finger-picking, never the plectrum. Also, I want to develop an Afro-jazz style and use Wes Montgomery and Charlie Christian-type chords in it."

I like to think that, for a career and life, he has done precisely what he set out to do."

Josiah Osei Agyeman, Texas, USA

"The hallmark of Koo Nimo's legacy is his selflessness, caring nature, and what he did for others. I still have vivid memories of Agya Koo Nimo teaching indigent children from my local Kumasi neighborhood who did not have the opportunity to attend school.

I may not have fully appreciated it at the time, but forty years later, I am grateful for the value of education he instilled in me. He would give us ten pesewas if our grades met his expectations and would be waiting for us early on Saturday mornings if we needed help with mathematics or reading.

He silently helped many children like me overcome harsh experiences, choosing not to ride on his successes. He sacrificed his time, being the father that many of the children didn't have. Always warm and always plainspoken, the man I knew was ambitious and motivated young people like me to dream, never allowing notoriety to overshadow his sense of belonging.

Much of his great work for others will go unnoticed, but Agya Koo gladly took on the daunting task of being the voice for a community in the 1970s, with a patience and sincerity that only he could offer. He never overlooked the fact that it is the little things in life that often make the biggest difference.

As a musician, I am sure it has been a great source of joy for him to do what he loves, but I consider it a privilege to have witnessed his inspirational work over the years and to see how he has never lost his joy in his art.

Agya Koo Nimo has been a blessing to the world of cultural music for decades and to his family, both near and far. What has been most refreshing is how, despite his accomplishments, Agya Koo Nimo still plays music with a cheerful heart and is most proud of his culture.

A great man he has been to many and an even greater uncle."

Laurel Sercombe, Seattle, USA

"The ethnomusicology program at the University of Washington in Seattle was pleased and honored to have Koo Nimo in residence as a Visiting Artist during the 1998-1999 and 1999-2000 academic years. As an archivist on the Ethnomusicology staff, I had the pleasure of getting to know Koo Nimo and his wife Comfort during those two years. Koo Nimo attracted an enthusiastic group of students to his studio, where he introduced them to the popular "highlife" tradition and his own style of palm wine guitar music.

In his first Seattle concert in April 1999, he also performed kete music from the Asante court and showcased the traditional atumpan drum ensemble. We knew that we were in the presence of a master musician, a scholar, and a gentleman.

Because I was present in the department every day, I grew accustomed to the wonderful sound of Koo Nimo's music filling the hallway as he shared songs and stories with his students and instructed them on guitar, drums, and bells. When his students joined him on stage in concert, they demonstrated their devotion and appreciation for Koo Nimo's teaching, and he was clearly proud of their achievements.

Koo Nimo also honored me as an archivist by entrusting copies of many of his recordings to our ethnomusicology archives. Our Koo Nimo collection now includes more than 30 recordings, including his Seattle performances, published documentaries, solo recordings, interviews, and recordings made in Ghana focusing on ceremonial and court traditions.

I'm grateful to Koo Nimo for the gift of his presence with us in Seattle and for his generosity in documenting his tradition in a form that we will be able to share for many years to come."

Professor Abena P.A. Busia, New Brunswick, USA

"In my mind, still lingering, a mixed-race group of foreign students dances into the night from the verandah of your modest house onto a street. It is remarkable only because you - teacher, folklorist, poet, guardian of our culture, always ancient, ever new - inhabit that space. You sang for my father when it mattered most. Thank you. And decades later, my students learned, first graciousness, then simple wonder.

Who does not know your chosen name, you who have sung from chop bars to the courts of kings? Prophets with a calling must reinvent themselves, take on new names with passion as a mantle of inheritance; the double portion of the burden, the double blessing. Not overtaken by events, you have borne us well.

Your palm wine music records an ageless history for the generations and makes us high on life. In your tongue, what at first seems passing, temporal, and ephemeral accumulates, like individual grains of sand becoming the spectacular architecture of anthills, slowly, unseen, until the landscape is unimaginable without them. Such is the stringed accompaniment of your world of words; the soundtrack of our lives.

Generosity is an uncommon tongue in a universal language, and your inner sanctum is a sanctuary to belonging. In your home of books, music, and memories, the ordinary is transformed: history is living magic, and today is a kaleidoscope of experience.

You took in strangers and shared, with laughter, the story of a people in texts and the texture of cloth, in jests and gestures, and in dances that tell so many stories, until we were no longer guests in the house. For to teach dance and gesture is to discover intimacies both communal and sacred. And joyous. The brilliance of the laughter is what is shared: life is what you make it."

Professor Royal Hartigan, Massachusetts, USA

"My good friend Agya Koo Nimo is someone I have known since 2012, during a research trip to Ghana, West Africa. His personal qualities and skills as a composer, scholar, and performer give him a unique persona and abilities that enable him to contribute to global music-making.

I have experienced firsthand his ability to create new works for guitar and ensemble through his compositions. His personal fluency with people from diverse cultural and linguistic backgrounds has allowed Koo Nimo to transcend language barriers and communicate effectively with scholars, professionals, students, and laypeople.

He consistently brings a brilliant mind and an open attitude to his composition, music research, performance, and his interactions with people in general. His strengths lie in composition and performance in both unique contemporary and traditional contexts: understanding the deep structures of traditional African music, palm wine guitar and ensemble styles, highlife/jazz, and storytelling with guitar and vocals, including spoken word, poetry, and song. He has created a new contemporary cross-cultural style with its own integrity, making clear the connections between traditional African music and dance, Ghanaian guitar and ensemble, and African American jazz.

Koo Nimo's approach reflects a true respect for cultures, their artistic expression, and their use of materials in a way that brings authenticity to the final form of his work.

As a performer, Koo Nimo is an excellent and experienced guitarist. He has written many original, cutting-edge compositions and arrangements for his own ensemble, which incorporates both traditional and Western-style instruments. His body of work is a refreshing voice on the global music scene, avoiding the common pitfalls of commercializing his music for status or personal gain.

In his work as a composer, researcher, and performer, Koo Nimo feels a responsibility to share his knowledge and works with others, colleagues, listeners, and laypeople, and interacts with an intellect and humanity uncommon in today's market-driven world. His ability to successfully work with people from diverse social and economic backgrounds, as an absolute egalitarian, has motivated many of his colleagues to accomplish more than they believe they are capable of and to believe in themselves. His openness to others and unconditional love of music and people make him a legend and a leading voice in the Ghanaian, West African, and global music scenes.

Unlike some in the performance, composition, and academic disciplines, he is motivated to develop outcomes for people's betterment and will work beyond the expected or required to accomplish this goal. His integrity is among the highest I have experienced in my career as a musician, composer, and educator. His particular combination of composition, ensemble leadership, performance ability, commitment to music as an end in itself, and to the people for whom he plays, make him a true master of contemporary arts and culture."

Kwabena Ofosu Mensah, Kumasi, Ghana

"It was in July 1984 that I first met Agya Koo Nimo. The meeting took place at the Commonwealth Institute in Kensington, London, where Koo Nimo and his Adadam Agofomma, along with other Ghanaian traditional music groups, were performing as part of the Commonwealth Cultural Festival that year.

It took me just one hour to realize that I had met a man of great cultural and intellectual depth, honesty, linguistic eloquence, and artistic excellence. Above all, I was listening to a virtuoso of traditional Asante guitar and music. This was an unforgettable experience.

In the era of 'burger' highlife, with artists like George Darko and Lee Doudu leading the way and the quest for the commercialization of Ghanaian music restarting, the traditional music played by Agya Koo was, and still is, so compelling that I released *Agya Koo Nimo — Osabarima* on compact disc (CD) in 1990 under my Adasa record label, licensed from Apogee Records. Indeed, Koo Nimo was the first Ghanaian artist to have his songs released on CD.

I have interviewed Agya Koo on numerous occasions and published these interviews in several newspapers and journals, including the now-defunct *West Africa* magazine. My article in the March 1985 issue of the London-based *Black Beat International* magazine on this great cultural and Ghanaian guitar music icon was appropriately titled, "Koo Nimo: The Repository of Asante Music and Culture."

When I later joined the staff at Kwame Nkrumah University of Science & Technology in Kumasi in 1994, both Agya Koo and I naturally resumed sharing ideas and visions. This collaboration has continued to this day. On numerous occasions in the past, I had asked Agya Koo to record more songs and/or write for posterity. I believe this project partly fulfills that dream."

Chris Lesser, Melbourne, Australia

"I first met Koo Nimo in 1985. I had traveled to Ghana with a colleague, Tom Fryer, on a research trip to record music and collect data for an honors thesis. We were to meet up with our then teacher, Kobla Ladzekpo, from Anyako. In case we failed to connect with Kobla, our contingency plan was to seek out Koo Nimo and study with him. We had learned about Koo through academic articles on African music and decided he was the most appropriate person for our purposes, next to Kobla.

As it turned out, in the subway on our way to the airport from London, we fortuitously met a gentleman, Kofi Agyeman, whose father worked at the same university as Koo and who lived very near him. After arriving in Accra, Kofi helped us in our search for Kobla, albeit without success. Three days of fruitless searching convinced us to go with Kofi to Kumasi and meet up with Koo Nimo.

Tom and I spent several weeks studying with Koo and his group, Adadam Agofomma. We were impressed with the breadth of his general musical knowledge and the depth of his understanding of traditional music. For us, it was a period of very productive interaction with musicians and dancers, and a highly educational exposure to Asante culture. Koo was very hospitable and inclusive, and his understanding of Western music was invaluable to our research progress. His standing in the community became apparent to us from the deferential manner in which people related to him, and from seeing the reach of his musical and academic network.

It became evident that Koo was not simply a traditional musician, but a worldly and well-versed proponent of Ghanaian traditions and culture who was widely recognized and respected. We were especially impressed that Koo was such a champion of traditional music while at the same time deeply connected with Ghanaian popular music history.

In 1989, I returned to Ghana to collect data for my postgraduate degree. I stayed with Koo in his house, and he welcomed me as a guest in his family. In 1992, my performance group, Adzohu, sponsored a visit to Australia by Koo and the master drummer in his group, Noah Owusu. Koo and Noah toured with Adzohu up the eastern coast of Australia, from Melbourne through Sydney to Byron Bay and Brisbane, as well as to Adelaide, holding performances, conducting public workshops, and teaching university classes. All who came into contact with Koo were impressed with his statesman-like nature and his affable and engaging disposition. Koo loved Australia, both the people and the country, and he especially loved our well-made roads.

Many teachers and performers of African music and dance in Australia have since traveled to Ghana, either to study as individuals or to take students on study tours. They nearly always visit Koo to receive instruction and see performances. I too have returned to Ghana many times, either on my own or with students, and I always stay in Australia Corner in Koo's house. His house has become my home in Ghana."

Dr. Thomas Kruppa, Berlin, Germany

"I got to know Koo Nimo and his Adadam Agofomma ensemble when attending various functions at the Kwame Nkrumah University of Science and Technology in Kumasi in 2000. When I was looking for an early learning music experience for my then-small children, I got to know him better, and not only did I find a great teacher, but over time, I also gained a very good friend.

Until I got to know Koo Nimo, I had no understanding of Ghanaian culture and tradition. As a great teacher, Koo Nimo taught us about the history and background of highlife music, which was being played in the ports of West Africa. He surprised us with the subtle rhythms of his own palm wine music and philosophical lyrics.

He introduced us to the famous five beats of the pentatonic scale, which were passing from West Africa to America and can be heard in jazz, blues, and modern pop and rock music. Whenever I notice these beats today, my thoughts go back to those first encounters with Koo, who explained the fundamentals of the music we hear today. He also introduced us to various musical instruments, such as the rumba box with its two or three metal tongues, the giant drums, and the mid-sized talking drums (fontomfrom). There was also the small squeeze drum, on which the player can change the tune by pressing its strings under the arm, and the banana-shaped bells. We were touched to learn about the seperewa, a traditional Akan string instrument, accompanied by songs, as well as the xylophone from the north of Ghana with its remarkable calabashes.

He told me that he had always wanted to teach children, to inspire the next generation by offering a unique environment full of traditional values, and to teach them the roots of their origins. We started with a handful of children from both Ghana and expatriate families every Saturday morning for one hour, introducing the kids to listening and performing together with people like George, Paa Willie, and Faustina.

The children became familiar with rhythm by experimenting with drums, xylophones, and bells, getting used to body movements, dances, and, as a highlight, storytelling. Koo Nimo started the story-telling with a proverb or parable, and the children were encouraged to share something important from their own world. This build-up of confidence made them think about the week ahead and allowed them to form new friendships, which they would always remember.

It was a special experience to see my friend performing outside Ghana in Wisconsin, USA. It was December 2012, freezing cold, when he performed after only one day of rehearsal with Madison's Atimevu Drum and Dance Ensemble at the University Concert Hall. For me, it was a perfect opportunity to experience firsthand how artists who had emigrated from Ghana translate and interpret values from the environment they had grown up in into the new world. The standing ovations for Koo and the ensemble were convincing proof of how music and art break down barriers and represent us as universal beings.

Finally, my children remember a wonderful time in their lives when Koo became part of their world. A big thank you goes to Koo, a true friend, for showing us that we are able to walk and work in different worlds and serve humanity."

Professor F.K.A Allotey, Accra, Ghana

"It is a great pleasure to write a short note on Dr. Daniel Amponsah, popularly known as "Koo Nimo," a former Chief Technician of the Faculty of Science at the Kwame Nkrumah University of Science and Technology.

As Chief Technician of the Faculty, he worked directly under me during my tenure as the Dean of the Science Faculty for twelve years. He was very knowledgeable, hardworking, and a pleasant person to work with. His talent and prowess in music were discovered by Dr. J. L. Latham, a British Visiting Professor to the Faculty. It was Dr. Latham who sponsored and promoted Koo Nimo's great works in music, particularly African traditional music.

Dr. Amponsah was also keen to learn some mathematical aspects of music, and he frequently came to me to study the theory of harmonics and Fourier series. His music took him to several countries across Africa, Europe, and the United States.

In 2015, the two of us appeared in an hour-long Dutch documentary film entitled *Multiverse*, which explores science, culture, and indigenous knowledge in Africa."

Professor Linda Day, New York, USA

"As a professor of African Studies at Brooklyn College, I was awarded a Fulbright Fellowship to Ghana in 1999 and subsequently began organizing Study Abroad seminars to Ghana for City University of New York students. I am delighted to say that I have had the privilege of working with Daniel Amponsah, Agya Koo Nimo. It has been a difficult task to put into words the impact this man, this teacher, this creative force, has had on me and my students.

When I brought my first group of American students on a Study Abroad program to Kwame Nkrumah University of Science and Technology in 2002, I knew they would be keenly interested in learning about Ghanaian music and performance traditions. So, I asked our Faculty Host if she would recommend someone to give the students a lesson on Ghanaian music. She immediately suggested the name "Agya Koo Nimo," and that was the beginning of a magical, wonderful relationship with a man who has become central to my students' understanding of, and love for, Ghana's cultural heritage.

That first year, on the appointed day, my students went to a classroom at the university and found about twelve members of the Adadam Agofomma ensemble, with all of their instruments wrapped in stunning adinkra cloths, ready to take the students on a journey of discovery. I realized that we were in the presence of the same company of performers whom Henry Louis Gates had introduced in his series *Wonders of the African World* as the best representatives of traditional Asante court music.

I was immediately overwhelmed with gratitude that my students would have the opportunity to learn from this master musician and his ensemble. And indeed, they listened, they watched, they felt the power of the rhythms, and they worked hard trying to copy the moves of Agya's dancers. This active learning event, one that captured all of their senses, was undoubtedly the highlight of the lessons we had at the university. My students and I were transported into a world where tones, rhythms, gestures, and movements carried meaning and messages passed down for generations. We were mesmerized.

We have been blessed to continue this tradition of music and dance workshops at Agya Koo Nimo's home studio. The hours spent at the studio, designed in the style of a traditional Asante dwelling, are some of the very best experiences of cultural immersion, participatory observation, and active learning that my students have ever enjoyed, whether abroad or at home. His courtly manner and warm hospitality are legendary.

In sum, Agya Koo Nimo has been central to the success of the Brooklyn College Study Abroad program to Ghana and has had a tremendous impact on the Brooklyn College Abroad students and faculty who have been privileged to know him, work with him, and learn from him. I am happy to attest that he is a national and international treasure, and it is a personal joy to have been able to call him a friend and colleague for all these years."

Mrs. Valerie Sackey, Accra, Ghana

"Somewhere in the 1970s, a motley crew embarked on a trip from Kumasi to visit Boabeng and Fiema, the famous 'monkey villages' in the Brong Ahafo region of Ghana.

There were four of us packed into an old VW Beetle: Hannah Schrekenbach, a German architect who had come to work in Ghana for the Public Works Department and the University of Science and Technology; Koo Nimo, the quintessential Asante man with all the best attributes of that category of humanity, but none of the negative ones, a guitar, and myself.

When we reached Techiman, we turned right onto the road to Nkoranza. The spectacular rocks near the village of Forikrom caught our interest. Hannah stopped the car by the roadside, where a small footpath disappeared into the long grass, and said, "Let's see if this leads to the rocks." After pushing our way through the long grass, we found ourselves in a cassava farm. However, the path continued to the foot of the rocks and disappeared into a narrow channel worn by both many feet and rainwater rushing down the rocks.

We climbed higher and higher, becoming aware of a deep humming sound, as if the rocks were vibrating. Bees were flying in and out of holes and cracks in the rock. In some places, honey oozed out, filling the air with its scent. Suddenly, we emerged into an amphitheater hollowed by erosion into the top of the rocks. The wind-sculpted walls of the amphitheater had arches and windows through which we could see the cassava farm far below. In the center stood a large mango tree, heavily laden with ripe yellow fruits, blushed with pink.

We stood in silence, gazing at the magical scene. Then Hannah said to Koo, "Play something." He replied, "I will play you a good old Presbyterian hymn," and sat down on a rock under the tree to tune his guitar. He played just one chord - and all the ripe mangoes rained down!

In this strange and secluded spot, no children had come to rob the tree, and we saw no birds. The tree was sheltered from the wind, so the fruit had reached the point of extreme ripeness at which the vibration of just one chord from Koo's guitar shook them loose! With mangoes lying all around his feet, Koo began to play the hymn, "Glorious Things of Thee Are Spoken." But to Hannah, the tune of that hymn meant something else. She came from a divided Germany; her family was in what was then East Germany, behind the Wall. And she began to sing, in a deep contralto that brought down a few more mangoes, "Deutschland, Deutschland über Alles," her national anthem.

On the way back from Brong Ahafo, the little VW found itself behind a small tro-tro, which had the words "Still Koo Nimo" written on its rear window.

"Look," I said to Koo, "the driver is a fan of yours."

Just then, we entered the town of Nkinkansu, and the tro-tro stopped to let a passenger get down. As we passed, I said, "Let's stop just beyond the town, wave him down, and give him a surprise."

So, we parked by the roadside on the steep hill just south of the town, waited until the tro-tro came in sight, and waved for it to stop.

Imagine the surprise and delight of the driver when Koo introduced himself! The passengers got down and begged, "Play something! Play something!" And so, we held a highlife jamboree in the middle of the road.

It was probably a foolishly dangerous thing to do, but remember, this was in the lean years of the 1970s when there was very little traffic on Ghana's roads. A traveler could wait for hours before a vehicle came into sight. However, in the middle of the musical celebration, a huge articulated lorry came hurtling at top speed down the hill from Nkinkansu! Everyone dived into the tall elephant grass by the roadside as the truck rushed past.

Then we all picked ourselves up, dusted ourselves off, shook hands with our newfound friends, said goodbye, and climbed into our vehicles to continue on our way."

Dr. Michelle P. Afrifah, Accra, Ghana

"Never insult a crocodile while you are standing in the river."

This quote by Agya Koo Nimo is one that has stayed with me for many years and is one that I frequently refer to. I have always been fascinated by this man, whose wealth of wisdom, knowledge, and advice is unparalleled.

His love for music and the guitar adds to his charm. As an old soul, I find his perspectives on culture, history, and society captivating. In a time when traditions, folk songs, myths, and legends are fading away, he has remained a source of authenticity for many - and hopefully, for many more to come. I have been fortunate enough to bask briefly in his glow.

Through life's many challenges, I will always remember his words of wisdom, but especially the one about the crocodile, which cautions us to reflect on our positionality before making reckless decisions.

The time I have spent with Agya Koo Nimo has been uniquely memorable. He is a great man, and I am proud to call him not just a mentor but a friend."

Nathaniel Braddock, Sydney, Australia

"To write about Koo Nimo is a humbling experience—what can I say that has not already been echoed by hundreds of other musicians? Ghanaian musicians call him *"Papa,"* and they speak of him with unquestioned respect and love for this man and his musical authority. To me, a white American guitarist, he is a connection to another land, another age, and to the roots of the African guitar music I love.

I met Koo during his visit to Chicago, where I had helped arrange concerts and masterclasses for him. We sat down for a lesson, and he asked me to arrange a band to accompany him at the concerts, announcing that I would play second guitar for him. This was a great honor, and I would stay by his side as a fellow teacher during the masterclasses. The entire Ghanaian community came out for the concert, and my students filled out the rest of the audience. This was a frigid, snowy week in January in Chicago.

The next time we met was in August in Koo's hometown of Kumasi. His car pulled up to collect me at the circle, and his band member ushered me into the back seat, where he was sitting dressed in the elegant and austere black kente that the Ashanti wear for state affairs and funerals. I felt intimidated by his authority, now my real lessons would begin. I stayed with him for a week, living in his guest room as many students had before me, sharing the meals prepared by his wife, Comfort, and having long lessons on his front veranda, which, unlike most Ghanaian compounds, has no exterior wall. His house is open to the street and to the world.

Our sessions there were a mix of guitar technique, the history of palm wine music, reflections on his childhood hearing the Kumasi Trio play, and brief interruptions when he would call the children in the street over for some grandfatherly discipline. We also had conversations about President Obama and modern politics. While I write here of his authority, he is also warm and welcoming, keen to share the music, his home, and eager to listen. I was sad to leave. While I call him teacher, I also call him Papa and friend.

I long to sit on that porch on a bright morning again."

Katieana Amponsah, Houston, USA

"I have been fortunate to call him Grandpa and have enjoyed his company, music, and words of wisdom during the few times we have been together. Strangely, when he spoke, his words always reminded me of one of his earliest songs, "Efie Ne Fie," which I first listened to.

Everything I have seen and heard from my grandpa - from a man who would listen quietly when I spoke and was genuinely interested in what I had to say, makes me appreciate conversations even more. While he read the books and articles that surrounded him, he always took the time to encourage me to seek God first, honor my parents, respect myself and others, and strive to be great at everything I do.

I have been studying and playing the piano and violin for a few years, and there will be moments when I play a certain chord, and I will immediately remember the times I listened to Grandpa talk about how children from his village near Kumasi, as well as people from all around, came to learn to play the guitar. The children were excited, too, and had their chance to hear his counsel.

I found out that the words to his music were wise sayings and proverbs, not always simple to understand. My father translated and explained the meanings, but he also told me that I had to listen very carefully to truly understand, just like how you have to pay attention in life to understand the world around you.

The lyrics were something I have always been so curious about, but the music itself is so beautiful that it doesn't matter if a person understands all the words. There will always be much of my grandpa's life for people to read about, so I always think it is very fortunate that I got to sit next to him, listen to his songs, and hear him talk about life."

George Ankuma Mensah, Kumasi, Ghana

"Meeting Koo Nimo has been such a wonderful experience. Fate and destiny, I would say, brought us together, for it wasn't long after my admission into university that I met my idol—a man I had admired so much as a young musician and aspiring guitarist, but could only see on television.

I had the chance to meet him for the first time in his office when I decided to take a music course at the Centre for Culture and African Studies. However, since I had exhausted all my credit hours for that semester, I was denied registration. But Papa would not let me go. He said he knows talent when he sees it.

I eventually became a member of his Adadam Agofomma group and his family. It was during this time that some of his guitar students were introduced to a variety of new musical influences, including jazz, classical, Latin, and palm wine music. His unique voice and classical approach to playing the guitar are astonishing to watch, let alone hear. Better than anyone, he is a true master of the palm wine guitar style and exceptional when it comes to using adages and idioms in compositions.

Papa, as I usually call him, has not only mentored me in guitar playing but in all aspects of life. He believes that there is enough sleep after death, and he spends half of his salary buying books and much of his spare time reading.

Agya Koo Nimo is the embodiment of humility; he respects everyone's views but will never give in to mediocrity. It is my wish that God grants him many more years to continue impacting lives and for people to get to know him even better."

Ethan Kogan, Illinois, USA

"Has it been a few years now? I feel, then, like a three-year-old. I have just learned to say my own name, and I am still feeling my way up and down stairs; still struggling to count. A few years since I shook your hand! A few years since, I played the talking drums that crowded the corner of your living room. I do miss those moments.

And was it only two weeks? The time, which passed so beautifully while I lived in your home, hasn't left me: neither the night air nor the morning sun. Nor that perfect square the rain painted on your cement floor - streaming, as gracefully as it did, through your open roof. And an open roof?

Still, I aspire to what I saw in your wry smiles as an attraction - perhaps, to the clever, the playful, the uncommon. That you believed in me for those two weeks that I cannot forget.

On your table, the first time we met, sat Aristotle's *Politics*, John Blacking's *How Musical Is Man?*, and Kwame Gyekye's *Essay on African Philosophical Thought*. Perhaps a cup of tea, too, and we spent that day on your porch, talking of this and that from the morning - could it have been 8 a.m.? - until the sun had set. Your photographer and her husband, your old dancer, came by as well. He played the premprensiwa, and you played your guitar and sang. That day - so much joy, that day.

You treated me with considerable kindness and deep hospitality. You possessed a curiosity and humility that I appreciated and which relaxed me. Do you recall the Goethe quote you repeated so often to me? "Death is a commingling of eternity with time; and in the death of a good man, eternity is seen looking through time." You would cry, "What could he mean?" and laugh, looking at me for an answer. Genuinely looking at me, searching! And I was puzzled, and you were puzzled; and I, puzzled doubly, asked myself: How is this great man puzzled? Still, at his age, he allows himself to be puzzled, and to smile.

The others who speak about you, they know much more about you than I do, I am sure. I'm sure there are wonderful stories to tell. We touched briefly; so of you, for you, and to you, I can give only my gratitude. It takes a unique soul to make that impact on a young man, and in such a fleeting encounter.

"You will be a great musician," you told me last night. The words wrapped themselves around something in my heart, and something in my heart wrapped itself around the words. Neither will let go; and the rain still paints perfect squares on the cement. I think of you still, and often, and dance still and often to your music, which flows like water."

Quanda Johnson, New York, USA

"I had just received my Master's in Music degree from the Conservatory of Music at Brooklyn College and had determined to attend the Summer Seminar in Ghana to deepen my understanding of African culture and musical traditions. During our orientation sessions, Professor Day told us that we would have a lesson and demonstration with Daniel Amponsah, more commonly known by his honorific title of Agya Koo Nimo, Ghana's preeminent folkloric musician, while we were there. When I heard I would have the opportunity to study under a true West African master of song, dance, and theatrical presentation, I was stunned.

To say I was excited by the mere possibility would be an understatement. I had heard of griots, musicians who have the ability to absorb and recite the entire history of a specific family or clan and relay the information at will through song and verbal pictures. Although Agya Koo Nimo may not consider himself a griot in the traditional sense, this is how I view him. He carries the folkloric cultural history of Ghana in general, and of the Asante specifically, deep in his heart and mind, and is able to relay it through song, drumming, and dance.

When Professor Day brought my colleague Adele Balderston and me to Koo Nimo's home, we exited the taxi to the ancient sound of drums - a sound I've associated with Africa since my earliest memories. In that moment, I knew this experience would surpass any other I've had in my life. I lifted my eyes to the drummers on the veranda and saw a small, distinguished man with the wisdom of the ages stamped on his face, moving down the stairs toward us. First, he greeted Professor Day with a warm hug and then graciously accepted Adele and me in turn. My first impression: here was a man among men - brilliant, embracing, and generously offering us his time and talent.

Indeed, that day, one of the first things Agya Koo Nimo said to me was, "Dance is life, and life is dance," and I knew that this internship was going to draw together many, many threads of my creative, personal, and professional life.

A watershed moment occurred on a Sunday afternoon, and on Tuesday of that same week, our entire class was treated to a concert and dance lesson by the Master himself. Robed in his black and white kente cloth, he looked like a sage, and I tried to hang on to his every word. Something he said touched me deeper than anything else. He said, "I'm going to give you everything I've got." In a time when scholars and artists are reluctant to give "everything" for fear of losing intellectual property or being taken for granted, here was a seventy-nine-year-old man telling our entire group that he was leaving it all on the proverbial table and was going to give us "every-thing I've got."

Agya Koo Nimo is so much more than an originator of palm wine music or a definer of genuine highlife. He's so much more than a biochemist who has poured his scientific brilliance into his students for thirty-eight years. He is more than a folklorist or a chronicler of Ghanaian/Asante culture. He is a gift to the world. Just thinking of him puts a lump in my throat. He is probably the most genuinely good and guileless person I've ever had the honor of meeting on my journey through life.

His allowing me to share a little of my gift with him buoyed my life so much while I was in Ghana. Not only for me and the others who have had the pleasure of hearing and seeing him, but he is a national treasure for Ghanaians. My hope is that they know how fortunate they are to be passing through life while Agya Koo Nimo is in the world."

William Boah, M.D., New York, USA

"My uncle Koo Nimo has been an integral part of my life for as long as I can remember. Though many of his words may escape me over the years, I will always remember the life I saw in the man I looked up to, and the musician I was so blessed to stand close to. Everything I aspired to be as a young boy was reflected in what Koo Nimo saw in me, and he strongly encouraged me every day. As a relative, my perspective on his talent and music was different from that of his fellow entertainers.

I remember Koo Nimo was the last person I stayed with before I went off to secondary school at Prempeh College in Kumasi. At the time, he lived in Suntreso, South Junction, Kumasi, which was about a mile's walk from my school. I was barely thirteen years old when he first talked to me about doing my best in everything I did, as if the world were watching my every step. It was as if he was doing his best to give his young nephew a glimpse into the psyche of a man who was determined not to live an ordinary life. Perhaps he had a much clearer sense of his destiny and what God had called him to do with his gifts, unlike anything I had seen from others. There was such resolve and a stubborn connection to his dreams that could only come from a role model eager to teach a young boy.

The Koo Nimo I knew could very well have become a pianist, as he had done at Adisadel College. He could have easily switched to a career as a spokesman for the Asantehene, having spent a great deal of time learning about Asante culture and language. Because he was such a brilliant conversationalist, there was never a day that went by without my listening to him talk about the events around us and share his unusual observations.

If there was one person I wanted to be like, it was Koo Nimo. It wasn't because of the guitar, nor was it because of the music or the fame. I was quickly evolving into a boy who focused on what my future could be, and I saw how being around Koo Nimo had infused my own passions with hard work, commitment, and a quest for knowledge, even when no one was watching. He told me not to be like him, but to do my best to be better than he ever could have been.

My uncle has been my mentor and a man I have looked up to throughout my own career. I will never become a guitarist, but whatever I have become in life, Koo Nimo's encouragement, prayers, and selflessness made it possible. "Truth is reproducible, but a lie will always evaporate," he told me. That is the kind of virtue that guided my uncle's life, and it is one I hope to carry forward through my own children. For all this, I thank Agya Koo Nimo, a great musician, and an even better man - someone I am fortunate to call *Wofa*."

Professor Kofi Asare Opoku, Accra, Ghana

"Whenever I think of Koo Nimo, an Akan drum text comes to mind:

Ɔdomankoma bɔɔ adeɛ,
Bɔrebɔre bɔɔ adeɛ.
Ɔkyerɛma yɛyɛ no brɛbrɛ,
Ɔkyerɛma yɛyɛ no gye adeɛ di.

Since the Creator made things,
Since Bɔrebɔre created things,
People have treated drummers with respect,
People have offered drummers courteous hospitality.

In Akan culture, musicians and master drummers, reverently called the Creator's own drummers and craftsmen, are regarded as eloquent spokespersons for the Supreme Being. They are therefore adoringly revered and deferentially respected. It is in this gleaming and widely acknowledged light that I see Koo Nimo - a towering example of our ancestral ingenuity and a living embodiment of the proverb: "The progeny of a chameleon will never lose the ridge down its back."

Firmly grounded in his Akan traditions, Koo Nimo never compromises his artistic integrity. By remaining true to his authentic self, he calmly and with serene dignity continues to put something compellingly beautiful into our world in this age of mortifying imitation.

Koo Nimo's uniqueness lies in the fact that, having embarked on his own distinct path in life, he has refrained from comparing himself with others. He has moved beyond any hesitancy or fear to be who he truly is - a preeminent contemporary exponent of the beauty, grace, wisdom, and depth of our artistic heritage of music. In his music, Koo Nimo has given us a vision of ourselves and what we could become. His music has ennobled us beyond description, and his presence among us in this generation will forever be held as a precious gift from the universe to be deeply treasured."

Eugene Yaw Asare Amponsah, Washington, USA

"I grew up as the ninth child in my family, and with such a wonderful father, I couldn't have asked God for anything more. As long as I can remember, he valued his children's education greatly and had a tremendous sense of awareness of the traditions and culture of the Asante people. I was born into the epicenter of a truly special culture, whose value my father did everything he could to share with me. He filled our house and garage with both Western and African musical instruments, and there was not a day that went by without the chance to see some of the most talented musicians sitting on our porch. This is how I learned, and it was the foundation of the platform my father provided to children - not just me, not just my brothers and sisters, but to anyone willing to learn.

I have always admired and revered my father so much that I wanted to follow in his footsteps and carry on his musical legacy. So, I spent most of my time playing music and honing my skills - with every tune and every beat of the drum serving as a glowing reminder of my father's own work.

When I was ten years old, he gave me the opportunity to travel and perform with his renowned Adadam Agofomma ensemble. Little did I know that he was laying a daring foundation for me to carry on the musical tradition, ensuring that the message and inspiration of Agya Koo Nimo would live on beyond a brief moment in our history.

In 1991, I was on stage with my father when he asked the master drummer of his group to pass his drumming sticks to me, so that I could play at the end of every performance. He wanted that moment to symbolize the passing on of our traditions to another generation.

This was the greatest gift my father gave me as a ten-year-old boy, and one of the best moments of my life has been to record and perform a song with him as a musician.

I am Agya Koo Nimo's son, and his influence on my life has given me the opportunity to cherish the art of music and continue to do so through my father's eyes."

Dr. Andrew L. Kaye, Ph.D., New Jersey, USA

"It was in Accra, in June of 1985, that I first heard the name Koo Nimo. I had just arrived in the Ghanaian capital with the aim of gaining some understanding of the changing musical landscape of modern Africa. On the third day of my visit, at the garden bar of the hotel where I was staying near Kwame Nkrumah Circle, I met a tall and imposing man wearing traditional African robes. "Ah! You want to understand our music? Then you must find Koo Nimo! He is our Homer - the Poet of Kumasi - and a veritable Wizard of African Guitar."

Over the next several days, I heard the name "Koo Nimo" (this is how I initially spelled it in my journals) repeated by several others. According to their accounts, he was variously described as an old wise man with a beard, a bearer of ancient folk wisdom conveyed through genial story-songs; a dynamic innovator in modern highlife; or, as a mechanic at the Accra lorry park said with a laugh, "Koo Nimo? He is up-up-up," making a gesture with his hands, waving them upwards. "Man, his music is high. He is King of Up-up-up."

When, one week later, I finally met the great musician at his office at the University of Science and Technology in Kumasi, I learned that this storied folk hero was also the institution's Chief Lab Technician in Biochemistry. On the occasion of our first meeting, he was draped in a white lab technician's overcoat, sitting humbly at work amidst papers and vials filled with chemicals of all colors.

"Andrew Kaye? Oh yes, I was expecting you. My friends at GBC told me you would be coming."

We immediately embarked on a lively conversation that ranged from American jazz and Brazilian music to my work with American folklorist and writer Alan Lomax. He was familiar with Lomax's writings and shared some of his concerns: "I agree with Lomax that we must preserve and promote our musical heritage. Our children are not being educated to appreciate their culture, and they are losing contact with their roots."

From that day forward, I was privileged to spend much time with Koo Nimo, in future visits to Kumasi and Accra, as well as on the road in the USA, where I helped arrange his New York City premiere at Lincoln Center in July 1988. Anticipating the concert, the *New York Times* hailed "Koo Nimo" as one of Africa's "premiere palmwine guitarists," and a capacity crowd, including the American pop musician Paul Simon, was in attendance.

I feel privileged for the times I have spent with Koo Nimo and his extended family of musicians, friends, and admirers. I share, with many of them, a deep appreciation of the magic he brings to the guitar strings, the lyricism and meaning he imbues in his poetry, and the rhythms he creates with his Adadam Agofomma (Roots Ensemble). With his music, he creates a unique sonic world that embraces not only the ancient rhythms and harmonies of Africa but also a personal sensibility that can appeal to listeners anywhere. For me, Koo Nimo and his music are a gift to the world that, like the music of Mozart, Bird, or Jobim, will sing on, and dance on, for all time."

Professor Kofi Agyekum, Accra, Ghana

"I knew Agya Koo from afar when I was a student in the 1970s. I enjoyed most of his songs that were played on GBC 1 radio. My favorite tracks were "Momfa Nnaase Mma Yehowa," "Abenaa

Mesuro wo Gyamfite," "Gyamena Buoo," "Adesua Ye Ya," among others. I enjoyed these types of music and songs because I loved their Ghanaian cultural aspects. His music covers all areas of human experience, including health, environment, education, agriculture, language, and history.

My interaction with Agya Koo became closer when I took an oral literature course at the Linguistics Department of the University of Ghana. Fortunately, one day Professor Yankah invited him to our class as a resource person, and I had the opportunity to meet him face-to-face. I was overwhelmed by his performance and oratory in the Akan language. I learned a lot about Akan history, folktales, and music from Agya Koo.

Even though he may not hold a degree in Akan or Linguistics, he is practically educated in the Akan language and culture, especially in folk songs and proverbs. He is well-versed in the lexicon and stylistic features of the Akan language. Agya Koo is not only fluent in Akan, but he also has mastery over the language, its culture, and its context of usage; he understands very well the cultural grammar of the Akan language.

All his skills in the Akan language are like precious stones reflected in his music. Agya Koo combines Akan history, especially Asante history, in his music. He also employs Akan folktales, proverbs, allegory, symbolism, and other literary devices in his work. The way he crafts the folktales and the flora and fauna characters shows that he has proper knowledge of the behaviors of these plants and animals. His music taps into both the utilitarian and aesthetic aspects of the poetic language of Akan. I believe his songs not only entertain his listeners but also teach Akan morals, values, ethics, religion, culture, discipline, and history. He is one of the musicians who has upheld the indigenous tunes and themes of Akan music, maintaining the Yaa Amponsa rhythm.

Agya Koo is an Akan scholar who continues to build his knowledge of the Akan language and culture. Sometimes, he calls me to explain some lexical items that he feels he does not understand very well. This clearly demonstrates that he is a humble, diligent, and honorable man. In such conversational interactions on the phone, I also learned a lot from Agya Koo.

Agya Koo Nimo is a living legend of Akan culture. He is a repository of Akan culture, language, religion, and history, walking daily as an encyclopedia of the Akan people. He has, at his fingertips, the A-Z of the ethnography and cultural ideology of the Akan. Even though I did not work with him on a daily basis, I have gained so much from his music and from our face-to-face and distant interactions. His services to me have been priceless, and I deeply appreciate his extraordinary benevolence toward me.

May the Almighty bless Agya Koo.

Asanteman da wo ase.

Ghana da wo ase."

CAREER/AWARDS

- 1979 - 1990: President, Musicians Union of Ghana (MUSIGA)

- 1979 - 1990: Interim Chairman of Copyright Society of Ghana (COSGA)

- 1980: Member - Board of Directors of Ghana Broadcasting Corporation

- 1980: Visiting Senior Lecturer, Music Department, Cape Coast University, Ghana

- 1984 - 1990: Member, Education Commission of Ghana

- 1984: Played a role in "Repercussions" produced by Dennis Marks

- 1985: Honorary Life Member, International Association for the Study of Popular Music (for Performance of Ghanaian Guitar Idioms)

- 1988: Dubbed "The Repository of Asante Music and Culture" (Vide July, 1988 WKCR 89.9FM, Columbia University, New York, USA)

- 1988: Played a role in a film, "Crossing Over" in Trinidad and Tobago commissioned by UNESCO. The Film was adjudged the best video documentary in Trinidad/Tobago (1989) and Martinique (1990)

- 1991: Received the Prestigious Asanteman Award from Otumfuo Opoku Ware II, Asantehene

- 1992: Doctor of Letters (Honoris Causa), Kwame Nkrumah University of Science & Technology, Kumasi

- 1995: Member, National Folklore Board, Ghana

- 1997: Head of State Grand Medal (Civil Division) Service to Ghana

- 2001: Honored by Ghana Association of Michigan for Outstanding Contribution to the World in Music

- 2001: Honored for Dedicated Service to Ghana in promoting the Ghanaian Cultural Heritage throughout the world by Ghana Association of Tennessee, Nashville, USA

- 2001: Outstanding and Dedicated Service Award by TEK Biochemistry Old Boys of Meharry Medical College, Nashville, USA

- 2003: Awarded Key to the City of Miami, Florida, USA by Mayor Alex Penelas

- 2004: Living Legend Award by National Theatre of Ghana (MUSIGA)

- 2005: Sunshine Artiste Music Award

- 2005: Du Bois-Padmore-Amu Awards for Lifetime Achievement (African American Heritage Award)

- 2005: Otumfuo Opoku Ware II Jubilee Foundation Award

- 2007: Awarded National Living Human Treasure (Music Division) by Ministry of Culture and Chieftaincy, under the auspices of UNESCO

- 2007: Member of Volta Award by H. E. J.A. Kufuor, President of Ghana

- 2009: Established Koo Nimo Cultural Resource Centre with the collaboration of the Ghana Cultural Fund

- 2015: Played a role in the documentary "Multiverse"

RECORDINGS

KOO NIMO with I. E.'s Band, *Queenophone Records, 1954*

- Ghana Mann (Calypso-Twi)
- Anoma Kole (Highlife-Twi)
- Go Inside (Dagomba-Twi)
- Tema (Highlife-Twi)
- Obi Diε Aba (Mambo-Twi)
- My Dear Comfort (Highlife-Twi)

KOO NIMO with Gyasi's Guitar Band, *Ghana Film, 1967*

- Owuo Tɔn Ade a tɔ Bi, Written by Koo Nimo, Vocals: Koo Nimo and K. Gyasi
- Owusu Sε Mamma, Written by Koo Nimo, Vocals: Koo Nimo and K. Gyasi
- Nana Yaa, Written by Koo Nimo, Vocals: Koo Nimo and K. Gyasi
- Ɔdonsɔn, Written by Koo Nimo, Vocals: Koo Nimo and K. Gyasi

KOO NIMO and the Kumasi Adadam Group, *Philips West Africa, 1969*

- Okomfo Anokye, Special release for Macelane. Guitar: Koo Nimo; Premprensiwa: Kwao Safo; Claves: J.K. Barwuah
- Samanadze (Abena), Special release for Macelane. Guitar: Koo Nimo; Premprensiwa: Kwao Safo; Claves: J.K. Barwuah

OBI AWARE SEM, Abena Akyigyina, *Ghana Film FIC, 1973*

- Asew
- Ose M'Aye
- Ataa Oblanyo
- Ohia Yε Ya
- Nana Afredua

AGYA KOO NIMO, *Apogee Solid State – Ghana, 1976*

- Fiada Me Ne Ko, Osa Barima (A Good Friday Song)
- Nana Otuo Akyampon (In Memory of Kumawuhene)
- Aburokyire Abrabɔ (Overseas Life)

- Owusu sɛ m'amma (The Driver's Lament)
- Naa Densua (The unheedful wife)
- Akora Dua Kube (The old man plants a coconut tree)
- Ɔdonsɔn (Let Love Prevail)
- Nipa bɛhwɛ yie na efi dɛe wahu (Forewarned is forearmed)

KOO NIMO, with Dr. K. Gyasi and his Noble Kings, *1982*

- Robert (Mensah) Wo Gyaa Yɛn (Hi-Life in Akan)
- Gol' Coas', by K. Gyasi, Kojo Donkor and Koo Nimo, Leader/ Trumpet: Tom King. Guitarist: Koo Nimo, Organist: Kojo Donkor
- Yɛrebreɛ Ayɛ Dɛn (Hi-Life in Akan)

ODONSON NKOAA, *Polygram West Africa, 1982*

- Ɔdonsɔn Medley (Da oke, Akosua Dampo, Owuo tɔn ade a tɔ bi, Soya adwuma yɛden)
- Asamado
- Wiase Nsem Dɔɔso
- Nocturne (Tribute to Ebenezer Laing)

GHANA OSEE YIE, *Faisal Helwani, Recorded at Studio One, 1985*

- Agya (Owuo tɔn ade a tɔ bi)
- Ohia Yɛ Ya
- Ghana Osei Yie
- Salamatu
- Ɔdo Akosomo
- Dampa (Adampa)

KING OF UP-UP-UP, *Boah, Kaye & Osei Tutu, 1988*

Guitar and Vocals: Koo Nimo; Guitar Kofi Twumasi; Percussion and Seperewa: Noah; Vocals and percussion: Abena Manu, Odei Obeng

- We Build Ghana Strong (Akokɔ mɔn, birekuo mɔn)
- Which Way to the Future? (Yɛbɛye no dɛn ni)
- Nipa Nkrabea (Destiny)
- God Listens to my Music
- Elephant's Winter Cocktail (Aburokyire abrabɔ)
- Seaboy in Love (Seaboy money na puer)
- Hello, Hello, Hello (Mito na lu lu no)

- Okomfo Anokye
- Friday Night Penny (Dagomba medley, Abɔtare, Friday night you ask me penny)
- Too much pride brings trouble (Kwakuu donsu don)
- Time changes everything (Kete demu odede montie)
- Yaa Asantewaa Woman Power (Efie ne fie)

KOO NIMO AT LINCOLN CENTER, USA, *Aquaitone – Brooklyn, 1989*

All songs written by Koo Nimo and instrumentations provided by Khodjo Aquai. Lead, Vocal & Guitar: Koo Nimo; Rhythm Guitars: Prince Twumasi, Kwame Nkrumah; Background Vocals: Abena Manu, Glenda Ifill, William Obeng; Percussions: Noah Owusu, William Obeng, Buggs Niles; Drums: Noah Owusu, Friday Pozo; Keyboards & Synth: Khodjo Aquai

- Nana Nyame Boa Me
- Yesu Wuo (Nyame Sunsum)
- Yaa Asantewaa (Efie ne fie)
- Okwantuni (Kwantumi ye mmobo)
- Ohuruie
- Kete Damu (Kete damu odede montie)

OSABARIMA, *Adasa Records London, 1990*

- Aburokyire Abrabɔ
- Owusu Sɛ M'amma
- Otuo Akyeampon
- Osabarima (Fiade mo ne ko)
- Naa Denusa
- Ɔdonsɔn
- Akora Dua Kube
- Onipa bɛhwɛ yie

TETE WOBI KA: The Past has Something to Tell, *Human Songs Records, 2011*

Koo Nimo: Guitar, Vocals, bells, talking drum, shaker; Osei Kwame: Seperewa, vocals, drum, bell, Kofi Annan: Drums Yaw Asare Amponsah: premprensiwa, talking drum, Marc Collier: Shaker, and Rick Welty: bell

- Abena
- Ohia Yɛya

- Enne Yɛ Anigye Da
- Boniayɛ kae Dabi
- Abubɛ ne Atebɛ
- Asotoo
- Osei's praise song
- Moma Yɛnsom no
- Ennua

HIGHLIFE ROOTS REVIVAL, *Riverboat Records, World Music Network, 2012*

Executive Producer: Mary Hark, Recorded and Produced by Ben Mandelson, Special Consultant: Bill Kubeczko

- Sɛ wonom me — Tsetsefly You Suck My Blood
- Owusuwaa
- Old Man Plants a Coconut Tree
- Integrity (The Cat and the Dog)
- Life Is What You Make It
- Medley: Nation Building/Adampa
- Medley: Ananse Song Story/Bear What is The Matter with You/ Horn Bill
- Praise Song for Otumfuo Osei Tutu II
- Yareɛ Yɛya (To Be Taken Ill, How Painful)
- Efie ne fie
- Adowa/Palm Wine Set: You Will Be OverTaken by Events/Listen, Listen and Listen Again

PALM WINE MUSIC IN THE 21ST CENTURY, *A Zaria Music "Ghana" Production, 2015*

Executive Producer: Dr. Adrian Nii Odoi Oddoye Snr, Akai House Clinic, Recording Engineer: Francis Kwakye, Producer: Jonas Bibi Hammond

- The Destiny of Man
- Time has its Boundaries
- Divorce is not the Answer
- Mummy where is my Daddy
- Inheritance
- Life Overseas
- Osabarima
- Hate

- Sawmill Song
- Buy When Death Sells
- Naa Densua

THE NATIONAL SYMPHONY ORCHESTRA OF GHANA, *A Zaria Music "Ghana" Production, 2015*

Executive Producer: Dr. Adrian Nii Odoi Oddoye Snr, Akai House Clinic, Producer: Jonas Bibi Hammond, Project Coordinator: Allotey Bruce-Konuah

- Osabarima
- Aburokyire Abrabɔ
- Naa Densua

INDEX

www.ingramcontent.com/pod-product-compliance
Lightning Source LLC
Chambersburg PA
CBHW021849090426
42811CB00033B/2193/J